# The Quest for Consciousness

When Llewellyn Publications asked astrologers across the country what topics they thought should be considered in our New World Astrology Series, most of them selected themes that somehow explore consciousness.

What exactly did they mean by "consciousness"? It is an elusive concept to define. The definition of consciousness for the scientist who's busy locating the firing of neurons in the brain lacks insight into the spiritual component of the term—"mind" awareness is much more than the charting of brain activities. In our era, we cannot overlook the living, expanding, feeling, freeing dimensions now ascribed to consciousness. Consciousness must be more than just physical awareness and mental alertness—more even than spiritual sensitivity or creative expressivity. Consciousness can be thought of as self-realization, with all the integration of mind, body, and spirit that implies.

As Tad Mann—one of the essayists in *Exploring Consciousness in the Horoscope*—has said, "We need to go beyond the physical, material world in order to contact our higher, spiritual self . . . Wholeness within ourselves is a prerequisite for wholeness in our world." But how to achieve consciousness, and thus wholeness and completeness?

Here are gathered together the thoughts of ten astrologers on the nature of consciousness in the horoscope. Why astrology? Because astrology offers an exciting set of tools with which to integrate your inner self with your external realities, and to thus approach the goal of consciousness. Since the achievement of consciousness and the study of astrology share an identical goal—to help people fulfill their potential—then anyone interested in self-realization will find the reflections of these noted astrologers on the interrelation between the two topics not only valuable, but fascinating.

## To Write to the Authors

If you wish to contact the authors or would like more information about this book, please write to the authors in care of Llewellyn Worldwide, and we will forward your request. Both the authors and publisher appreciate hearing from you and learning of your enjoyment of this book and how it has helped you. Llewellyn Worldwide cannot guarantee that every letter written to the authors can be answered, but all will be forwarded. Please write to:

*Llewellyn's New Worlds of Mind and Spirit*
P.O. Box 64383-391, St. Paul, MN 55164-0383, U.S.A.
Please enclose a self-addressed, stamped envelope for reply, or $1.00 to cover costs. If outside U.S.A., enclose international postal reply coupon.

## Free Catalog from Llewellyn

For more than ninety years Llewellyn has brought its readers knowledge in the fields of metaphysics and human potential. Learn about the newest books in spiritual guidance, natural healing, astrology, occult philosophy, and more. Enjoy book reviews, New Age articles, a calendar of events, plus current advertised products and services. To get your free copy of *Llewellyn's New Worlds*, send your name and address to:

*Llewellyn's New Worlds of Mind and Spirit*
P.O. Box 64383-391, St. Paul, MN 55164-0383, U.S.A.

Llewellyn's New World Astrology Series
Book 12

# EXPLORING CONSCIOUSNESS IN THE HOROSCOPE

edited by
**Noel Tyl**

1993
Llewellyn Publications
St. Paul, Minnesota, 55164-0383, U.S.A.

FIRST EDITION, 1993

**Cover Design by Christopher Wells**


Library of Congress Cataloging-in-Publication Data
Exploring consciousness in the horoscope /
    edited by Noel Tyl.
        p.    cm. — (Llewellyn's new world astrology series ; bk. 12)
    Includes bibliographical references.
    ISBN 0-87542-391-4
    1. Astrology. 2. Self-realization—Miscellanea. 3. Consciousness—
Miscellanea.   I. Tyl, Noel, 1936–. II. Series.
    BF1729 S38E868   1993                              93-34544
    133.5—dc20                                           CIP


☺ Printed on recycled paper.


Llewellyn Publications
A Division of Llewellyn Worldwide, Ltd.
St. Paul, Minnesota 55164-0383, U.S.A.

# The New World Astrology Series

This series is designed to give all people who are interested and involved in astrology the latest information on a variety of subjects. Llewellyn has given much thought to the prevailing trends and to the topics that would be most important to our readers.

Future books will include such topics as astrology's special measurements, astrology and sexuality, astrology and counseling, and many other subjects of interest to a wide range of people. This project has evolved because of the lack of information on these subjects and because we wanted to offer our readers the viewpoints of the best experts in each field in one volume.

We anticipate publishing approximately four books per year on varying topics and updating previous editions when new material becomes available. We know this series will fill a gap in your astrological library. Our editor chooses only the best writers and article topics when planning the new books, and we appreciate any feedback from our readers on subjects you would like to see covered.

*Llewellyn's New World Astrology Series* will be a welcome addition to the novice, student, and professional alike. It will provide introductory as well as advanced information on all the topics listed above—and more.

Enjoy, and feel free to write to Llewellyn with your suggestions or comments.

## Other Books in this Series

## Forthcoming

# Contents

## Noel Tyl

For over 20 years, Noel Tyl has been one of the most prominent astrologers in the Western world. His 17 textbooks, built around the 12-volume *Principles and Practice of Astrology*, were extraordinaily popular throughout the 1970s, teaching astrology with a new and practical sensitivity to modern psychotherapeutic methodology. At the same time, Noel presented lectures and seminars throughout the United States, appearing in practically every metropolitan area and on well over 100 radio and television shows. He also founded and edited *Astrology Now* magazine.

His book *Holistic Astrology: The Analysis of Inner and Outer Environments*, distributed by Llewellyn Publications, has been translated into German and Italian. He is one of astrology's most sought-after lecturers throughout the United States, and his international lectures are very popular throughout Denmark, Norway, South Africa, Germany, and Switzerland, where for the first three World Congresses of Astrology he was a keynote speaker.

Most recently, Noel wrote *Prediction in Astrology* (Llewellyn Publications), a master volume of technique and practice, and edited Books 9, 10, and 11 of the Llewellyn New World Astrology Series, *How to Use Vocational Astrology*, *How to Personalize the Outer Planets*, and *How to Manage the Astrology of Crisis*. In the spring of 1994, his master opus, *Synthesis and Counseling in Astrology—The Professional Manual* (1200 pages of analytical technique in practice), will be published. Noel is a graduate of Harvard University in psychology, and lives in Alexandria, Virginia.

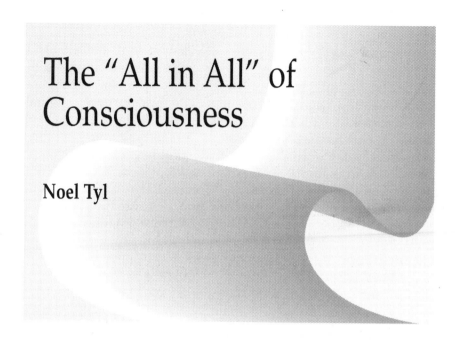

# The "All in All" of Consciousness

## Noel Tyl

What an elusive, illusory concept consciousness is! The philosopher grasps it one way, the scientist another, the psychologist another, the spiritualist still differently. And there are yet other approaches from other points of view and from other cultures: zen motorcyclists have a view which the great consciousness guru Alan Watts would have espoused; a kamikaze pilot fulfills himself at a high level of consciousness within an ethos with which we occidentals can not identify; the follower of Islam who dies in Holy War is at one with Allah; and, in dedication to "cost consciousness," even politicians and corporate executives deal with the concept. *And*, when Llewellyn Publications surveyed astrologers across the country, asking which themes we should include in this series of volumes, lo and behold, most astrologers specified at the top of their lists themes that explore consciousness!

The simple etymology of consciousness is from the Latin *conscius* (com + scire) which translates "to know with" or to be mutually aware, or more modernly, "perceiving, apprehending, or noticing with a degree of controlled thought or observation." Then, very quickly, as if to be rescued from vagueness, we are zoomed in on the word "aware," the dictionary's synonym for conscious. Indeed, practically everywhere that the word "consciousness" appears, the word "awareness" is not far behind in context.

1

That's the easy part. There are a slew of subtleties attached that are not covered by the dictionary: there are all *kinds* of consciousness (social consciousness, Christ consciousness, Krishna consciousness, visual consciousness, self-consciousness, spiritual consciousness, etc.). There are levels of consciousness, elements of consciousness, consciousness factors, a rise or alteration in consciousness, and even *locations* that stimulate or are actually thought *to have* higher values of consciousness; e.g., the consciousness movement (!) in the United States has long been dependent upon influence from the East; there are the consciousness-facilitating reputations of Sedona, Arizona, Findhorn in Scotland, Stonehenge, and a host of other sites in Brittany, Machu Picchu in Peru, Delphi, and many more.[1]

What does the concept of consciousness *really* mean? If we are talking about controlled thought or observation as the dictionary does, we are talking about systemized ways of looking at things—schools of thought, if you will. That's the concrete base of the Rationalism movement born early in the 17th century from which our present-day scientific view of the world emerged. But there is more than that: what about the "soft" spots we feel in the concept of consciousness; the importance of the spirit, of inspiration and growth? These are the points of diffusion—and confusion—in our current management of the concept of consciousness.

We have inherited a special understanding of consciousness from the 1960s, the "Flower Power" movement, the coming of the Maharishis and the assimilation of their teachings, the pervasion of chemicals to alter consciousness to some exalted state (a recall of practically timeless Shamanistic practice). Consciousness has wrapped itself around dimensions of development, change, liberation, self-realization, and even the divine. This has occurred at many levels, from shallow pipedreaming to ecstatic transcendence.

Consciousness has come to envelop realms of emotion, imagination, dreams, mystical experiences, previous lives, and lives to

---

1  On the planes of holy sites and sacred architecture, incorporating the inspiration of a living Earth with the wisdom of transformational humanity, a marvelous book, *Earth Memory* by Paul Devereux (Llewellyn Publications, 1992), is packed with observation, discussion, fact, and fulfillment: "Geomancy is the geography of consciousness . . . Sacred geometry encodes into structures the ratios of creation to mirror the universe, to create a microcosm of the macrocosm." (page 129)

come. All these aspects of the mind—the enigmatic swirl of consciousness—defy scientific explanation. Neuroscientists pursuing networks of large sets of interacting neurons or hypothecating the number of atoms in the human cortex that is needed to allow self-reflective consciousness still throw up their hands at the remoteness of any satisfactory theory to include "mind" awarenesses within the charting of "brain" activities. Perhaps William James, the father of American psychology, put it best a century ago with his observation that *consciousness is not a thing but a process.*

In an overview of consciousness, we can not overlook the scientific postulate, "I think, therefore I am" *(Cogito ergo sum).* This is certainly a major statement of consciousness, i.e., the process of knowing that one is alive; a controlled thought and iron-clad observation. It was the analytical fundament for the philosophy of René Descartes (1596–1650), *the* basic truth which no one could possibly doubt. It was his base upon which to build more complicated truths and a full system of knowledge.

Descartes, reclusive, mathematics and geometry genius credited with founding Rationalism and scientific method (along with Francis Bacon), saw that everyone everywhere had different ideas about all subjects. He felt that *the* truth would not come out of creative criticism or analysis of all the disagreements, so he discarded all ideas and theories, and determined a basic truth that was completely beyond doubt. On this base, he built a system of controlled thinking, ontological thinking (based upon being or experiencing), that he eventually expanded to prove the existence of God and the existence of matter.

Descartes extended his systemization of thought to the conception of a mechanistic universe, to the conception that every individual thing, no matter how large or small, is a self-operating machine functioning on the force initially given to the universe by God. Descartes taught that self-evident truths had *no relation to sensory experience* and were simply part of the mind from birth. While Descartes' philosophy fits our "hard" dictionary definition of consciousness (or better: our dictionary preserves Descartes thinking), his glib axiom cools for our purposes of understanding the "soft" development of consciousness concepts four hundred years later.

In our era, we can not possibly overlook the living, breathing, expanding, feeling, freeing dimensions now ascribed to con-

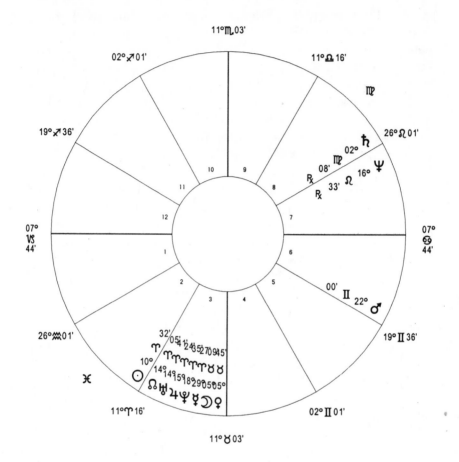

**René Descartes**
March 31, 1596, LeHaye, France
2:00 AM LMT
01E23  49N28
Source: Taeger-Archives, Bauer Verlag
Freiburg im Breisgau, Germany

---

NOTE: Descartes' birth data is consistently recorded in the major international data sources as shown above for 2:00 PM, LMT, or for 2:15 PM.
The presence of eight significators in the 3rd House is an extraordinary
emphasis of his cerebral focus and his genius for structuring perceptions
(the Moon-Venus conjunction). Mars-Venus rulership of the 3rd-9th axis
is most telling, as is the Saturn rulership of the Ascendant and the
absence of any emphasis in Water.

sciousness. I started to make a list of people I thought had "high consciousness." The list betrayed itself by scientific standards: I was citing my opinion, based upon "soft" concepts more than upon "hard." The people were cerebral types, spiritualists, occultists or artists who were cerebral, spiritual, or occult. For example: Helena Blavatsky, Alice Bailey, Annie Besant, Anton Mesmer, Madame Curie, Gustav Mahler, Ernst Ansermet, Pierre Boulez, Richard Alpert (Ram Dass) Timothy Leary, the Maharishi, Dag Hammerskjold, Ansel Adams, etc.

But who is to say that these cerebral, occult, spiritual, or artistic celebrities are *not* representatives of high consciousness—as we know consciousness today? I studied their horoscopes, but there was "no cigar," so to speak, to help astrology harness consciousness through measurement. Consciousness had to be more than just the dimensions of mental alertness, occult sensitivity, spiritual comfort, or creative expression.

I even looked at the less popular figures in history, from our point of view: Hitler certainly was a man of high consciousness (and was saintly to many millions), Emperor Hirohito was descended from the gods, Rasputin was a self-proclaimed occultist of the highest order and an advisor to the Czarina, Stalin had enough consciousness to frame a new World Order, etc. But there was no astrological profile of consciousness sneaking out of the horoscopes in the terms we might expect. Do we know what to look for? Are we looking for a "thing" instead of a process? How do we find a process, anyway?

The answer—the bond among all the people on my list, the bond among any of all of us—finally came to me: consciousness is *having it all together,* to function individualistically, freely, confidently, surely; consciousness for us is self-realization to one

---

This is a horoscope without squares and without oppositions, i.e., no diversion from the phenomenological focus on the 3rd House which dominated Descartes' extremely reclusive life. There was awareness of little else. Yet, foreign countries were very important in his life: while born in France, he was a military mercenary in several countries until age 31 when he confined his life to secluded quarters in Holland for 22 years. At age 53 he went to Sweden for his last year of life, summoned by that country's Queen Christina to show her "how to live happily in the sight of God."

degree or another. Somehow, leadership and celebrity very often do accompany self-realization. Perhaps well-exercised consciousness is recognized and acclaimed by society intrinsically.

There are many ways to pursue consciousness, to get it all together. That is the process. That is the quest. That is the path.

Ralph Metzner is a clinical psychologist with credentials that go back through Oxford and Harvard and collaboration with Timothy Leary and Richard Alpert on *The Psychedelic Experience.* His book *Maps of Consciousness* (Collier Books, New York, 1971) is a beautiful consciousness-sensitive overview of the I Ching, Tantra, Tarot, Alchemy, Astrology, and Actualism. Metzner points out that "the conflicts and disunity in the other world mirror the fragmentation and separative chaos within our personal nature . . . Our *yoga,* our way of truth, has been science: systematic observation and experimentation. Using this method we have gained considerable understanding of and control over the external forces of Nature. We have made no corresponding progress in our understanding of the laws of our own inner nature."

This idea is echoed beautifully by Tad Mann (who has contributed to this volume) in his *Millenium Prophecies* (Element Inc., Rockport, MA, 1992). In discussion of Jung's personal preparation for unification with God, i.e., psychic wholeness, Mann adds: "We need to go beyond the physical, material world in order to contact our higher, spiritual Self. And wholeness within ourselves is a prerequisite for wholeness in our world."

The 16th century French philosopher, Montaigne, who died just four years before Descartes was born, wove an important thread of insight throughout his *Essays* that called attention to our need to unify our inner world: that the distance between us and others equals the distance between us and ourselves.

The inner world/outer world idea is a primal idea, less mechanistic than the Cartesian premise but certainly as axiomatic now. It is an idea regularly remembered. When Socrates said "Know thyself," he was quoting the oracle at Delphi. The *Bible* presents many doctrines of self-awareness and evaluation, including the Commandments and the Beatitudes. In *Hamlet*, Polonius preaches, "To thine own self be true." But now, out of the 60s, the idea of inner-world health, if you will, is accompanied by ways for adjustment, ways *to achieve consciousness,* togetherness, self-realization, wholeness, completeness. Again, just as with "I think, therefore I am" and "Know thyself," a lot of potential is indicated and a lot of work is expected.

It is particularly interesting to me how folk-talk capsulizes philosophic axioms and carries them forward in time. For example, the Existential movement popularized in France in the 1940s as an umbrella for the theories of Sartre, Kierkegaard, Nietzsche, Dostoyevsky, Heidegger, and Jaspers used human consciousness and the mental process as points of departure for an assessment of being. The movement maintained that the concept of man having an essential self is an illusion. Rather, a man's self is nothing except that which he has shaped for himself up to any point in time. Think how these great theorists would applaud our folk-talk snippet of wisdom, "Do your own thing!" Or "Shape up!" The impact of the movement endures.

What about the quest for the Holy Grail, the ideal of purification through dedication and effort, the holiness of getting there, the making of an effort to crystallize one's life, that has haunted history for two thousand years? Is our folk-talk exhortation "GO for it!" not out of the same mold?

These cryptic truths reflect an *implied* philosophy. Quick communication facilitates teaching. Culture conditions behavior.

We have, "If it makes you HAPPY!" a kind of free-passage permission for action, i.e., no one should deny another's right to fulfillment.

And then, the powerful, sobering admonition under stress: "GET IT TOGETHER!" Or the highest applause: "So-and-so's really got it together!" which implicitly *includes* having done one's own thing, having shaped up, having arrived, having fulfilled one's Self, having raised consciousness.

There's "where are you coming from?" which questions self-development, and seeks to determine purpose, cause, and effect. In other words, *how* are you getting it together, for what reasons?

The esoteric teachings in our awareness—schools of controlled thought or observation, even though of "soft" things—identify the "teacher within." Metzner puts it beautifully, "For the kingdom of heaven is within you, and the goal of the path of evolutionary growth and development, according to the most ancient and sacred teachings, is to learn to follow the inner direction of the Higher Self, so that we can externalize the divinity within, and it will `be on earth as it is in heaven.'"

When I encountered William James' reference that consciousness is not a thing but a process, I immediately recalled a discussion I had years ago with the much-loved, now gone astrologer Isabel Hickey. We were talking about spirituality (read "consciousness" here) and we both decided that spirituality was not an end in itself but a *means;* indeed, a process. And now, studying these thoughts all together, I begin to feel many of the internalized "procedural" teachings and checkpoints in my personal life: among them, "Do this in remembrance of Me" and "what are you going to do when you grow up?" *The process, the means, the actualization of consciousness, has got to be the programming we do to justify our life.*

## Getting It Together

Coursing through all schools of esoteric thought, all wisdom-teaching systems, is the concept of unification, the wedding and fusion of opposites. Just as night yearns for day and day for night, so the duality of *yang* and *yin* works through change to unify into the *Tao*, the way of life. The reconciliation of opposites into a threefold unity is a core concept of all consciousness teachings (including the Trinity concept within Christianity).

Throughout extraordinarily extended metaphor, the alchemists worked entire lifetimes to imitate the work of Nature, to recreate what they found within Nature *and* within man, i.e., the process of transformation. The alchemists used the word "spagyric" to describe their art. This word comes from Greek roots that mean "to take apart" and "to bring together."[2] In all their symbolism, the alchemists worked sacramentally to blend the Sun and the Moon, the male and female principles—Sulphur and Salt, respectively—through the agent of Mercury, which is consciousness. Here again, the polar opposites, within the process of unification, re-form into a threefold unity.[3]

---

2   Also very important is the oft-quoted alchemical maxim *"Solve et coagula"*: Latin for "dissolve and coagulate," i.e., break it down and get it together.

3   In some texts, only two forces are described, with Sulfur as male and Mercury as female. Preference in texts and commentary respects the Sulphur-Salt-Mercury trinity.

In Tantric philosophy, the union of opposites *(yuganaddaha)* within one's self is the highest state of illumination and knowledge of the universe. Again, we see the union of male and female—Siva and Sakti among Hindus, Prajna and Upaya among Buddhists—within one's consciousness and within the body; we meet awareness of Brahma, the Creator.

In Tibetan Buddhism, we encounter the philosophical diagram of overlapping circles: the solar circle, representing universal consciousness and the inner world of mind, and the lunar circle, representing empirical consciousness, outer-world appearances, overlap to form the area of the *manas* (human consciousness). These circular *yantras* become a high art form for the Tibetan Buddhists. Metzner points out that the circles can be regarded as externalizations of the state of inner wholeness and the center point of creative energy. Psychologist Carl Jung observed that patients who were beginning to reintegrate scattered psychic components, to reunify self, would begin to see circular or mandala-like forms in their dreams. This led Jung to formulate the notion that the mandala is an "archetype of psychic integration."[4]

In astrology, we have the Hermetic doctrine "as above, so below," again the unification of opposites, which is achieved through teaching, through learning, through Mercury (Hermes, for the Greeks), the messenger of the gods.[5] Also in astrology's teachings we have the microcosm and macrocosm polarity related within the consciousness of oneness. We have the *I* and the *thou* of the Eastern and Western horoscope hemispheres; subjective preparation and objective experience of the Northern and Southern hemispheres, all meeting in the center of being. We have the dynamic concept of exactness (union), which is two planetary

---

4   Two equal, overlapping circles, the circumference of each passing through the center of the other, is called in the Latin of western teachings the *vesica piscis* the "vessel of the fish." It is an extraordinary construct in that its geometry forms proportions and further constructions that reach the sublime in sacred geometry, including the hexagrammatical basis for "Solomon's Seal" (the Star of Israel) The *vesica piscis* was the secret symbol for Jesus in His lifetime and some two centuries thereafter, and was emblematic of the Age of Pisces.

5   Hermes Trismegistos (Hermes thrice-master), also the Egyptian personage/god/teaching principle called Thoth, had thirteen profound teachings written in Phoenician upon an emerald tablet *(Tabula Smaragdina)* "As above, so below" is quoted by occultists more often as "As above because of what is below; as below because of what is above" suggesting a reciprocal causal correspondence that is very powerful indeed within astrological consciousness

symbols coming to partile within aspect measurement (echoing the Lunation symbolism of fecundation). We have the overall drive of life which is to fulfill potentials, to meld with time. *Synthesis becomes consciousness.*

Is it any wonder that we describe disorientation, getting off the track, or feeling lost as disintegration, as falling to pieces, as dis-ease? We learn that raising consciousness comes to the rescue through reintegration, through getting things together, through reprogramming a justification of life. We study astrology and other disciplines to find the meaning of life and our part within it, to bring our inner self together with our external reality, in appreciation of the spirit. Consciousness for the scientist, postulating and locating the mechanistic firing of neurons in the brain, appears coldly incomplete without the light of spiritual awareness.

A recent newspaper article dealt with these issues in a report about success and failure in social programs. For twenty years, the founder and president of a national neighborhood help agency observed a phenomenon: virtually all successful social programs studied over a twenty-year period had had in common a leader with a strong *element of spirituality* (read "consciousness"?).

Social workers have long been trained not to get emotionally involved, to maintain a separateness from work situations as assurance of professional efficiency. What we see in this separatism is the separation of opposites, the helpers from the needy, the light from the dark. In contrast with the norm, the spiritually enriched leaders went *into* situations and unified fragmented forces; they brought people together within themselves and with one another. The spiritual dimension was profoundly effective. The meaning of life was being taught by the leaders and exemplified in their living style. The implications for insight into social service were summed up this way in the article: "The hunger in America is not a hunger for things but a search for meaning."[6]

Since the 60s, consciousness movements and teachings have become fashionable. They have molded the lives of many, many millions of people.[7] Our world religions seem to have lost the

---

6  We can easily cite the lives and style of service of Albert Schweitzer, Mother Teresa, and members of the Peace Corps as corroboration of this report.

7  Just yesterday, I met with a client, a Catholic priest. In asking him details of a recent period that suggested "enlightenment" (Jupiter/Saturn, Uranus/Neptune contacts) I learned that he had been "initiated" into Transcendental Meditation.

light: they have become rickety structures of bureaucratic formalism, and, in the West, the potential for spiritual rejuvenation through teachings of timeless wisdom has grown enormously.

The concept of New Age, of course, refers to the dawning of the Age of Aquarius, the astrological sign of man on the threshold of discovery. In the unification of opposite signs, we see the god-spirit of Leo infused within man (Aquarius); we discover the god within, conscious of the divine potentials within selfhood. This is the quest of Actualism, still another wisdom-teaching system, described by Metzner as "a teaching formulated for the twentieth-century mind." It creates a powerful light of its own, the *Agni Yoga*, the union of opposites by fire, actualizing man's divine potentials and objectifying them in creative expression. Here the "fire" seems close to the alchemical process of constant refinement; illuminating darkened areas of consciousness and burning out obstructions to the free-flow of energy from inner sources.

## The Astrology

Reapproaching horoscopic measurements, trying to discover that key of consciousness, I focused first on Mercury. The mind would surely lead the way! Mercury was consciousness for the alchemists and the Rationalists; Mercury had to come through for astrologers.

What could be the process facilitated by the brain to suggest the propensity to consciousness development, to getting things together? Each of us has propensity potentials toward so many things, and, indeed, that is what astrology is all about, understanding these propensities and their development within time. We can already see propensities to such extremely individual concepts like confusion, inspiration, creativity, anger; diabetes, bad backs, migraine headaches; the arts, technology, the priesthood, etc. Why not the propensity for consciousness development as we understand it in modern terms? Is there a predisposition there in the natal horoscope?

Of the first twenty-five horoscopes I studied—of persons whose reputations suggest "having it together," being of special consciousness development—three had Mercury peregrine, i.e., not in major aspect with any other planet nor in a sign of accidental dignity, which ordinarily suggests that the life-function of the peregrine planet will dominate behavior: Jesus[8] (Mercury in Aquarius), the Ayatollah Khomeini (in Taurus), and Mahatma Gandhi (in Scorpio). For each of these socioreligious leaders, the mental faculties were extraordinary, of course, affecting the course of history and socioreligious vitality; but a simple measurement such as this one, even though it is relatively rare since Mercury is always so close to the Sun and forms conjunctions with it frequently, can not be applied to any generalized analysis beyond that for an individual. There are many highly conscious people with busily aspected Mercurys.

Joan of Arc, Pope John XXIII, Pope John Paul II, Martin Luther, Michelangelo, Ram Dass, Dag Hammerskjold, and Pierre Boulez all have Mercury configurated with Neptune and, often other planets. Our astrological understanding of Mercury-Neptune contacts involves sensitivity, imagination—in fact anything cerebral from daydreaming to delusions of grandeur! While these dimensions can certainly be part of the consciousness process as we know it today, there are many people with Mercury-Neptune contacts who have very little of life together. This singular measurement can not capture the all-pervasive registration of consciousness.

Pope John Paul II, Saint Bernadette, Franz Liszt (the brilliant pianist and composer who ended his life as a Franciscan monk), occultists Annie Besant and Alice Bailey, Isabel Hickey, and Swiss conductor Ernst Ansermet have Mercury configurated with Jupiter and, often, other planets. While Jupiter symbolizes the vital process of assimilation, key to our understanding of unification within consciousness, there is nothing extraordinary or consistent in this small sample of measurements.

We can note that Pope John Paul II has his Mercury-Venus conjunction (idealism) square to a Jupiter-Neptune conjunction (religiousness and spirit) which defines an enormous portion of his horoscope, a cluster-by-aspect if you will. There is the enormous cluster in Descartes' horoscope (page 5). Martin Luther had *eight* planets within 56 degrees (Jupiter, Mars, Saturn, Venus, and Sun within a Pluto sextile with Mercury-Neptune). Mass-murderer Henri Desire had an overwhelming configuration for us to

8   March 1, 7 B.C., 1:21 AM, LMT in Bethlehem (35E13, 31N42) rectified brilliantly by Don "Moby Dick" Jacobs. See Tyl, *Prediction in Astrology* (Llewellyn 1991) or request a full study from The Joshua Foundation, San Francisco CA.

ponder: a Sun-Moon-Jupiter-Neptune conjunction in Aries, squared by Uranus, with Mercury peregrine!

Do these dramatic clusters suggest that *parts* of horoscopes may "get together" to form overwhelming points of focus for the life, raise self-awareness (consciousness) in special, even functionally autonomous ways, perhaps as extraordinary zeal, mania, even obsession, to make one's way in the world, to make history?

Again, my small sampling—those above and others with other Mercury aspects, other clusters—reveals my culturally inculcated bias that consciousness is close to spirituality, to religiousness, to aesthetic states. I bring in mass-murderer Landru just to jar that profile, as we must when we consider *all* the other people born at these same dates and places at close to these same times who did *not* emerge to public recognition but had some kind of consciousness togetherness along the lines of the famous. We can ask, "does consciousness always make a lot of noise?" Is it always recognized by society? Can someone be well aware of one's self, have it all together, have a zealous focus to make life extraordinarily meaningful, i.e., live a life of higher consciousness, and just go about everyday life normally? As I discuss this elusive concept with you, am I reaching out to discover what I want to see? Since we live in the same culture and at the same time, are you thinking along the same lines as I am?

For almost a quarter of a century since I first read Alan Leo's *Art of Synthesis*, I have been intrigued with his cryptic statement that "Neptune allows the soul to leave the body." My enduring question has been, "For what reason?" Does the soul have anything to do with consciousness, let alone Neptune? Is "consciousness" what Leo meant when he referred to "soul"?

Every practicing astrologer has seen over and over again that people decide to go into spiritual studies, get to the bottom of things, take on responsibility for greater development of consciousness, find religion, dissolve personality and reform it (remember the alchemist's *solve et coagula*) under strong transit and/or Solar Arc passage of Neptune over sensitive points in the horoscope.[9] The ego is somehow dis-assembled and put back

---

9   These types of changes are not exclusively Neptunian, of course; they manifest in correspondence with other measurements involving other planets as well. However, Neptunian contacts appear to predominate in transformational behaviors.

together again. Usually, something strange happens. New awareness emerges. Alan Leo knew this and focused strongly on Neptune for symbolic correspondence.

Certainly an extreme incidence of transformation, of vision, of ultimate consciousness—in terms of religion, the spirit, the soul—would be repeated objective experience of the divine personage of God. We come close with Bernadette Soubrious, who had repeated visions of the Virgin Mary, mother of Jesus, at Lourdes, France between February 11 and March 4, 1858. The visions were confirmed and ratified by the Catholic Church in 1862, and Bernadette was canonized in 1933.

Saint Bernadette's natal horoscope shown here does not reveal any dramatic focus on Neptune natally, nor by Solar Arc or Transits (not shown) at the times of the vision.[10] What does stand out is a peregrine *Jupiter* in mutual reception with Uranus (Jupiter being the former ruler of Pisces). And this Jupiter received the Solar Arc conjunction from the Midheaven early in 1858 during the visions, a semi-square Solar Arc from Uranus exact in December, 1857, and a strong transit from Uranus at 25 Taurus early in 1858.

Here we have a strong case for the spirituality (consciousness?) dimensions of Jupiter symbolism. In our small sample of horoscopes, nearly 38 percent had conspicuous Jupiter involvement. Hitler, with his visions of grandeur and mania, had Jupiter conjunct a Capricorn Moon, trine the Taurus Sun. Suicide-sect leader Jim Jones had Jupiter conjunct Pluto, this conjunction square his Moon, Venus, and Uranus, opposed his Saturn. The modest, introverted Englishwoman Alice Bailey, the medium channel for "The Tibetan," Djwhal Khul, for some 30 years and ten thousand pages in nineteen books of esoteric philosophy, had Jupiter square her Mercury, sextile her Venus, trine Mars, and conjunct Saturn.

But Saint "Mother" Cabrini, the Italo-American missionary canonized in 1946, has a commonplace Jupiter—and Neptune, and Mercury. Similarly: occultist, medium Helena Blavatsky; and also Timothy Leary.

While fascinating, the hunt for a consciousness key, a lean astrological profile for the propensity to consciousness develop-

---

10 Although meaningless to our discussion, we may note that the planet Neptune was not discovered until almost three years after Bernadette's birth.

ment, is frustrating. We do not find often enough what we expect or think we should be looking for. We are unsuccessful in finding a grand process within sharply defined symbolisms. I recall theologian Paul Tillich sharing benignly and confidently his grasp of God as "the all-pervasive creative principle." In all his God-consciousness, Tillich captured what *we* are looking for: the unifying sensibility that flows through everything, that underlies completeness, that causes and crowns the miracle of life.

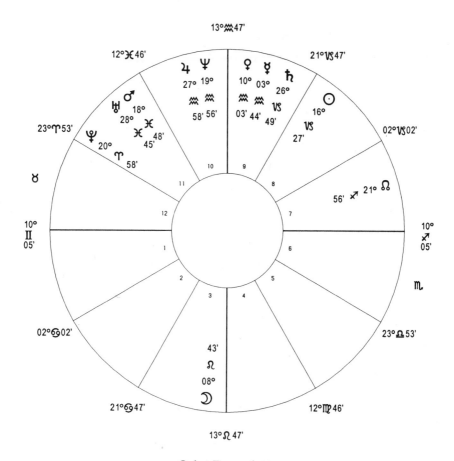

**Saint Bernadette**
January 7, 1844, Lourdes, France
2:00 PM LMT
00W02   43N07
Source: Taeger-Archives
Bauer Verlag
Freiburg, im Breisgau, Germany

This consciousness principle can be whatever an individual makes it. It can make as much noise as a society will allow in recognition or condemnation, in beatification or denigration. It can weld like-thinkers together or drive them apart to come together again in another formation. This is survival. This is progress. This is evolution.

Jupiter signals again for us the importance of assimilation, getting all things together for reward, as the opportunity of life. Jupiter is the reciprocal of Saturn, the dimension of time, the concept of necessary controls that eventually culls the focused from the diffused, the found from the lost, and confirms wisdom. In terms of consciousness, all of our horoscope speaks afresh at a pervasive level of integration, at the level where our behavioral faculties work efficiently and surely to fulfill the light of the Sun reflected upon the Moon. Our minds (Mercury) take our life energy and sense of individual needs (Sun and Moon) into a social arena to relate to the world (Venus), and our energy of self-application (Mars) keeps us on our individual growth path. We arrive at different plateaux at different times with different senses of fulfillment. We gradually assemble the parts of the kingdom within, and the New Age dawns for us, each in his own time. We know the circle.

Every wisdom-teaching system declares the goal of consciousness to be the fulfillment of potentials, the refiner's fire fashioning the essence of selfhood. In the *Nicomachean Ethics*, Aristotle sets happiness as the goal of life. He sees pleasure, fame, and wealth as valueless in pursuit of the highest happiness (read "consciousness"?). Instead, he commends man to the contemplation of philosophic truth because—and this undoubtedly was inspiration to Descartes—it exercises man's peculiar virtue, *the rational principle*. Aristotle as well defined greatness so simply and powerfully as the fulfillment of potentials.

In conclusion, I must introduce one other premise: consciousness may not be exclusively in the horoscope as an individual's special propensity and birthright. Paul Devereux (*Earth Memory*, Llewellyn, 1992) suggests that consciousness is a medium, a field; that it is not "skull-centered"; that it is processed rather than produced by the brain.

*Then* Devereux goes on to suggest that consciousness is not restricted to humans, but can occur in *all* matter. Intriguingly, this means that a rock is not solid and inert, that the Earth itself is alive, that the Earth is also conscious. He asks "Is the Earth sentient?" and I ask about the other planets as well: are they conscious? Is that how astrology really works? Is that what Hermes meant, "As above *because* of what is below; as below *because* of what is above"? Is the study of ubiquitous consciousness the frontier for astrology in the new millennium?

The French visionary Teilhard de Chardin has suggested that we humans became sentient when the Earth passed on a quantum of consciousness to its own evolving biosphere, i.e., to humans, animals, all other things. Taking these thoughts seriously, we learn that consciousness can exist separately from the human brain, and indeed, maybe this is what Alan Leo was trying to say about the soul leaving the body.

Questions then arise about our interaction with *other* structures of consciousness. Could this potential be at the vortex of our global anxiety about Earth environment? Getting it all together for consciousness development certainly will have to include all that is without as well as all that is within. For me, as my horoscope gets its parts together at new levels over time, the master teaching of St. Paul becomes particularly meaningful: "God is All in All."

When I was concluding this introduction, two very human statements came to my consciousness, almost as journalistic grace notes for this text. First, I saw on television an anthropological study of an Indonesian burial of a man aged 116 years, a special man, a celebrated artist whose ears had heard the explosion of Krakatoa, perhaps the greatest eruption of Earth consciousness ever. A family member spoke happily about the dead man to the camera: "It's not enough to have been clever and also spiritual: he was also *complete!* He gathered his friends around him and . . . and he just let go! . . . It was a conscious death."

And second, a television commercial for high-tech basketball shoes featured a celebrated professional star whose specialty (fulfilled athletic potential) is jamming (dunking) the ball down into the basket. To establish brand-consciousness for the shoes, he glared strongly into the camera and said, "I jam, therefore I am."

In this volume, ten fine thinkers in astrology have come together to share with you reflections on the elusive quicksilver of consciousness. They embrace the spiritual. They respect the practical. All of us are aware that consciousness feeds our awareness of existence; that, while it defies scientific method, it is vital for life. And we know that not knowing all in our horoscopes keeps all of us consciously human.

**Ed Steinbrecher**

Ed Steinbrecher is the author of *The Inner Guide Meditation: A Spiritual Technology for the 21st Century* (Sixth Ed., Samuel Weiser, Inc., 1988) and the director of D.O.M.E., the Inner Guide Meditation Center, Los Angeles, CA. D.O.M.E. stands for *"Dei Omnes Munda Edunt*/All the Gods/Goddesses Bring Forth the Worlds." He is a discoverer-developer of the Inner Guide Meditation, and pioneered and perfected the astrological concepts used with the meditation, such as the Shadow figures, "Alien" patterns in the Horoscope, astrological role reversal in women's charts, the physics of partnership and marriage, and using the horoscope to distinguish false from true Inner Guides.

Ed is editor of D.O.M.E.'s periodic journal, *White Sun,* and a frequent contributor, and co-author of the text for the *Life\*Scan Astrological Personality Profile,* a personal computer analysis of the horoscope. He travels extensively, lecturing, teaching, and initiating into the Inner Guide Meditation, and appears regularly on television and radio interviews. He works with thousands of people in the psychology, psychiatric, social work, health, and counseling professions, as well as those in entertainment fields.

The Inner Guide Meditation is a blend of Jungian analytical psychology and Western metaphysics utilizing astrology and images from the Tarot.

# Seeing the Horoscope as a Map of Practical and Spiritual Oneness

**Ed Steinbrecher**

Every spiritual tradition has at its base the concept of Oneness or Unity, of God or Spirit being supreme and including *All That Is*. The ancient East has resolved the paradox which Oneness creates in the concept of *yin* and *yang*, the feminine-masculine, magnetic-electric, cold-hot, black-white, dark-light interchange experienced throughout the universe and in every life. In the East, especially in Taoist tradition which survives in the *I Ching*, or *Book of Changes,* yin and yang were understood as equal in importance, one always being included in the other, each interacting with and balancing the other in myriad energy cycles and patterns through time and space.

We in the West, unable until recently to see the truth in paradox because of a lack of spiritual tools and a heritage of book burning and oppressive dogma, divide our perceptions of reality with the mind, not the intuition, and see reality linearly through the mind's eye of logic, separation, and moral judgments, instead of as holistically interacting energies. The Western mind interprets the reflection it sees in the outer world of its own dual yin-yang aspect as evil versus good, as energies warring with instead of complementing each other, as competition instead of cooperation, as Devil fighting with God. The result of this view is the reality we have created with the mind running the show—the reality each of us experiences day by day.

Astrology is the only system I have found that describes this experienced reality *as a whole* and allows the monkey mind itself to obtain new information so that it can correct its intellectual errors and retrain itself. Oneness is a fact, not a theory. The horoscope shows this Oneness and demonstrates that everything is connected to everything else to anyone open enough to learn its language and perceive its truth.

When I speak of "mind," I am talking about Gemini and the 3rd House of the horoscope. Without the support, balance, and structure of the other three Cadent or Mutable Signs and Houses— Virgo/6th House, Sagittarius/9th, Pisces/12th, Gemini becomes psychotic, the state we find our culture in today. Gemini is the sign of duality, left-right brain functions. Castor and Pollux, the Twins that Gemini represents, are the active and passive aspects of the mind which have a binary Yes-No function, like a computer. Gemini perceives everything from this dualistic, logical, straight-line, absolute point of view. To Gemini everything is multiple, or at least dual.

The mind is designed to separate the Oneness into single, unique parts. It has no other perception but itself reflected in all it sees. When Gemini/3rd House looks out into the world, it sees its partner and opposite, Sagittarius/9th House. Thus, unconscious Gemini sees a dual God and/or a dual creation—right-wrong, win-lose, good-evil, God-Devil. It has the mentality of the Army Corps of Engineers: "Make it straight, orderly, and add cement. Get rid of the disorderly, unpredictable organic things, like plants and animals. Put in a parking lot." Unconscious Gemini would fill the world with computers, technology, digital sound, artificial intelligence, car phones and other new ways to keep people from being together face to face and from feeling. But conscious Gemini looks at the Sagittarius area of Spirit and sees God whole as male-female, Mother-Husband (not Mother-Father) God, with all the apparently warring opposites as polarities, two aspects of one unity. Like their own balancing forces, Pisces and Virgo, Sagittarius has the overview, while Gemini sees the pieces; again, two aspects of one pole, both absolutely necessary for perceiving a whole.

Although the word "God" has strong patriarchal associations, throughout this essay I will use it to mean Spirit and All That Is as Mother-Husband God, a wholeness that includes both masculine and feminine as equals. Even the "Great Spirit" of the American

Indians is mainly a concept of masculinity, of Father Sky. The *neters* of the ancient Egyptians, which they experienced as the many aspects of the One God, represent, in my judgment, the most sophisticatedly correct God-concept I have discovered, but this concept seems too esoteric for use at present. I use Mother-Husband God, because it includes both the masculine and feminine bodies of God, not just the feminine. It is Cancer/Mother-Aries/Husband (feminine and masculine) instead of Cancer/Mother-Capricorn/Father (feminine only). Where Father/Capricorn is consort to Mother/Cancer, Wife/Libra/Partner is consort to Husband/Aries/Ego in both men and women. Aries, not Capricorn, is the Husband/Begetter, as Cancer is the Mother/Conceiver. The consort roles are secondary and passive to the primary roles.

Our realities are sustained by six astrological poles, three male and three female. One end of each pole is masculine, the other feminine. The three Fire/Air poles make up the masculine Spiritual/Mental bodies of each of us; the three Earth/Water poles, the feminine Physical/Astral bodies. Each male pole is balanced by the female pole that squares it, the pole of the same element. Hence, the Aries/masculine–Libra/feminine Cardinal male pole is balanced by the Cancer/feminine–Capricorn/masculine Cardinal female pole. The Leo/masculine–Aquarius/feminine Fixed male pole is balanced by the Taurus/masculine–Scorpio/feminine Fixed female pole. And the Gemini/feminine–Sagittarius/masculine Mutable male pole is balanced by the Virgo/masculine–Pisces/feminine Mutable female pole. When the male poles are not acknowledged as balancing instead of antagonizing the female poles, no four-body balance can be achieved, and disaster results, as we see in our world.

It must be remembered that the consciousness of the astrologer must be taken into consideration when considering the horoscope as a map of practical and spiritual Oneness. The astrologer who is atheist or agnostic, who has never experienced being touched by God or who acknowledges only the earth plane to be real, regarding spiritual matters to be ephemeral, is limited by logic and practical, earth-plane experience, and cannot be expected to comprehend the spiritual-intuitive and mystical-psychic aspects of a horoscope any more than a blind person could discuss the hues and shadings of color. One can only perceive from one's level of consciousness and awareness with the equipment one has been given or has developed. If you have no eyes, you cannot see.

My approach to astrology is anciently traditional, with a major shot of pragmatism. If it works, use it, no matter what the theory. If it doesn't work, dump it, no matter how hoary its tradition. I believe that when the modern planets, Uranus, Neptune and Pluto, were discovered, they disconnected the old rulers of Aquarius, Pisces, and Scorpio from those Signs and completely took over rulership of said Signs. But, as in life, many astrologers cling to the old rulerships, not necessarily in belief, but in practice. Hence I see many Saturn-based astrologers in my reality, seemingly controlled by the ghost of the old rulership. Uranus taking over Aquarius did not automatically make all astrologers into Uranian astrologers. Humanity seldom changes as fast as the universe changes. So it is useful to recognize these two breeds of astrologers, the Saturn-based full of fears, "shoulds," judgments, fate, conservatism, seldom if ever speaking of spiritual matters, and the Uranian, based in spirituality, trust of the universe, cooperation, freedom, options, and a holistic view.

When looking at the horoscope as a map of the Oneness, it becomes imperative to include all aspects of that Oneness. I find too many old-school astrologers leaving the spiritual aspect of a horoscope out entirely or treating it separately under the title of "Esoteric Astrology," perceiving it to have no practical value for everyday life concerns. To me this is like talking about the solar system and leaving out the Sun, ignoring the Source from which all comes and which centers and balances all the interacting parts. This division is a continuation of the old Christian separation of Earth and Spirit, "pie in the sky by and by" that has nothing to do with mundane life on the planet, a view of the physical earth plane as evil, and a promised heaven as the only good.

This separation cannot be made if the horoscope and the person it represents is to be truly understood. Spirit is as practical to your life on the planet as food, God is as much of a player in your reality as is your partner or your mother-in-law. To separate God from the rest of reality continues the unconsciousness that each of us experiences in our everyday lives. We in the counseling fields bring all our unconsciousness and hangups to each person we work with. Each of us sees only out of our own narrow views and understandings of reality.

It is useful to remember this each time we work with another in a counseling mode. *There is no such thing as being objective.* No objective universe exists that will ever be experienced by anyone alive on the planet. An objective universe is a false premise that we have built on for far too long. If we are to change and heal the universe each of us experiences, each of us must take total responsibility for everything—no blame, but total responsibility, understanding "responsibility" to mean the ability to respond to and act on the messages seen outside of oneself that are harmful or destructive to the Oneness. Each of our universes is always in perfect balance, but some of the balances create extreme pain for the individual ego having to experience such balancing.

## The Four-Body System

God in the horoscope *permeates all the horoscope,* as the Fire Body in each of us permeates our lower three vibrational bodies. The four-body system that makes up each human being corresponds to the four elements of the horoscope: Fire, Water, Air, and Earth.

The Fire Body corresponds to the Fire Signs, Houses, and Planets of the horoscope. It is the Spiritual Body, the life-giving, love-giving, creative aspect of ourselves. Because the Sun is contained in this body, it carries the primary purpose of the life, what each of us is here to do during this incarnation. It is the least dense of the four bodies, is yang or masculine, and has the highest vibration. When the Water or Astral Body is awake, developed and able to see auras, the Fire Body is seen as a beautiful egg-shape body of light, color and flowing energy patterns.

The second body in terms of density is the Air Body. This is called the Mental Body and is comprised of the Air Signs, Houses and Planets. The three modes of thought take place in this body: logic, comparison, and gestalt (Gemini, Libra, Aquarius). It is a yang, masculine body which connects all the other bodies through the Mercury/Gemini "Messenger of the Gods" function. When seen psychically, it appears as a silver-grey or bluish egg-shaped light body, densest and most brilliant next to the skin of the physical body.

The next body in denseness is the Water or Astral Body. This is the love-receiving, magnetic, receptive, psychic, feeling body.

All feelings, both sensory and emotional, are perceived by this yin, feminine body. This is the body you are in, in dreams or visual meditations. It is the body you are in during an out-of-body experience. It is the body you are in after you die. It has the ability to float, fly, walk through walls, and teleport. It looks just like the physical body in form, but being astral it has the ability to change its shape. This is the body which determines others' reactions to us because of its watery, magnetic, emotional nature. Therefore, no matter how physically beautiful you might be, if you feel ugly or you feel bad about yourself, this body becomes ugly or distorted to reflect these feelings, and it will cause others to respond to you accordingly.

The great actors and actresses understand and take advantage of this transformational ability of the Astral Body. They consciously change this body, through feeling, into the roles they are playing. They train themselves to astrally become the characters they are acting out. When the Astral Body becomes the character, the audience and the other actors have no choice but physically and emotionally to respond to the character the Astral Body has become, not the actor or actress taking the role.

It is interesting to experiment with this body in your everyday life. If you have lunch in the same restaurant every day where the staff knows you, or if you are in a work situation where the same co-workers interact with you day after day, experiment with taking on a new Astral Body role. Feel yourself to be someone totally different from who you are.

For example, feel yourself to be an ancient old man or a ten-year-old girl, and experience how the outer people respond to you in totally new ways. Demonstrate to yourself the power of transforming the Astral Body under will. And if you dislike how others respond to you in general, examine yourself to find out how you have distorted your Astral Body up to now, and bring healing and change to restore its natural beauty, harmony, and balance.

The densest of the four bodies is the physical Earth Body, a yin, feminine body. It is comprised of the Earth Signs, Houses, and Planets. It has no life of its own, but gains its life from being interpenetrated by the upper three bodies. It is our anchor to the earth plane, the pot in which each of us is cooking in this life, the vehicle through which our Solar Centers express love and creativity, the temple that houses the Gods and Goddesses or Archetypes within.

The four bodies are equally important and equally holy. One is not better than another. The Earth Body and Earth Plane are just as important and holy as the Fire Body and the Spiritual Plane. To view them as hierarchical in value, the higher being better than the lower, damages the Oneness and creates difficulty and pain in your life. No longer is it useful, if ever it was, to think of one thing as better than another. Is the brain better than the heart? Male better than female? Black better than white? Straight better than gay? When we think in these separatist, erroneous ways, *our lives and realities go out of balance and destruction results.*

In terms of vibrational sequence, the four bodies go from the least dense Fire Body, through Air and Water, to the most dense Earth Body. These can be understood as two units. Fire and Air forming a masculine, yang energy body, Water and Earth forming a feminine, yin energy body. But when we are born, these masculine-feminine bodies hook into one another, forming a sequence of vibration differing from the sequence described above. The Air Body moves in between the Earth and Water Bodies, and the Water Body goes in between the Air and Fire Bodies, in much the same way the yin-yang symbol is constructed. At the death of the physical body, the inner three bodies remain together for a time. (Hence the ghosts and astral entities that are perceived from time to time by psychics and astrally sensitive people. At the second death, the Astral Body separates from the Fire-Air Body and dissolves. At the third death, the Air Body is absorbed into the Fire Body, and the life experience cycle is complete.

An understanding of the physics involved in the four-body interaction is useful for any astrologer attempting to communicate the reasons for the occurrences of different life events and experiences. Nothing happens by chance. Your entire reality is a message to you about yourself, no one else. Events or people you label as negative or evil represent your unconscious inner energies. Those you label as positive or good represent your more conscious inner energies. Each person and situation in your reality shows you an aspect of yourself. Reality is in fact a Oneness, *your* Oneness. There is no way to avoid a reality your own inner energies are creating and sustaining.

Let me take a moment to clarify a confusion about the word "intuition." It seems that the human psychic function has become so embarrassing to the rational Gemini mind that has currently taken over our society that the word "psychic" has become taboo, and the word "intuitive" has taken its place. When I use the word "intuitive," I am referring to the Sagittarius/9th House active spiritual function which comes in words, concept, or knowing.

Psychic information, a receptive spiritual or mystical function, can be felt or visualized. For wisdom and psychological health, psychic/Pisces/12th House function must be balanced by the common sense/applied theory/Virgo/6th House function; these two must be balanced and work with the intuitive/Sagittarius/9th House function balanced by the logical/theoretical/Gemini/3rd House function. Without each function balanced and working with the other three, imbalance, pain, and psychological problems result.

## Horoscopic Factors

A horoscope is a map of the solar system at a specific place on the earth at a specific time: the birthplace and the first breath. It represents the holographic projector and film, the gross physical body and living cells that create and sustain the personal reality of the one specific person whose horoscope it is. It contains everything and everyone in that person's reality, from the point of view of that individual's ego persona or Point of Ascendant.

As soon as birth occurs, the potent archetypal energy-forms described by the signs, houses, and planets in the infant's horoscope begin to project out onto and manipulate all the individuals and events in the infant's reality: mother, father, siblings, doctor, nurses, grandparents, neighbors, strangers, and to receive and respond to their projections in turn. What the infant will draw out of each of these role players, either positive or negative, will be described in the infant's horoscope.

For example, a domineering, arrogant older brother will be unconsciously taking the role and living out Leo on the infant's 3rd House; Pisces on the infant's 10th House will require that Father be an escapist or weak in some way in the child's perception; the Sun in the infant's 7th House will draw magnanimous strangers throughout the infant's lifetime.

Everyone related to each one of us through blood, law, or role lives out for us a specific aspect of the Oneness that our horoscopes describe; each carries a specific message about how the section of the life or house of the horoscope that he or she represents is doing. It's all you, inside and outside. If you don't like the message the outer world carries for you, *only by changing yourself will you get the outer world to change.* No one outside of you is able to change as long as your unconscious projections on them are insisting they remain just as they are, even if you, the ego, hates how they are and desperately wants them to change.

Some years ago I was talking to an astrologer-colleague about this concept of Oneness and of everyone living out an aspect of us to show us ourselves, and she was heartily agreeing. But in a later conversation, when she began talking about her ex-husband and his hateful behavior toward her, I reminded her that that might be the message to her about herself. She angrily responded with, "Well, you can only take this so far!" Wrong! It must be taken *all the way,* to total responsibility, if you want your experienced reality to heal and change.

It seems difficult to own the Oneness. It is especially difficult *to own* those deeply suppressed or repressed aspects of ourselves that show themselves seemingly totally apart from ourselves as the murderers and thieves and other negative role players of the world. Who wants to acknowledge the Hitler or the Judas or the Manson aspect of oneself? But each of us is *everything,* has every potential of action. What we see outside ourselves is inside each of us. Each of us must acknowledge and take responsibility for his and her abilities to rape, pillage, maim, or murder, as well as the abilities to heal, love, give, and transform. A consciously aware being knows that he or she has the ability to do all these things, but the hurtful, destructive actions are just never chosen as expressions in life. When you experience the Oneness and it becomes fact for you, whom or what would you consciously choose to injure or hurt? It would be like the heart hurting the liver leading only to disease or death.

My only purpose as an astrologer is to help people recognize and begin their own unique spiritual paths. Although I am traditional in my approach, I keep up with current fashionable theories and techniques in astrology, and I use them when they make my current approach simpler, easier, and more accurate in terms of experienced reality. I find practical skepticism and a pragmatic approach to be useful tools for sorting out the truth from the nonsense in my reality. Truth is not fragile. It withstands severe testing.

I use geocentric tropical astrology and the Koch House cusps, finding these to coincide most accurately with my own and my clients' personal reality experiences. I have not found any life experience that this traditional approach does not account for, and with twelve signs, twelve houses, eight planets, the Sun and the Moon as infinitely interacting factors, astrology at its most basic is a complicated language. Therefore, I find no use in my practice for asteroids, Chiron, invisible planets, chart comparison, mid-points, or any mass-market religious system. In my experience, these seldom, if ever, lead to increased spiritual consciousness, freedom, or new choices for me or for those I have observed and worked with.

### The Gender Factor

There is one factor I use that is seldom addressed. This has to do with the fact that almost all the ancient texts from which our Western astrological knowledge has been derived were written for and about men, as women were regarded as mere chattel in those times. I find that the astrological rules regarding rulership, exaltation, detriment, and fall by both sign and house must be reversed for women, as well as how each house of the horoscope will accept and project energy. Men and women accept and project energy in opposite ways. The astrological factors a woman will assimilate and accept easily into consciousness, a man will not, and vice versa. For example, a man will easily make conscious and harmonious in his life a Mars in Aries or in the 1st House, where this same factor in a woman will cause acute crises and pain initially, and a woman with Moon in Scorpio or the 8th House will delight in her feminine, lunar principle, where a man with this lunar position will initially be plagued with negative, painful experiences with women who take the mother role for him. This fact is most easily observable in fraternal twins of opposite sexes who have almost identical birthtimes and who experience diametrically opposite life experiences. What begins as conscious in the female twin, begins as unconscious in the male.

### The Lack of Free Will

An uncomfortable fact that I embrace is that *free will is not a given*. We do not begin our existences with free will. If we did, no astrologer could ever read a horoscope. It would be impossible.

But it seems to me that we can evolve free will, step by step, by becoming conscious and aware. I have found that the more unconscious a client is, the easier his or her horoscope is to read and the more robotic or mechanical that person is, a person who reacts without any true conscious ability to act.

Our clever minds mask our lack of free will and conscious action by rationalizing after the fact. We respond puppet-like as the planets and signs move against our horoscopes, pushing our action buttons and causing our reactions. We then rationalize why we have done such and so, as if we had logically thought it all out in advance, but in my experience, as I have become more aware of myself and the energies that create and sustain me, more choices have developed in my life. Where twenty years ago life would lay ·a problem at my feet and give me only one door to go through, only one choice, after twenty years of meditating, choice seems to have expanded and I now have many more doors to choose from. This motivates me personally to continue the process of self-exploration, meditation, and change, scary though it may be, and to experience those fleeting moments of free will, which may only be my conscious cooperation with the Divine. At least I find that my horoscope has become less predictable, more difficult for my fellow astrologers to read. And this taste of freedom is exactly the bait I need to keep me moving toward consciousness and God.

When sitting down initially with each client, the astrologer must make an intuitive guess as to just what the client has done with his or her given horoscopic pattern up to that moment. What level of consciousness has the client achieved up to now? Just where is the client in his or her spiritual journey? How aware is the person of why he or she is alive, what must be done in this life? These questions can only be answered by the astrologer's intuition and spiritual insight. No amount of logic can answer them.

Although my central purpose in counseling others is spiritual, one doesn't begin at the top in helping others fully develop their spiritual paths and unite with God. You start from the ground up, as if you were building a house, a temple for God's dwelling. And ground means just that, the earth plane. How is the client's health? Diet? Is the work being done helping or hindering personal evolution? Is time being utilized efficiently? Is the client clear about Yes-No patterns, personal rules? How does the client deal with authority? What is the relationship with co-workers or employees? Is there willingness to give up marijuana use? What is the relationship to money and possessions? Are there food hang-ups? Focus is put on all the Earth Body areas, Earth Signs and Houses, and an examination of how Saturn and the earthly aspects of Mercury and Venus are expressing in the client's reality.

Many clients wonder why, when they have come to work with me on enhancement of their spiritual paths, I seem only to want to talk about what they are eating or how they are doing at work. I try to explain that building oneself spiritually is exactly the same as building a house, as we have discussed: it must be built from the bottom up. If constant money worries or pains from physical problems, catastrophic work situations, or fears are absorbing their attention, these things must be attended to first. In addition, spiritual change means physical change. If you want union with God, you must change your body in order to handle the experience.

When these physical plane things are under control, the next step is to train the monkey mind to act under the will and the heart, and to not push the ego around or constantly divert the spiritual goal with endless prattle. When thought is following and not leading the heart, then the emotions must be addressed next.

The metaphor of walking on water can be interpreted as having the emotions in such a solid, supportive condition that they furnish a strong base for the ego to operate from instead of trying to drown it. Attention to these aspects of the three lower bodies strengthens the ego persona so that it can endure transformation and union with the God force. Mother-Husband God is powerful. It is dangerous to those unprepared to receive its energy. You cannot safely miss steps. *Enoch walked with God and was not!* The union of the feminine-masculine God force with the ego is a harrowing horror to the unprepared and the most rapturous joy for those prepared to experience it.

## Inner Guides and Archetypes

In working with people, I rely exclusively on each individual's own personal Inner Guide to function as teacher and protector for the person. I alter my role as outer guide in initiation/meditation sessions in accordance with their Inner Guides' advice and principles, and I attempt to be as open as possible for use by the potential initiate's Inner Guide in my outer work with the person. The method of reaching one's Inner Guide is described at length in my book, *The Inner Guide Meditation: A Spiritual Technology for the 21st Century* (6th Edition, 1988, Samuel Weiser, Inc., York Beach, Maine), so I won't go into it here, but I do want to talk about how to recognize the true Guide from false guides in the horoscope and to mention all the other inner world speakers each of us must deal with in one way or another.

There are many inner speakers. Beside the false guides, there are the twenty-two Archetypes that are pictured in the Tarot, which represent the twelve Signs of the Zodiac, the eight planets and the Sun and Moon: Uranus/Fool, Mercury/Magician, Moon/High Priestess, Venus/Empress, Aries/Emperor, Taurus/ High Priest, Gemini/Lovers, Cancer/Chariot, Leo/Strength, Virgo/Hermit, Jupiter/Wheel of Fortune, Libra/Justice, Neptune/Hanged Man, Scorpio/Death, Sagittarius/Temperance, Capricorn/Devil, Mars/ Tower, Aquarius/Star, Pisces/Moon, Sun/Sun, Pluto/Last Judgement, and Saturn/World. These are the twenty-two aspects of God available to our everyday ego experience. They are the potent spiritual forces that create and sustain our individual realities. They pattern and relate to one another in each of us according to our horoscopes, and each has specific needs and expressions through us. Those in conflict at birth create the pain and difficulties of our lives, those in harmony, the joy, ease, and luck we experience.

Each speaker has a voice within us. Some contradict others or war within us. In addition to these twenty-two inner speakers or voices of God, we also have the false guide or guides. As an inner figure, it is represented by the 3rd House of the individual's horoscope as the 1st House or Ascendant of the false guide. The false guide is a personification of the mind and the rationalization system. This is the voice that usually comes through those who channel an inner entity for others. The false guide has no power to protect the ego. Neither does it help develop the individual's spiritual path, no matter how "spiritual" its words may sound. True Guides do not channel. Your Guide is not here to teach me or others. He is here to teach only you. False guides are not necessarily "evil," but they often correspond to the negative, unconscious aspects of Gemini/3rd House. They are often clever but superficial. They are tricksters. They lie or distort the truth. They volunteer information unasked and judge others readily. They encourage us to choose sides, and encourage our base competitive, non-cooperative aspects. But the most important aspect of a false guide is his or her inability to make spiritual progress and evolution safe. They encourage us to skip steps. They inflate our egos and tell us how special we are, how much better we are than other people, how we are right and others are wrong. No true Inner Guide would ever display any of these behaviors.

### Your Personal Inner Guide

The most important of the inner speakers when beginning on your own spiritual path is your own personal Inner Guide. He is described by the 9th House of your horoscope as his 1st House or Ascendant (utilizing geocentric astrology, Koch House cusps). Your first Inner Guide (there are six, all told) is always an unknown male figure in both men and women, probably because his ego corresponds to a male Sign, Sagittarius, a male House, the 9th, ruled by a male planet, Jupiter. (Some extreme feminists, perhaps because of a lack of understanding of the differences between Archetypes and Guides or that masculine and feminine energy must be equal and balanced, seem to have trouble with this fact, but the Guides lovingly and patiently endure their prejudice.) And when they do persist in meditation to insist that their first Guide be female, they end up with an Archetype—the High Priestess in Tarot and Moon in astrology, generally—for their guide, and their chauvinism becomes more acute as their lives and their difficulties with their masculine principles go more out of balance inside and out, requiring even more unconscious, negative behavior from the males in their realities.

As the first Guide is always male, so the fourth Guide is always female, corresponding in both men and women to a female House, the 12th, a female Sign, Pisces, ruled by a female planet, Neptune. (The second and third Guides are generally, but not always, male figures, and the fifth Guide is the same sex as the person. I have no solid experience with the sixth Guide to share at present.)

To see your initial Inner Guide's horoscope within your own, you turn your horoscope so that your 9th House becomes a 1st House, using the Koch House cusps. Thus you are looking at a twelve-house horoscope from the point of view of your 9th House. If you have your Sun in your natal 7th House in Capricorn, your first Inner Guide would have his Sun in his 11th House in Capricorn, hence he will have an Aquarian expression of his Capricornian solar nature. If your natal Moon is in Leo in your 3rd House, your Inner Guide's Moon would be in Leo in his 7th House. And the sign on your 9th House will be your Guide's Ascendant or Rising Sign, the Sign that conditions your Guide's appearance and personal ego expression. But the true test of one's true Inner Guide is the test of love. There is total unconditional love from one's Inner Guide. He totally accepts you and never judges you or others. If you don't feel that love and acceptance, you are not with your Inner Guide.

Working with your Inner Guide is important, both spiritually and practically. Your Inner Guide projects into and tries to work through anyone you select as a 9th House teacher figure. You will judge the outer world teacher to be as good or as bad a teacher for you in accordance to how well he or she allows your Inner Guide to express through him or her.

But outer teachers, therapists, counselors, and gurus are unfortunately always at least one step away from the Inner Guide source within yourself and carry the overlay of all their own karma, their horoscope patterns with all the consciousness and unconsciousness they include. How much truer and time-saving to work directly with your own Inner Teacher instead of filtering him through outer world teachers.

Additionally, no one knows you as well as your Inner Guide. He has been with you at least since you were born, knows all that you are, all your secrets and potentials. He knows not only your past and present, but all your future possibilities. He loves and accepts you wherever you are and never will judge you or others. He never interferes with your free will, except to try to keep you alive. And he knows the direction and goal of your spiritual path, what the safe steps are that you must take to be yourself and unite with God. Where could you find a more perfect Teacher?

In addition to the twenty-two pure Archetypes, these twenty-two potent spiritual energies can combine and recombine to make an infinite number of distinct and different forms. I have found it useful to invite some of these combination forms into visual consciousness and to interact with them in practical ways. Some I have found to be generally useful to most people. A primary combination figure is that of the Solar Center. It is composed of the Sun, its Sign, plus any planets conjunct the Sun, plus their Signs. For example, the Solar Center of someone with Sun conjunction Jupiter in Capricorn would be made up of three Archetypal figures, the Sun/Sun, Jupiter/Wheel of Fortune and Capricorn/Devil, combined into one male figure, because one's Sun Center is a masculine, yang form.

Another primary figure is that of the Lunar Construct or Inner Mother. She is composed of the Moon, her Sign, plus any planets conjunct the Moon and their Signs. In a Moon in Leo with no conjunctions, she would be a combination of the Moon/High Priestess and the Leo/Strength energies as one female figure, because one's Lunar Construct is a feminine, yin form.

### Shadow Figures

Two Shadow figures are also useful to work with. The Shadow side of the ego is pictured by turning the horoscope upside down so that the 7th House cusp becomes the Ascendant of a twelve-house horoscope. The Shadow develops in our inner planes as each of us develops an ego, between birth and seven years of age. The ego begins to develop as we begin separation from the Oneness at birth. The ego identifies with and is constructed out of certain elements of the All, and it rejects others. All the "I" elements become the ego. All the "Not-I" elements form the Shadow.

In Jungian analytical psychology, the Shadow is understood and worked with as a same-sex figure, but I have found working with both a same-sex and with an opposite-sex Shadow figure to be more useful. One's Shadows act to balance the ego inside and out. They contain all our unconsciousness, so that what is unconscious to your ego is conscious to your Shadows. If each of us has two built-in unconscious partners who know everything we don't know and see everything we don't see, what incredible allies they might be for us if we get to know and interact with them.

The male Shadow figure represents the active aspect of the Shadow side; the female, the receptive. I encourage those I work with in meditation with their Inner Guides to meet their two Shadow figures and make them literal life partners, equal partners, neither the ego nor the Shadows getting 51 percent of the votes, and to work with them as if they were actual, out-in-the-world practical partners. This begins the grounding that spiritual work requires and eases all one-to-one interactions in the outer life. Our Shadows are always attempting to balance our lives anyway. How much better for us if we get to know them and learn to cooperate in the balancing.

Let me give an example of how I work with people. Say I am working with a man for the first time who has been exclusively career-oriented his entire life. Suddenly, he has an inner urge to explore astrology and spirituality, and someone has mentioned my name to him. He calls for an appointment, having no idea of exactly how I work. I tell him that, before we can get together, I need him to do some family research. I ask him to research the pregnancy sequences on both sides of his family (no dates necessary), beginning with his maternal and paternal grandparents, then his parents, aunts, uncles, cousins, siblings, and the sequence of any pregnancies he himself has caused. I also ask that this be done with his partner's and/or ex-partner's families. I tell him it is important in this research to attempt to ascertain where abortions, stillbirths, or miscarriages come in these sequences, as these count as one slot each, and, if there are twins in the family, which was first-born, to make sure all sequences are as correct as possible. I tell him to do the best that he can in this research and to bring the written results to our first initiation session.

In the first session, I plug the entire family and all other role players into the specific house of the horoscope each belongs in by the traditional rules (Partner/7th House, Mother/4th House, Father/10th House, Sibling/3rd House, Child/5th House, as the building blocks). Many people initially react negatively to this aspect of how I work. The man might tell me that he's not the least bit interested in his family, has spent his life disconnecting from them, and, with the exception of his current wife and children, doesn't even want to think about the rest of his family or spend any time in our session focusing on any of them. I try to explain that these people related to him by blood, law, or role are important, not personally, but as barometers of specific aspects of his personal reality. Each shows him a different aspect of himself. It has nothing to do with his feelings toward or about any one or all of them. It is a way to see himself, outside of himself, without fooling himself. And it demonstrates the Oneness and connectedness of everything.

As he proceeds to meditate, change, and make conscious specifically different areas of his life, all the relatives and role players that are barometers of each life section will also change.

They will change *in fact*. It won't be that he just feels different toward them. They will begin to do new things, giving evidence to the man that the area they represent is becoming more conscious. For example, as he works with his two Shadow figures, he will find all his 7th House, outer-world Shadow figures changing and transforming—his wife, his ex-wife, his business partner, the child of the second pregnancy he caused, his third brother or sister (technically, the child of his mother's third pregnancy or the third pregnancy child of his father, not counting himself), the person suing him. *All of these people will show him the results of his own inner work with his Shadows, by taking more positive role behaviors toward him or by going out of his life.*

Let's look at how a transiting planet might communicate its degree of consciousness as it visits a client's natal 4th House. Let's say that Mars is the visitor. The client may report numerous crises, all happening at the same time: he has developed a stomach ulcer, his first child has badly cut his foot requiring stitches, he blew up suddenly at his second child for no apparent reason, his mother had a migraine attack, his father hurt his lower back, his house almost burned down, his boss's wife left him, and his friend was hospitalized with appendicitis, all within days of each other, each event having to do with the 4th House. The message here is clear. He was not conscious of the needs of the archetypal Mars force within his own Oneness, and, when Mars visited, he reaped the rewards of this unconsciousness.

## Communicating with the Archetypes

The Archetypes do express. They will take any expression we allow them. They operate by the spiritual physics of the universe, by universal law. There is no Jehovah sitting on a throne saying, "Punish that person" or "Reward this person." It's all up to each of us. We reap what we sow. We harvest the results of the degree of consciousness each Archetype has within us. Wherever we are unconscious, we will draw pain and negative experience. If we work on the Archetypes that cause our pain or negative experiences, and if we change ourselves to allow them to express in new ways, they do so. The same Mars energy that causes anger, violence, and competition when it's unconscious, brings the joy of life, exploration, and new starts when it's conscious. Mars doesn't care. It's an Archetype. It has an infinite spectrum of expression within its own archetypal limits on all levels of reality, in all the bodies of our four-body systems and throughout the universe.

Let's examine how the Archetypal energies communicate their consciousness status to you, house by house, in your horoscope. When you learn the language of astrology, its symbols and those outer world players that carry the messages of your astrological forces, the Archetypes, you can begin to experience the Oneness of yourself. Each symbol and each outer barometer carries specific information about you and your consciousness. Learning to read and experience the Oneness is essential to your union with the Divine. Remember, when I talk of a person as a barometer, I am talking about his or her ego as you perceive and judge it.

**The 1st House** of the horoscope is your ego or persona, whom you see in the mirror and who you think you are. But we don't seem to see ourselves as the whole of the 1st House, only as the Point of the Ascendant. Therefore, a woman with Libra Rising and Mars in Scorpio in the 1st House will see herself as peace-loving and harmonious, but others (7th House) will respond that she is somewhat pushy and aggressive. When she gets this feedback consistently over the years, she will come to believe it, even though she still can't quite see how she manifests the Mars behavior.

The 1st House also corresponds to your eyes and sight in general, your head, your physical brain, your upper jaw, your blood and your muscles. It describes or has to do with how you start things, your friends' cars, your outlook on life, all new ventures, your partner's lower back, your mother's profession, your boss's home, your mother's career, your anger, and your lover's and your children's spirituality, especially your first child's. Its barometers are your maternal grandfather, your paternal grandmother, your second child's partner (remembering to count any miscarriage or abortion as a pregnancy slot when numbering your children), your fifth child, your mother's authority figures, your partner's ex-partners, your first sibling's friends, your third sibling's partner, and your fifth Inner Guide (the same sex as you).

All of these people and things show you how your ego is doing. Female barometers show you the receptive aspect of the life area they vibrate to: the male show the active aspect. Eye problems or headaches could be message that the ego is unconscious about something that involves it directly, that you are not seeing something about yourself that others see easily.

**The 2nd House** corresponds to your ears, mouth, lower jaw, chin, vocal cords, neck, throat, and the base of your skull. It describes or has to do with your income, earnings, stocks and bonds you may possess, food, movable possessions, jewelry, talents, abilities you can exchange for money or food, your friends' homes, your third child's health, your father's first sibling's car or other vehicle, your lover's profession, your first child's profession, banks, banking, the general health of your spiritual teachers, secrets of your first sibling, budgets, debts owed to you, the kind of voice you have and how it sounds, hearing, listening, your partner's sexuality, what your partner owes, your father's creative expression, your first child's profession, and the spirituality of your coworkers or employees. Its barometers are all bankers, your father's second sibling, your mother's second sibling's partner, your lover's father, your first child's boss, your first child's mother-in-l.aw, your fourth child's father-in-law, your boss's first child, the partner of your mother's second sibling, your mother's friends, and your sixth Inner Guide. Thus a money problem could be the message that you don't listen or that the food you are taking in is totally wrong for who and where you are.

**The 3rd House** corresponds to the hands, arms, shoulders, lungs, the bronchi, nerves and nervous system, and all the connectors of the body. It describes or has to do with your thinking, logic, rationalization system, how you speak and use your voice, writing, gossip, lying, information, theories, your questions, your curiosity, journals, how you learn, your manual dexterity, the educational experiences you will have in grammar school and high school, your car or vehicle and how you drive, the media, paper, books, magazines and periodicals, newspapers and the news, computers, the mails, tape recorders, telephones and communication devices, letters and correspondence, the written aspect of agreements, automatic writing, channeling, your father's health, your second child's spirituality and college experience, your partner's spirituality, your boss's health, your employees' or coworkers' views of you, and short trips you take. Its barometers are your sixth child, your third child's partner, your first sibling, and your siblings in general, the kind of teachers you will have in grammar and high school, the kind of students you would have, how you are as a student, the partner of your partner's first sibling, your coworkers' or employees' fathers, your neighbors, acquaintances, your first child's friends, your friends' children in general, the first child of each in particular, the partners of your spiritual teachers and your friends' lovers. Thus car troubles could be a message that something is wrong in your logic box, that your mind is not functioning as it should. New cars always correspond to new ways of thinking or an influx of new ideas.

**The 4th House** corresponds to the stomach, breasts, uterus, womb, all the protective coverings of the physical body, like the pleura of the lungs or the eye's casing, and how a woman carries a child during pregnancy. It describes or has to do with your security needs, the things you feel support you, your emotions, your home, your city, your country, conditions at the end of your life, your old age, your real estate, all containers, domesticity, your friends' health, the sexuality of your spiritual teachers, your second child's career and view of authority figures, your partner's view of your mother, your third child's sexuality, your partner's career, your first sibling's income, your heritage from the past, the collective mass of humanity, your first child's secrets, how all things end for you, memory and your genetic roots. Its barometers are your family in general, your mother, your father-in-law, your second child's mother-in-law, stepmothers, foster mothers, your partner's boss, your father's third sibling, your father's first sibling's first child, your second child's boss, your co-workers or employee's friends and your boss's partner. A problem with memory or your stomach might indicate something not worked out with your mother or living in an environment that doesn't work for the whole of you.

**The 5th House** corresponds to the heart, upper back, and circulatory system. It describes or has to do with your ability to give love, your self-expression, your creativity, your inner child, your hobbies, your acting ability, how you play and what is fun for you, all games and recreation, happiness, vacations, romance, gambling for amusement or pleasure, clubs that have to do with pleasure (yacht clubs, for example), your first sibling's car or vehicle, your father's sexuality, your mother's money, your boss's sexuality, love affairs and all the things that bring you joy. Its barometers are lovers (if you don't live or conceive a child together), your children in general, your first pregnancy child or the first child you father, your second sibling (counting all miscarriages and/or abortions), your friends' partners, your partner's second sibling's partner and your partner's friends. A heart condition could be a message that the love-creative flow is blocked and needs expression, that you're not having any fun.

**The 6th House** corresponds to the intestines, colon, and the assimilative function. It describes or has to do with your practical, common sense and how you apply what you know, as well as your work methods, facts, tools, jobs you take (as differentiated from your 10th House career), your selectivity, your working conditions, labor unions, the armed services, your general health, your diet, your critical abilities, your ability to analyze, magic of all varieties, your mother's car or vehicle, your pets, domestic animals, your father's spirituality, your first sibling's home and family life, your first child's income, your lover's money, your second child's secrets, your third  child's career, your hygiene, cleanliness in general, cloth and clothing, craft abilities, healing abilities, purity, the option of virginity, medicine, nutrition, and vegetable gardens. Its barometers are all tenants, all service people (waiters, waitresses, mechanics, physicians, market clerks, etc.), your first sibling's father-in-law, your mother's siblings in general, her first sibling in particular, your third child's boss, and your fourth child's partner. A constant problem with co-workers could indicate that your diet is wrong for you, or that you are being careless about how you work.

**The 7th House** corresponds to the lower back and lumbar region, the kidneys, the loins, and the ovaries. It describes or has to do with all your one-to-one relationships, comparative thinking, contracts and agreements, alliances, marriage and divorce , your lover's car or vehicle, coworkers' money, lawsuits, flowers, politics, your fourth child's sexuality, your friends' spirituality, your father's career and reputation, peace and war, your father's second sibling's health, your first child's car or vehicle and your social affairs. Its barometers are your second pregnancy child or the second child you father (generally the most difficult), all astrological clients, anyone you counsel, all business customers, politicians, arbitrators, rivals, robbers, marriage partners, marriage ex-partners, business partners (only while they are legal partners), roommates (only while they are roommates), your third sibling, your peers, theatrical agents, your paternal grandfather, your maternal grandmother, your third child's friends, lovers you live with or conceive with (whether the pregnancy comes to term or not), jury members, open enemies, those who sue you, competitors, all strangers (anyone who has no other role slot), your boss's boss, and any opponent. Lower back pain might be the message that you are out of touch with your own Shadow side and that all one-to-one relationships need your attention.

**The 8th House** corresponds to the genitals, reproductive system, excretory system, anus, rectum, bladder, sinuses, sweat glands and the body's immune system. It describes or has to do with irreversible change, transformation, your sexuality (as contrasted with your love-giving ability), sexual passion, astral projection, astral experiences, obsessive-compulsive behavior, your partner's money, neighbor's pets, employee's and coworkers vehicles, other people's money, debts you owe, taxes, death and the dead, kundalini experiences, dowries, inheritance, legacies, insurance, your detection abilities, your nosiness, your second child's money, your first child's home and family life, your second sibling's home and family life, your third sibling's money, your first sibling's health, the occult, rebirth, your rage, leather and dead bone, sexual experiences and/or abuse, wills, grants, bequests and money available to you from others. Its barometers are your mother's second sibling, your father's friends, your friends' bosses, your father's second sibling's partner, the director of a group you belong to, your stepmother's children in general and her first child specifically (if your father didn't adopt her children), your first child's father-in-law and your fourth child's mother-in-law. Sinus problems could be a message that your sexual flow is clogged in some way or that you are using your sexuality unconsciously.

**The 9th House** corresponds to the liver and hepatic system, the sciatic nerves, buttocks, hips and thighs. It describes or has to do with your concept of God, your unique spiritual path, your intuition, philosophy, religion, wisdom, life direction, your trial and error learning abilities, your mother's health, your experimental abilities, procrastination, self-indulgences, experience in foreign lands, churches and temples, long journeys, your partner's car or vehicle, your third sibling's car or vehicle, your second child's car or vehicle, immigration, publishing, higher learning (past the high school level), experiences at colleges and universities, prayer, meditation, prophetic abilities, and hunches. Its barometers are your first Inner Guide (a male), all counselors and spiritual teachers, college and university teachers, your coworkers' or employees' mothers, your friends' friends, your lover's first child, your first sibling's partner, your partner's first sibling, your third child (generally the easiest), your first child's lovers, your grandchildren in general, your fourth sibling, and your first child's first child. Problems with procrastination might be cured by giving more rigorous attention to your spiritual area.

**The 10th House** corresponds to the knees, the living bones in general, the joints of the body, the skin, hair, teeth, and nails. It describes or has to do with your career, all professional matters, your reputation, your judgment of the outer world, the world's judgments of your achievements, honors that come to you, worldly success and attainment, time, schedules, your rules, what you say "No" to, your community standing, fame or notoriety, your fears and paranoias, the establishment, government, your lover's health, your friends' secrets, your second sibling's health, your first sibling's sexuality, your first child's health, your third child's money, your second child's home and family life, your place in society, your position in the world, and your material plane power. Its barometers are your second Inner Guide, your father, stepfathers, foster fathers, any policeman and policewoman, your boss, all authority figures, your mother-in-law, your second child's father-in-law, your employees' or co-workers' lovers, your mother's third sibling, and your mother's first sibling's first child. An arthritis problem might be a message that you are judging and separating from others in a way that is destructive to yourself, or perhaps that your time is too loosely or too tightly structured.

**The 11th House** corresponds to the ankles, calves, shins, the lower legs, the circulation and the body's electrical system. It describes or has to do with your end goals (the things you want to have done by the time you die), gestalt thinking, groups you belong to that have similar end goals to yours, corporations and all corporate structures, cooperation, humanity perceived as cooperating, evolving individuals, friendship, your father's money, your partner's creativity and self-expression, your employees' or co-workers' health, your mother's sexuality, your boss's income, your first sibling's spirituality, freedom, your hopes and wishes, co-ops and your objectives. Its barometers are your third Inner Guide, your friends, fellow members of any group you join having to do with your end goals, your fourth child, your first child's partner, your second sibling's partner, your second child's lovers, your first child's second child and your lover's ex-partner. Perceiving your partner as unloving might indicate that your own goals are too unconscious, that you haven't really sat down and decided where you want your life to go.

**The 12th House** corresponds to the feet, toes, and the lymphatic system. It describes or has to do with your deepest-level dreams, your psychic abilities, visions, mystical experience, all the Archetypes, dance, film, poetry, music, privacy, wild animals, rest homes, reformatories, hospitals, prisons, sanitariums, asylums, monasteries and convents, charity, compassion, seclusion, your synthesizing ability, the ability to see the common thread that runs through everything, secrets, drugs in general, escapism, illusion and delusion, sensitivity, maya and projection, fear where the cause is unknown, hoaxes, mediumship, intoxication, past lives in general, last life in particular, potential, intrigue, sleep, victim roles, prostitution, anesthetics, your lover's sexuality, your second child's health, your first sibling's career, your lover's sexuality, your partner's health, your third child's home and family life, your boss's car, your mother's spirituality, your friends' money, your first child's sexuality, your second sibling's sexuality and your father's car or vehicle. Its barometers are your fourth Inner Guide (a female) your employee's and co-workers' partners, your first sibling's boss, your father's siblings in general, his first sibling in particular, secret friends or enemies, your third child's father-in-law, your partner's and your second child's co-workers or employees, your first sibling's mother-in-law and your mother's first sibling's partner. Sleep disturbances or health difficulties in your partner could indicate that something is really wrong in your deep unconscious. Problems in the 12th House require time alone and meditation to correct. Peculiarly, often going to more movies in theaters clears up 12th House problems temporarily. Film theaters seem to fulfill the sanctuary needs that churches fulfilled in earlier times but don't seem to any more.

I have given these symbols and barometers of each astrological house, because I have found it useful for my own personal spiritual development to learn the Archetypes' symbolic language and expressions and to pay conscious attention to what the various barometers in my personal reality are doing and how they are handling their lives. The idea of Oneness begins as just that, an idea. One needs to get used to thinking in terms of Oneness. You begin your early life with the Gemini mind making reality seem clearly separate from you. Life seems to be happening *to you*, not *from you*. But, if your horoscope works, everything is a message to you about yourself. Nothing happens by chance. Modern physics is correct: reality is a hologram that your Archetypes project twenty-four hours a day. Each person and event carries a specific message to you from one or more of your Archetypes about an aspect of yourself. If you don't like the message, if what you are experiencing is difficulty and painful, the only way to change it is to seek out the sources and make the changes within yourself with the help of your Inner Guide.

If you accept and act on the message when it is still far away from you, it won't have to get any closer. But if you ignore the messages your reality sends you, it must get closer and closer, first as something happening to an acquaintance, then someone at work, then a distant relative, then a brother or sister, and finally, one of your own children. If you still don't listen, the unconscious Archetype has to hit you on the head in the form of an accident or a sickness you experience. Archetypes don't care. They are the impersonal forces of God, operating according to the spiritual physics of the universe. They will take any expression you give them, conscious or unconscious. It's up to you. Long before a sickness or disaster occurs, warning was given and ignored that a certain Archetype within you *needed consciousness.*

If you want a new reality, a healed planet, a cooperating, loving community, a government for all the people, you must change. You must change all the way down to the cellular level. You must give your Archetypes new expressions and allow all your outer barometers to take new, positive roles for you. And you must trust your Inner Guide and your Center to protect you and take care of you during your process of evolution and change.

The job each of us has now seems to be to spiritualize the material, to infuse the physical plane with the energy of spirit, so that the planet and her people can be healed. We are faced with the possible extinction of our species, and we have created governments too short-sighted and greedy to acknowledge this fact. The ozone layer diminishes, the rain-forests are being depleted, the oceans are polluted, AIDS is rampant, over-population gets worse, radioactive waste increases, and more. The earth is the outer symbol of our physical bodies; the ocean, of our physical blood. *We have the symptoms of the dying.* If the earth you experience represents the practical and spiritual Oneness that is you, where are you? How did you get in such bad shape? And what are you going to do about it?

Only by changing and healing yourself will you change and heal your planet. No amount of activism or protesting can change the reality message your Archetypes are sending you. You must bravely seek out the sources of the pollution, the greed, the lack of caring, the destruction, the sickness, the self-indulgence, the lack of control, the hate and separation within yourself. Then you must discover how you must change, what you must do that is new, to allow the Archetypes to express in a new, more conscious way in your reality. Only you can change the world, and only through changing yourself. The responsibility is total. There is no out. No one else is going to do the work for you.

No Aquarian Age is about to come along and save you. The Aquarian Age doesn't begin until 2813 AD when the Point of the Vernal Equinox touches the first star in the constellation Aquarius. You must still work with and learn the lessons of the Piscean Age, the lessons of compassion, sensitivity, charity, self-sacrifice, understanding of how reality is projected, overcoming of delusion, development of the psychic function and the recognition of the common thread that connects all humanity: *that we are one another.*

But you do have major helpers, teachers and protectors: your Inner Guides. Meet with your first Guide and begin your clean-up campaign. Heal and transform the inner Archetypes with your attention, respect, and love. When healed within, they will show you the results of their healing in your outer world.

**Steven Forrest**

An early fascination with telescopes and astronomy led Steven Forrest to begin exploring astrology. He received a B.A. in religion in 1971 from the University of North Carolina at Chapel Hill, and shortly thereafter he began to establish his astrological practice.

In 1984 Bantam Books released his first book, *The Inner Sky.* That volume was followed in 1986 by *The Changing Sky.* In 1988, with his wife, Jodie, he published the third volume of the "Sky" trilogy, *Skymates.* All three volumes are now available through ACS Publications, San Diego, CA.

Additionally, Steven has written technical articles for most of the major astrological journals, and composed the popular "The Sky Within" report writer for Matrix Software. His work has been translated into several languages, and he travels widely throughout the United States and Canada, lecturing on astrological topics. He has just completed his fourth book, to be published by ACS in 1993. Entitled *The Night Speaks,* it is an extended argument for the intellectual and philosophical plausibility of astrology.

Steven won the 1985 Professional Astrologers Incorporated Award for "Outstanding Contribution to the Art and Science of Astrology." He lives in the woods near Chapel Hill, NC with his wife.

# The Quest Motif in the Ninth House

**Steven Forrest**

In all the world's literature, there are a handful of stories, told over and over again:

- Boy meets girl . . .
- Looks bad for the good guys, but the good guys pull it off . . .
- Naivete draws betrayal, turns to wisdom . . .

You know the tales; you've seen them in theaters, read them, heard them, probably dreamed them. And even on the shortest list of these "literary motifs," one invariably encounters the theme of the Quest. In common with all the other fundamental human stories, the Quest motif is subject to endless embroidery, countless individual variations, and myriad narrative twists and turns. Thus, despite the ultimate symmetry of the tales, our interest never palls. Still we can distinguish two common elements which must be present for an account truly to qualify as a representative of the Quest genre.

- There is a "journey"; the protagonist is seeking something in the outer world.
- There is an inward transformation; the protagonist is faced with an opportunity to "die and be reborn."

Either of these two undertakings may be successful or unsuccessful. The second one may be conscious or unconscious, in either case. Yet always there are two levels: outward seeking and inward becoming.

Thus, the Knights of the Round Table seek the Holy Grail. Some of them find courage. Odysseus seeks home after his shipwreck and finds a tempering of his brash spirit. Frodo Baggins, the hobbit in J. R. R. Tolkien's *The Lord of the Rings* seeks the Cracks of Doom and finds wisdom, dignity, and self-respect.

- Outward journey; inward metamorphosis.

Rambo, by contrast, is typically an insensitive, self-absorbed phallocrat at the beginning of his film odysseys, and thus he remains as the credits roll. It may be a story, but it's not the Quest. One never has the sense at any point that there is a notable prospect for his attaining much beyond the level of the iguana on the evolutionary ladder.

- No possibility of inner transformation, no Quest.

My premise in the pages that follow is that this elemental part of our human story, the Quest Motif, is the blood running in the veins of 9th House symbolism, and that all other interpretations of that House derive ultimately from it.

Place yourself imaginatively in a little village in northern Italy in the fourteenth century. You are an astrologer, as was your father. You are of course also a Catholic; and in your opinion, God is a Catholic too. You could not find much argument on that score anywhere in local society. Your musty volumes of Ptolemy inform you that the 9th House represents "Far Journeys." Experience bears out the ancient wisdom: you observe that among your clients born with that house tenanted, there is an elevated tendency toward geographic mobility. Giovanni, the Baker, with his Moon there, once saw Rome. Bettina with her Venus in the 9th married a rich man from far Napoli and now lives on the slopes of Vesuvius in splendor. Ptolemy says its true, and practical astrological experience supports him. You are content; the 9th House means travel.

Now reincarnate. You are an illiterate bargeman in the Thames in the early nineteenth century. Gazing at the stars at night fills you with an urge to know and learn. Laboriously, you teach yourself to read, and begin your study of astrology. As your erudition advances, you encounter teachers. In a decade, you are practicing astrological divination in the homes of the wealthy and the connected. Your own birthchart, you learned long ago, displays a stellium in the 9th House.

And yet travel has not figured prominently in your biography. What *has* figured there? Stretching, learning, expanding . . . coming to know that the idea that "God is a Catholic" may fall short of the entire truth.

Life has many horizons, not all of them geographical. In fourteenth century Italy, and in fact in most places throughout history, the world for the majority of people was a narrow, one-dimensional place, at least culturally. Societies were relatively monolithic. Travel was perilous, prohibitive in cost, and socially almost unprecedented. Still if a man or woman felt a compelling hunger to *see something different,* there was essentially only one option: get out of town. Run away. And astrologers throughout history have observed an association between that itchy-footed quality and activated 9th House symbolism.

As the nineteenth century dawned, printing became cheaper and education began to be more democratically available. Astrologers shifted some of the interpretive weight from 9th House "Long Journeys Over Water" toward 9th House "Educational Endeavors." This accurately reflected, I believe, a real change in the way the basic archetype of the House was actually being experienced. Either way, the concern centered on stretching beyond one's accustomed horizons: "questing," in some sense of the word.

Nowadays, as astrology has come to be articulated in more psychological and motivational terms, the 9th House might be defined as the human desire *to break up routines.* There is something in us all that hungers for variety, something that craves adventure and fresh experience, something that winces at the thought of living a safe, boring life followed by a polite, solvent death. That, at least emotionally, is the essence of the House: a Questing spirit in you, me, and everyone else, something that likes the look of those white lines running down the open highway at dawn.

All the foregoing considerations draw on the mainstreams of astrological thought, but they flesh out only one of the two elements of Quest symbolism: the outward journey, which may be geographical, experiential, or intellectual.

What of the second dimension? What of the inner transformation? What of the Grail itself? Let's dig more deeply into the astrological lore we've inherited.

Horoscopic tradition, ancient and modern, underscores another piece of 9th House symbolism: religion and philosophy. Charles E. O. Carter adds, "It has bearing on man's moral ideals and conscience." (*The Principles of Astrology*, Theosophical, 1925.) And what do such concerns signify? To begin to frame an answer, let's ask another question: what is the *result* of our "questing" in the world—our travels, our cross-cultural experiences, our efforts, accredited or otherwise, toward educating ourselves? We begin to detect *patterns* in human experience. We begin, inevitably, to learn about life.

A fair distinction can be made between religion and spirituality, with the former being essentially an attempt to account reasonably for the latter. "Religion" and "Philosophy" in the 9th House sense always involve an effort to understand life, to impute meaning to it. And there, in a nutshell, we have the heart of the second dimension of 9th House symbolism: the Holy Grail we seek is nothing less than the Meaning of Life.

The Meaning of Life! At the phrase, cynics groan while the eyes of the innocent grow misty and knowing. Perhaps the most elemental observation regarding the worldview implicit in astrology is that each person's experience, each person's reality, is different and distinct. That principle applies here in letters a mile high. For each of us, the Meaning of Life is a personal, individual question. And yet, for all its seeming abstraction, a pressing one. Life without meaning is—meaningless. Human beings cannot sustain energy and verve without feeling some larger sense of purpose in their existences.

After speaking of all our basic animal appetites and of our more obvious emotional hungers, the psychologist Abraham Maslow writes, "Even if all these needs are satisfied, we may still often (if not always) expect that a new discontent and restlessness will soon develop, unless the individual is doing what *he*, individually, is fitted for. A musician must make music, an artist must paint, a poet must write . . . he must be true to his own nature." (*Motivation and Personality*, Harper and Row, 1954, pg. 46) This kind of "meaningful" life, for Maslow, is inextricably bound to following one's own path through the world, and more basically, simply to knowing that path.

"Knowing one's own path"—aiding individuals in their efforts in that department is arguably the core purpose of the entire astrological edifice. Certainly, we cannot separate any discrete area of planetary symbolism and say, "This represents Joe's path, and the rest does not." The 9th House is not the "path" per se; that's the whole chart taken in concert. The 9th House represents *how to find* one's path: a far more definable and distinct question. Certain kinds of "quests" in the outer world seem alchemically to trigger in particular individuals a sense of having arrived at a view of life and one's place in it that consistently and satisfyingly "fits." In that observation, we come to the practical core of 9th House Quest symbolism in its second, more inward level.

In Tarot symbolism as interpreted by Dr. Arthur Edward Waite (1857-1942), one card is called "The Fool" and is given the number zero. It depicts a young man "off to seek his fortune." He carries his belongings in a sack at the end of a stick borne over his shoulder; he gazes heavenward; in his left hand he carries a white rose. He is about to step over the edge of a cliff. Soon he will discover the implications of that fact, and presumably his beatific expression will undergo a cataclysmic reorganization. The image is entertaining. It can almost be read as a cartoon. And yet the idea it represents is profound, and right in the crosshairs of 9th House symbolism. There is at the beginning of any enterprise an inevitable naivete which only experience will cure. "The Fool" thus does not symbolize stupidity, but rather ignorance—two qualities which are often hard to distinguish, but which are utterly distinct both in origin and prognosis.

In terms of our "paths," in terms of our own knowledge of who we actually are, all of us start out life as Fools in Dr. Waite's sense. We must, in the eternal phrase, "seek our fortunes," although fortune here has a larger significance than the one which might arise intuitively in the mind of Donald Trump. It is more akin perhaps to the word "vision"—some set of core principles, more felt than understood, which are invariably reflected in those existential choices which prove meaningful and satisfying for a given individual, and which are notably removed from those choices, however moral and practical, which prove transitory and forgettable.

Reading the literature of astrology as it existed before, say, the Beatles, one is generally struck by its lack of psychological sophistication. There are exceptions, of course: Dane Rudhyar's work, that of Grant Lewi. But generally there is a blissful ignorance regarding problematic emotional states, let alone one's relationship with the unconscious mind.

• This attitude, so distinct in the literature earlier in the lifetimes of people now living, was almost universal in the previous century and before. The older fashions in astrology tended to be practical and concrete; Mars in the 1st House meant red hair and a scar on the face, period. There was some psychological typing of people as "Saturnine" or "Mercurial" but very little of the depth analysis which is currently fashionable.

That astrology has undergone a psychological revolution in the last few decades is a truism. For whatever the value of my own opinion, I applaud that development and have done my best to further the trend in my own "Sky" trilogy. But we must strive to avoid the near-unavoidable pitfall of imagining that all history is an attempt, through the glass darkly, to see what we now observe so clearly and unprejudicially. Modern "psychological" astrology reflects the zeitgeist of the era as unerringly as do four-thousand-year-old etchings on Mesopotamian clay.

• Assurbanipal, King of Assyria (668-626 B.C.), was informed, "When Mercury culminates in Tammuz, there will be corpses." (Toonder and West, *The Case For Astrology*, Penguin, 1973). Similarly, a modern individual might with equal authority be told that, "Intense inner frustration and a feeling of weakness and powerlessness are two of the more difficult side-effects of Mars-Saturn contacts, and it often becomes necessary for the individual to impose his will on others in a forceful way because he is so afraid that he will be imposed upon and controlled himself." (Liz Greene, *Saturn: A New Look at an Old Devil*, Weiser, 1976, p. 117).

Can one perspective be called "provincial" and "specific to its era" while the other is revered as truth beyond time or fashion? Intuitively, such an attitude seems dubious. And we search history in vain for evidence of anything of philosophical consequence ever being finally "settled."

Our present astrological bias toward psychological, internal, emotional concerns has had many rather obvious benefits. But it has, I believe, inhibited our ability to understand clearly the logic of the 9th House. For the Quest, as we have seen, has *two* dimensions, one inward and one outward. And without the outward extremities, the inner state is not realized. For modern practitioners, a temptation arises to imagine that if only the inner "Grail" were realized psychologically, then the outer journey would be recognized as superfluous and somehow "shallow," and that, I believe, is a fatal cognitive error.

A simple analogy: a client of mine with the Sun and three planets in the 9th announces her intention of journeying to India to study meditation and yoga. Good-naturedly, a friend afflicts her with the following bug-in-the-ear: "Gee, off to India to find God! I'm jealous . . ." Then, mock-wistfully, "I sure wish God had offices here in North Carolina!"

And of course, as we all know, God does.

The implication, equally clearly, is that there is something wrong-headed about anyone feeling the need to "go somewhere" to do "inner work." We may lose the car keys, but we never really lose the mind. Wherever we go, it's right there between our ears . . . and presumably available to adjustment.

Yet, for my 9th House client, the trip proved catalytic, leading to a professional reorientation. As is so often the case under 9th House symbolism, the outer Quest led serendipitously to inward understanding. I say "serendipitously" because the inward developments were not foreseeable in any way, or even very easy to link logically to the realities of the trip to India.

The critical point: the *mere act* of journeying, or otherwise moving outside the bounds of the familiar, shakes up old attitudes, disrupts customary patterns of thought, and unleashes the expression of previously-unconscious factors.

How? Through what mechanism? A complete answer may be unreachable, but certain observations can be made with confidence. We are all creatures of habit, our behaviors linked through time-honored patterns of stimulus and response to our accustomed environments. Place us in new circumstances, and old behaviors are less useful or relevant. The creative, adaptive intelligence is re-engaged. Inevitably, new and uncharacteristic expressions arise.

But we can go deeper. Napoleon is alleged to have said, "History is a lie agreed upon." I suspect he was correct, but he only hit upon the tip of the iceberg. The larger truth is that, to a great extent, "Reality itself is a lie agreed upon." The sentence is perhaps overly polemical, but the point is that each culture and each individual within that culture creates a "model of the world"—a "religion"—which is imagined to be equivalent to "The Facts," and which, from the perspective of history, is almost invariably recognized to be comically wrong.

This situation is not correctable. Translating reality into the perceptual coordinate systems of the human psyche is like drawing a sphere on a piece of paper: the best anyone, even Rembrandt, can do is get "close." Still, something eternal within us cannot help but build models, cannot help but "connect the dots." That pattern-seeking, pattern-recognizing, pattern-creating function in human psychology is represented astrologically by the 9th House. It is about *understanding,* and understanding is always to some extent fictional.

Yet we don't live in the "real world." We live in the fictional world we experience, the one in which we believe. We all, inescapably, live our religions. I go to a party, and upon observing a certain guest, my inner monologue may go something like this: "Hmmm . . . Virgo with Cancer overtones and a dash of Jupiter . . ." The Freudian might be thinking, "Anal, with mother-dominance themes and repressed grandiosity . . ." The broker, meanwhile, reflects, "$30,000-$45,000 . . ."

How do we get at those attitudes that underlie our view of the world? How do we change them, let them grow, shake them up? Short of the sort of psychopharmacological interventions Nancy Reagan was known to lament, how might we open wide "the doors of perception?"

Shock. That's the answer. The shock that arises when totally incongruous perceptions flood the psyche. The shock of the unexpected, the alien, the astonishing—9th House phantasmagoria.

Psychologists call it "cognitive dissonance." Seasoned travelers, open to adventuring away from the tourist buses, call it "culture shock." Researchers, the light-bulb of intellectual illumination going supernova over their heads, call it "breakthrough." Call it what you want, but it is the heart of the 9th House, the fire that drives it, the air it breathes, and the ground on which it stands.

Again: the Quest. The outer journey transforms the interior landscape. Experience drives realization, and shock throws it into hyperspace. Exotic, unexpected experience shatters assumptions—and the assumptions most prone to shattering are the ones least fundamental to one's elemental identity; that is to say, those assumptions that originate not in the soul but in the family, in the community, on the cultural roulette wheel.

There is another level to 9th House symbolism, darker and more sinister. As is eternally the case, no positive response to any astrological structure is ever guaranteed, only offered as a possibility. A man or woman might respond to the potentials woven into a 9th House configuration in an unconscious or unimaginative way, one motivated essentially by fear. And the result, regardless of the planets and signs involved, is always the same: a species of narrow-minded fanaticism inevitably comes to dominate that person's worldview. Depending on other horoscopic factors, that fanaticism may express itself noisily, even violently, or in smug, silent certainty. But without the leavening effect of the outer Quest, such rigidity will reliably appear, as certainly as air will rush to fill a vacuum, and for much the same reason.

Human beings do not choose to make sense of life; the function is autonomous, a by-product of brain functioning. As we expressed it above, something inside us all is compelled to "connect the dots," putting our perceptual field into some kind of order. You wake up in a strange room, perhaps a little disoriented. For a moment, your depth perception is awry. You see as a new-born sees: an orderless nonsense world of colors and shapes. Almost instantly, something "clicks" and the familiar three-dimensional interpretation kicks in. Welcome back to . . . is it reality, or is it the "lie agreed upon?" Either way, it is the brain reflex astrologers call normal 9th House functioning.

The point is, we all have 9th Houses. Every one of us carries an internal model of the world. Every one of us is "religious." It's as certain and as inevitable as our having an affinity for water, oxygen, and the sort of chocolate for which the Lord made our taste buds.

Back to connecting the dots. We all do it. But, like the old sky-maps with their fanciful constellations, there are lots of legitimate and compelling ways to link the same bright stars. Where Americans see a Big Dipper, the English see a Plow . . . and similarly, looking at the same burned-out ghetto, conservatives see liberal programs run amuck while liberals with equal sincerity and confidence see conservative programs run amuck.

Upon which 9th House lie will we agree? By reflex, we'd prefer not to agree on any lie, but instead to "know the truth." Ultimately, that may be an unreachable ideal. Still, it's a worthy one, and the North Star of any healthy 9th House Quest. Yet the mind is intellectual, the dot-connecter, while the "Truth" isn't about "dots." It isn't about cognitive constructions. "Knowing the truth" is actually an oxymoron, like "painting a symphony." We can't do it, yet it is in our natures to try.

Damned if we do, damned if we don't? Yes, but there's a saving principle: the more dots we connect, *the truer is our model.*

And what are the "dots?" Experiences: the life-blood of the outer Quest.

It is a reliable maxim that prejudice, dogmatism, and fanatical certainty thrive in information-poor environments. The surest way, for example, of maintaining an assurance that all Manchurians are odiferous dwarves with wicked smiles is to arrange never to meet one. Not all of us, praise the Buddha, are subject to an inclination toward that kind of racial typing, but what underlies it is in fact fundamental to us all: again, the 9th House hunger to "make sense" of this incomprehensible, miraculous world.

All horoscopes must, by necessity, contain a 9th House. Even if we are born with that sector of the chart untenanted, it will undoubtedly undergo frequent stimulation through the medium of the major transits, progressions, and arcs. And all of us must inescapably have a sign on the cusp of the house, and likely some significant midpoints, asteroids, comets, undiscovered planets and planetoids, not to mention heretofore unimagined points of astrological sensitivity, will lurk there, invisibly. It is relevant to everyone, in other words. But for those of us born with planets in the house, the Quest with its attendant joys and quagmires naturally has an elevated significance.

# Interpretation of 9th House Planets

A planet occurs in a client's 9th House. How do we translate the foregoing theoretical perspective, our discussion so far, into sensible, meaningful language for that person?

Planets are perceptual faculties. One can "see the world" through the eyes of Saturn, for example. Then, the volume is turned up on hard facts, one's awareness of risks, one's need for self-sufficiency and independence in the face of life's quandaries and dilemmas. Such perceptions are always there to be had, naturally. But it is the Saturn function in a person that actually sees on that wavelength. Such perceptions might go right by Neptune, as invisible and unnoticed as an electron. On the other hand, Neptune might well tune in loudly and clearly to a creative inspiration or an intuitive message—one that Saturn might miss.

*In a nutshell, the planet in the 9th House is the perceptual faculty most suited to the construction of a meaningful philosophy of life for that individual.*

Interpretively, there are several tacks an astrologer might take in developing and presenting that notion:

- He or she might present the 9th House planet as a wise "teacher" whose teachings, though perfectly suited to the person in question, are nonetheless flavored by the teacher's personality. In fact, the teachings and the teacher are inseparable.

- The astrologer might emphasize that the planet represents a state-of-consciousness which, if explored, will reward the client with a sense of inner guidance and inspiration.

- The astrologer might focus concretely on the planet as symbolic of certain particular experiences which, if cultivated, will reward the individual with feelings of purpose or meaning.

- The astrologer might make a short speech regarding the pitfalls of the "life of quiet desperation," then present the 9th House planet as savior and cure, a provider of motivation, energy, and encouragement—whichever tack is taken.

- The astrologer, for the sake of balance, should make some reference to the perceptual biases built into the 9th House planet and, in a spirit of caution, outline the particular species of dogmatism associated with that body.

In a typical counselling session, more than one of these attacks on the material may be appropriate. Each illustrates a different dimension of 9th House symbolism, some centering on the inner Quest, some on the outer. Always, one must remain conscious of presenting the fundamental principle, which is that while succeeding at the inner Quest is really the point, such mastery is inseparable from the outer Quest and utterly dependent upon it.

Let's apply these principles concretely to the analysis of an actual birthchart.

## Tristan Jones

Few human beings better epitomize the spirit of the Quest than the Welsh explorer, Tristan Jones, born in 1924. At the age of fourteen, he began working as a seaman aboard one of the last sail-driven merchant vessels plying European waters, *Second Apprentice*. At the outset of World War II, he joined the Royal Navy and survived the sinking of two vessels in cold North Atlantic waters. In 1952, still serving in the British Navy, now in Aden, he received terrible wounds and was discharged and told he would never again be able to walk properly. He overcame the diagnosis, and in the late 1950s, bought a derelict lifeboat named *Cresswell*, converted it to sail, and began to fit it out for a journey into the icefields off Greenland . . . but not before filling the ship's coffers through the device of a bit of smuggling. In his book, *Ice!* he writes in typical Jonesian style, "After all these years, I do not regret having done this. It helped keep some otherwise impoverished Hebridean islanders going for a few more months; it brought the delights of good Scotch whisky to many a benighted Frenchman . . ."

Between May 1959 and June 1961, Jones, along with his three-legged dog, Nelson, lived aboard the *Cresswell*, sailing up the west coast of Ireland, and on to Iceland where he became the first man to circumnavigate that country solo under sail. What followed was an extraordinary epic of survival as Jones spent the next two years alone, apart from brief contact with some Inuit people, locked in the arctic ice, barely surviving an attack by a polar bear, near-starvation, and the capsize of a mighty iceberg.

The list of his subsequent voyages and accomplishments is too lengthy to develop in detail here. Suffice it to say that he has sailed 420,000 miles . . . further than any living human being; he has crossed the Atlantic under sail twenty times, nine of them alone; he traversed the "green hell" of the Mato Grosso; he was jailed and tortured in Argentina for his role in helping a man escape that country during the dark years of fascist dictatorship.

Throughout his life, a chronic lack of money has been a consistent theme. All his early voyages were done on the proverbial shoestring. He's never been sponsored by a large funding organization, even after his books began to earn him recognition. One of them, *Adrift*, details his life among the "Bowery bums" of New York City while he was writing his first book, *The Incredible Voyage*, men whom he treats with an unusual degree of compassion, respect, and sensitivity. Once, by chance, I met a sailing woman at an astrology conference who had spent some time with him. We only spoke briefly, but the comment that sticks in my mind was her fond but puzzled observation that, "Tristan always winds up on the waterfront with the simple people . . . sort of the low-lifes, really."

In 1982, he lost a leg. Naturally, this would be a terrible blow to anyone, but to one of Jones' temperament and lifestyle, it is difficult to imagine the emotional devastation such a loss would engender. A nurse at St. Vincent's hospital in New York, where the amputation took place, asked him what he planned to do next. Characteristically, he said, "Bloody well sail around the world!" And, with his prosthesis, he began to do exactly that, but not before forming the Atlantis Society, an organization devoted to encouraging self-sufficiency and adventuresomeness among the disabled.

In the middle 1980s, *sans* leg, Jones set another record. He was the first to take an ocean-going vessel clear across the continent of Europe via the canals and the length of the Danube, emerging in the Black Sea. During the voyage, he took some eight hundred people, "leg amputees, arm amputees, the deaf, the dumb and the blind" aboard his trimaran. Dispirited, not only by the negative attitude of society in general, but even more so, by the attitudes of many of the disabled people he met, Jones wrote, "We disabled would have to try to meet a previously unmet challenge, to show the world that we might not only try to keep pace with the able-bodied, but that we might even *set them a challenge of our own.*"

What he did next with a crew of disabled Thai men and one young German was to accomplish something that had defeated even the Imperial Japanese Army during World War II: he took a vessel across the Kra peninsula of Thailand, previously considered impassable. The story, chronicled in Jones's most recent book, *To Venture Further,* is as much about the inner quest of the people involved as it is about their remarkable outer adventure.

Thomas Ettenhuber, the young German who accompanied him on the Kra voyage, wrote of Jones in the foreword to *To Venture Further,* "Tristan Jones is not an easy man to venture with into anything. He drives himself too much to be very tolerant of others' failings. He can explode, yet he is never unkind. He is, for others, a meticulously careful captain; no one on our venture, except himself, was ever injured. He is much more affable than his account, perhaps, shows. I know of few people who didn't feel better for meeting him."

Tristan Jones, as befits his nature, was born at sea under extremely colorful circumstances, "in a ship bucking crazily in a full storm . . . It was onboard the *S.S. Western Star,* on one of these tramping voyages from Perth, Australia, to Halifax, Nova Scotia, that I was born on May 8, 1924. The ship was approximately 150 miles northeast of the remote island of Tristan da Cunha, in the southern Atlantic Ocean . . . My dad told me that it was exactly at sunrise that he and the mate finally got my shoulders away from my poor mam, then my head last." (His was a breech birth).

I have applied the standard techniques of rectification to Jones' chart and have confirmed the "sunrise" birth to be accurate within a degree. His natal chart is Figure One.

Mars, the fiery War-God, stands out prominently—and unsurprisingly—in the House of the Quest, in independent, rebellious Aquarius. And Tristan Jones's actual quests have fit the overt implications of the symbolism quite precisely. He's displayed extraordinary courage and tenacity in his adventures all through his life, and has endured considerable pain and emotional travail in the process. But, as always, it's a dangerous interpretive ploy to begin with a planet as though it were operating in a vacuum. One might fairly say that it's dangerous to begin anywhere, since any starting point will involve some distortion of the whole. Still, the best policy, I think, is to begin with the basic symbolism of Sun, Moon, and Ascendent, and, with that foundation laid, build up toward an understanding of the rest.

Sun, Ascendent, and Mercury all share the eighteenth degree of Taurus, in a hard and nearly precise square to Neptune in Leo and the 3rd House. Traditionally, such a concentration at the

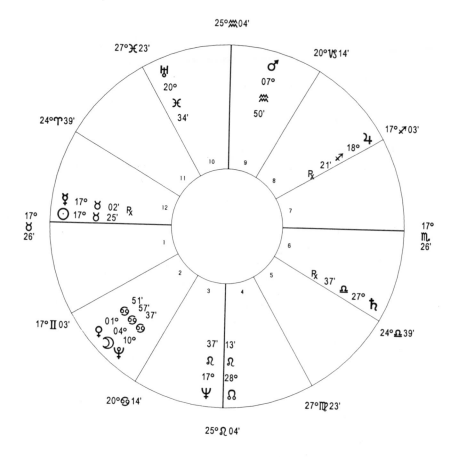

**Tristan Jones**
May 08, 1924.
150 miles N.E. of Tristan da Cunha,
at approximately 011W00 longitude by 35S00 latitude
5:30 AM-AZT (+2 hours)
NOTE: Please employ Placidus Houses

Ascendent would be interpreted as a sign of leadership qualities in the individual. This is, in fact, often the case, and Jones has done the large part of his voyaging in the role of captain, guiding and organizing a wide and diverse range of human types under circumstances that were sometimes quite stressful. That he has succeeded here supports the classical view of the Sun-Ascendent conjunction.

But we can carry the symbolism more deeply.

Leadership—what is it? Elementally, it is the making of choices for others. There may be an effort to achieve consensus; there may be sharing, reflection, and dialogue. But eventually the leader bears the burden of decision, and of responsibility for the decision. To succeed, the leader must be capable of making hard choices and of sustaining a commitment to following through on them, and this must typically be accomplished in an information-poor environment. When do we ever know enough to be utterly sure our choice is correct?

Thus, Jones's Sun-Ascendent conjunction tells two tales, one exoteric, the other esoteric. Outwardly, he manifests a remarkable degree of will, charisma, and natural authority. There is little that can stop him, and, through his Ascendent, he radiates that tough, tenacious quality. But inwardly, in the logic of his own spiritual journey, the emphasis is upon the *development* of those very qualities. This is the core paradox of astrology: we are exploring the very faculties we apparently possess; we are often most driven, most unsure, hungriest, least certain in the very areas where we are said to excel.

In Jones's case, the outward logic goes this way: what a forceful, courageous man . . . two years alone in the pack-ice . . . the distance to the moon and back under sail, much of it alone . . . he once pushed a yacht sixteen miles over rough ground on rounded logs rather than be turned back . . .

But: inwardly, psycho-spiritually, we must ask the question, "Why?" Why did he bother? What lessons might he teach his own deep psyche in the course of achieving those accomplishments? Many would answer simply: "His IQ hovers around room temperature." Or "He's bonkers." Well, stupidity and madness are not unknown on this earth, but Tristan Jones's birthchart suggests a more benign interpretation of his drive. What better way to teach himself the elemental First House lesson of Will?

The Taurean energies of the Sun, Mercury, and Ascendent add, of course, the fabled "stubbornness of the Bull" to Jones's psychic matrix. And Taurus being the most primal of the Earth signs, gives an affinity for Mother Nature, and thus supplies the locus of his Will-building adventures: the natural world of wind and water. [Note that Venus, ruler of Taurus, is conjunct the Moon in Cancer.]

Mercury, fused with Sun and Ascendent, and perhaps abetted by his Welsh heritage, silvers his tongue. Jones's prose is quite extraordinary, alternately comical, salty, and eloquent. The strength of his natal Mercury alone would suggest the presence of that articulate faculty. His poetic, metaphorical Neptune in the 3rd House of Communication adds an element of inspiration and imagery which the matter-of-fact Taurean material alone might fail to provide. In *Ice!*, for example, he writes, "Then, as she [the moon] rose higher and higher, the shadows on the ice piles withdrew, and soon all was pale white and black again, with the moon's face cold, ghostly, and deathly alone as she became smaller and smaller, to hang in the sky a crystal ball of ice, under the cold curtain of stars."

Jones's Moon lies in Cancer in the 2nd House conjunct both Venus and Pluto. The "Money" implications classically associated with 2nd House symbolism fit his biography. Like the Moon, his financial fortunes have waxed and waned. Jones has known the dire poverty of shelters for the homeless in New York City (Pluto), yet while extremely hesitant to "mooch," odd jobs have always come to him through friends (Venus). "Two good things about not having much money," he writes. "Your pockets don't get holes in them and you meet a lot of interesting people whom otherwise you might miss."

Gemini on the 2nd cusp resonates with his powerful Mercury and suggests that ultimately his most reliable source of income is achieved through Geminian means: publication and lecturing. This has proven to be the case during the last twenty years.

The 2nd House has a deeper layer of meaning. Money, compared to astrology, is a new invention. Long before money, people had 2nd Houses—and the need for Resources, which is the real focus of the symbolism here. Money is symbolic of more primary needs: food, shelter, clothing, a means of self-defense, membership in a community. If those needs are met, we feel competent to survive in our environment. Otherwise, we feel insecure—and for compelling reasons. Psychologically, the 2nd House then correlates with self-confidence *and* its polar opposite, self-doubt. Typically, those with powerfully focalized 2nd Houses feel an instinctive insecurity, a need to "prove themselves to themselves." And, if successful, that goal is achieved in part through the accumulation of appropriate resources—but here "resources" has more to do with talents, skills, connections, and tools than with a liberal line of credit.

Thus, deep inside the self-protective shell of the Crab, Jones' lunar emotional nature emerges as reflexively self-doubting and therefore driven toward accomplishment as a method of self-validation. This dynamic interacts explosively with the 1st House decisiveness and Taurean determination we explored a few moments ago.

So: Tristan Jones, the coiled spring. A powerful Will with something to prove—and a tale to tell.

The center of the symbolism is without a doubt Jones' Taurean 1st House, with both Sun and Mercury tightly within the orbs of the conjunction. And what is the ruler of Taurus? Venus . . . which adds more emphasis to that 2nd House restlessness and need for redemption-through-achievement.

But what planet has natural rulership over the 1st House? Immediately our attention turns to Mars, in the House of the Quest.

At first glance, the combination of fiery Mars with the adventuresomeness inherent to the 9th House seems perfectly natural. This, at the deepest archetypal level, is probably true, though no classical "dignities" are involved. There is, however, a deeper perspective.

Mars, in common with all planets, is simply, neutrally, an "energy." And that energy has many faces and can be directed in a variety of ways, some healthy, some less so. In astrological primers, we learn that Mars has to do with anger and drive, with pluck and spirit, sometimes with meanness or cruelty: the basic menu of adrenal emotions—fight, fright, and flight. To me, the primal Martial drama is that of the Hunter and the Prey, the critical point being that Mars represents *both* roles. Where Mars lies in a birthchart, the native is challenged to learn "Hunter skills:" Courage, Assertiveness, and the Right Use of the Sword . . . the stinger being that if he or she fails in that enterprise, then all that remains is for the person to be preyed upon by others. The energy won't go away, in other words; it will manifest: that is cosmic law. Our freedom lies in determining exactly how the Martial drama will materialize, whether we will "eat" or "be eaten." In plain language, the dark side of Mars equates with the Victim archetype . . . thus the enigmatic references in the old books to "scars on the face" or, in the case of Mars in the 9th House, "troubles and injuries in a foreign land."

Jones's Martial sensitivity suggests that an underlying evolutionary drama in his life revolves around mastering the virtues of Mars: specifically, *the development of courage*. Outwardly, Jones's 9th House Mars is appropriate symbolism for his venturesome life. Mars is fierce; and Jones has likewise been fierce in his endeavors. "Troubles in a foreign land?" He's had his share there too, from ships sinking underneath him in the Atlantic to near-maiming in Aden, from losing a leg in the United States to being kicked and beaten into unconsciousness by the South American gestapo.

Still, that kind of surface correspondence between astrological symbolism and personal, existential reality is the great snare of our interpretive art. It works; we are tempted to be satisfied. But might we go past description and achieve inspiration? Might we not only "delineate" but also illuminate, support, and encourage? That's where we enter the Mars symbolism through a new door: we recognize that Tristan Jones's obvious bravery is something of a smokescreen, and that it conceals a secret far deeper and far more engaging: he is Questing in this world, and his Holy Grail is the attainment of Perfect Courage—as unreachable in practice as Polaris, and just as useful for navigation.

Consider Jones's own words, taken from the foreword to *Saga of a Wayward Sailor*. "My arctic voyage . . . was probably among the most futile of expeditions. It was made for the wrong reasons, with the wrong boat, meager finances and unsuitable equipment. It was a classic example of how not to tackle such an effort. *Or so it seemed at the time*, before the realization that I had been exploring *human limits* finally dawned on me."

"Human" limits? The word is too general. Remember that Jones was alone on his arctic expedition . . . exploring his *own* limits.

The outer adventure; the inward transformation:  Quest symbolism. And isn't "exploring human limits" an eloquent expression of the best face of Mars—Courage, the Grail he seeks?

To the ancients, as we explored above, the 9th House represented Religion. Earlier, I spoke of any planet there as a person's
Teacher in the philosophical or religious sense. With Mars as Tristan Jones' Teacher, we envision him apprenticed in the archetypal
temple of the red planet, having signed up before his first breath
for a lifetime of tempering in the school of the Great Warrior, forg-
ing courage in furnace of extremity.

And if he refused? Certainly that was within his power. Then
the Martial force is compelled to manifest its Victim-face, and
Jones's view of the world—his "religion"—would have been
shaped around the perception of endless, insoluble difficulties
visited upon him by petty tyrants, victimizers, and abusers. In
short, the centerpiece of his universe would have been simple,
coldly fearful, hopeless, resigned, and mouse-like. "But," he
writes, "fear is only Nature's way of overcoming man's inherent
intelligence. Nature is wily when she wants to be, and the way to
deal with fear is to remember that it interferes with man's place in
the scheme of things as a logical, crafty, scheming, calculating son
of a bitch who won't let Nature take his mind over."

If Mars could speak, it would make a speech like that one.
But Jones's cautious Taurean and Cancerian qualities come
through too. "Concern is another thing altogether," he adds.
"That is facing up to the reality of any given situation. Worry,
often confused with concern, is Nature's way of getting her foot
in the door so that fear can come in, bringing panic with her . . .
Concern is the harbinger of solutions, the defeater of fear."

Mars is in Aquarius. How does this deepen our understanding of the configuration?

Always, in Aquarius, developmental themes revolve around
the process of individuation—the process whereby we separate
out who we really are from all the norms and expectations visited
upon us by family, community, figures of authority, and the various gods, demi-gods, and sundry tele-demons of modern society.
"I am what I am"—that's the Aquarian theme, when it's healthy.
When it's sick, all that glorious defiance gets channeled in pointless, symbolic directions. We see the "rebel without a cause:" contrary, eccentric, eager above all to defy and shock. But quite
clueless regarding his or her own positive values and direction.

Adding Aquarian energy to the 9th House matrix, we recognize that Tristan Jones's Grail-path would be that of the "out-

sider," which is to say that he would, if successful, seem "strange" or "weird" in his choice of adventures. He would want to do the unexpected, the extreme, the "impossible"—and to do it independently, oddly, perhaps even illegally. This quality underlies his highly Aquarian determination to undertake his voyages without "sponsorship," a fact of which he is apparently quite proud, to judge by the frequency with which he refers to it in his writing. Nowadays such an approach is most unusual; it is, of course, the norm for expeditions to be team efforts, funded by universities, governments, or organizations such as the National Geographic Society.

Jones's Aquarian independence has also led to some comical situations. Once, for example, he was told that it would take six months and a king's ransom in bribes to get permission to move his boat from the coast of Peru to Lake Titicaca. Despondent, he began drinking in a waterfront bar in Callao. There, he met an Indian, drunk also, but with a truck. They struck up a friendship, and soon his *Sea Dart* was loaded up and they were on their bouncing way into the Andes, quite illegally. On the journey, in the city of Arequipo, the mayor got word of their arrival and, on live TV, with Jones and his Indian companion standing solemnly alongside, made a flowery speech of welcome, intoning "for over two hours, and all the time *Sea Dart* sat on the truck, contraband, smuggled, paperless, probably being searched for high and low right now by the Peruvian customs service."

He got away with it, but as a result could not return the way he came. That problem led to his epochal struggle to move the boat down the bug-ridden, jungle rivers of the Mato Grosso to Argentina, where he fell afoul of the military junta and was lucky to escape, penniless, with his life.

Which leads us to consider the dark side of the 9th House Aquarian Mars.

Always, in the 9th House, a human being exercises a God-like quality: he or she creates a world. Not a physical one, exactly. But rather a mental construction whose atoms are assumptions and whose molecules are beliefs and attitudes. And then that human being closes around himself or herself that world like a translucent shroud, through which the images of the "real world out there" must pass. In Tristan Jones's case, that mental world he inhabits is necessarily tinged with Martial and Aquarian values and perspectives. This, we must assume, is good for him and relevant to his spiritual journey—if he keeps it healthy. A few paragraphs ago, we explored one dark possibility: he might have created the paranoid, oppressive cosmos of the self-identified "victim." By all appearance, Jones didn't do that, but any accurate, helpful astrological interpretation of his 9th House energies would have to include a warning along those lines.

Judging the spiritual qualities of others is perilous, but there is at least some evidence that Jones has at times slipped into the darker side of Aquarius, making perhaps too much of a virtue of doing everything the hard way, the backwards way, the marginal way, rather than accepting the benefits of counsel and cooperation from others. One can, for example, make the case that he did not explore sufficiently the possibility of moving his boat legally to Lake Titicaca, perhaps by seeking the help of the British embassy or of local Peruvian yachtspeople, explorers, and interested parties. Might he have gotten the paperwork he needed, and avoided the impressive but arguably rather pig-headed journey across the Mato Grosso and his subsequent "troubles in a foreign land" in Argentina? Always, with an Aquarian Mars in the 9th, one must guard against the tendency toward "us and them" thinking, seeing enemies and conspiracies where there aren't any, looking at everything through the distorting, combative eyes of the "Warrior" and the "Outcast."

If Jones or anyone else with the Martial 9th House configuration came to you asking counsel, what might you say? Perhaps such a person has fallen into one of the many attitudinal traps associated with the structure. Recognize first that it is in the nature of the "religious" dimension of the human psyche that we tend to see, not the world, but rather *what we believe to be true*. Perhaps the individual has slipped into believing that the universe exists to torment and oppress him or her. You say, "Actually, that's not true . . . it's merely an attitude—" The client cuts you off and launches into a lengthy and convincing list of the predations, betrayals, con jobs, lies, deceits, and injuries that had been visited on him or her in the last six months. What can you say? It's clear the person is convinced. Maybe by that time you're convinced too.

I don't believe that a frontal assault is the right tack. Try instead to emphasize the positive, and not because of some greeting card philosophy, but rather because it simply works better.

Don't try to argue with the person's "religion"—as most of us know, such arguments never produce much more than sour feelings. By "emphasizing the positive," in this case, I mean to talk about Mars as the Teacher, teaching Courage through the vehicle of an adventurous Quest. Emphasize that an adventure, scary and exciting, is built into the client's destiny pattern, and that, if undertaken, that adventure forges something brave, confident, and decisive in the spiritual psyche. Then, mention that, by the way, there is another, less attractive possibility, a lower manifestation of the Mars energy, quite unpleasant and quite unnecessary.

Would it work with Tristan Jones? Who knows? Arguing with a 1st House Taurean is not always rewarding. But, even in speaking the words, once, quietly, perhaps a seed is planted. And what more can an astrologer do?

The foregoing detailed analysis provides us with some principles which can be generalized to the interpretation of other 9th House planetary structures.

First, always think of the planet primarily as an idealized, archetypal state of consciousness, and remember that the final aim of the person's questing is *the full realization and integration of that high planetary function.*

Second, grasp and support the fact that looking at life through the "colored lens" of that planet is healthy and appropriate for the individual in question, and provides him or her with the most edifying and inspiring possible view of existence; for him or her, that is the religion that "works."

Third, emphasize that this planetary energy must be stimulated into development through outward experience, experience which will carry the person into exotic and unfamiliar directions geographically, intellectually, emotionally, and culturally.

Fourth, by considering the nature of the 9th House planet, state the nature of such experience.

Fifth, caution the individual against the fanatical or dogmatic extremes which might be associated with that planet.

And sixth, describe the negative, oppressive, or counterproductive worldview which might arise if the 9th House planet is not fed on a diet of moment-to-moment consciousness in at least the occasional presence of the Miraculous.

**David Pond**

David Pond has been a professional astrologer since 1976. He holds a B.A. in Education and a Master of Science degree in "Experimental Metaphysics" from Central Washington University. David has co-authored, with his sister Lucy, *The Metaphysical Handbook*. He is a contributing author in *Astrological Counseling: The Path to Self-Actualization,* volume six of Llewellyn's New World Astrology Series.

David travels throughout the western United States and Canada, giving workshops on integrating astrology and spirituality into daily life. David's daily life includes yoga, gardening, coaching sports, and enjoying family life with his wife Laura and their four sons.

# Experiencing Tranquility While Achieving Potential

## David Pond

As above, so below. This saying is certainly the most popular axiom used to justify the use of astrology. The microcosm reflects the macrocosm: as it is in the heavens, so it shall be on earth. As astrologers, we typically talk a great deal about this principle. However, is it what we teach? What do we experience when we go out into the night and observe the heavens? Is it not peace and tranquillity? We see the vastness, observe the changes that are constantly occurring, and, as we watch this celestial dance, a deep sense of tranquillity will often come over us. That is the "above," but is this our experience on earth, the "below"? Rarely. Change is certainly happening, but on earth it seems chaotic and discordant instead of graceful and harmonious.

"As above, so below" is not as much a statement of what is, as it represents what can be if we learn to live in accordance with the laws of the heavens. Astrology is the language of the heavens, and through its use we can decipher the code of how to experience tranquillity within dynamic activity. We witness this in the heavens and, as astrologers, we are here to help others find it in their lives as well.

It has been said that it is easy to find peace and tranquillity on a mountain top, but can you find it in the marketplace as well? Experiencing tranquillity and achieving potential are often thought of as contradictory. Our picture of those who have maintained tranquillity is often associated with dropping out of the rat race. We picture the yogic lifestyle in an ashram or monastery: attaining peace by turning away from the pursuit of ambitions. Conversely, our image of those who are pursuing their ambitions is the driven, type-A personalities, pushing at life by sacrificing peace. We have all seen people who represent both extremes and the question arises, "Is it possible to do both simultaneously?" This essay will explore this possibility, first philosophically, then astrologically.

## Uranus/Neptune Conjunction in Capricorn: The Evolution of Myths and Ideologies

The latter part of the 1980s and the early1990s have been witness to an incredible revolution in the political beliefs, ideologies, and myths that guide life on planet earth. The collapse of communism and the breakup of the U.S.S.R. are prime examples of the Uranus/Neptune conjunction. Ideals and myths (Neptune) that are no longer inspirational are going through a tremendous revolution/evolution (Uranus). Communism was not always an oppressive force. In the eyes of its originators, it was thought of as an ideal that could improve the life of the people. When it was no longer serving the people, the ideal collapsed.

We are now seeing the shadow side of many of the myths and ideals with which we grew up. When I was in primary school, a myth that was highly touted was the idea that science would one day be able to overcome nature and greatly improve the quality of life for everyone. It was thought that we could control the climates, harness the energy of the wind and sea, and generally subdue earth to do our bidding. We are now seeing the shadow side of this myth in the current ecological crisis that is upon us. We are seeing the cost of what happens when you do not live in harmony with nature. The rapid decline in the quality of our rivers, oceans, forests, and the air we breathe reflects our lack of respect for nature.

Another myth we have all grown up with is the "American Dream." The idea is that with hard work and effort everyone can acquire an incredible amount of material wealth. This myth, too, has a shadow side. The discrepancy between the "haves" and the "have nots" is setting the stage for a possible revolution. Even the people who have been successful at the American Dream of consumerism are realizing that it takes five to seven days a week of chasing dollars in order to win at this game—but where is the time to enjoy the fruits of such a labor-intensive life?

While old myths are being shattered, we are seeing the birth of new myths. The dominant emerging myth of our era is the Gaia Hypothesis. This is the view that Mother Earth is a living organism in and of herself. This concept has many ramifications and would greatly change the picture of what our role is on the planet. If Mother Earth is alive, then we humans are but cells of consciousness within her greater being. Like a cell within the human body, it is in our best interest not to conquer the body; instead, the idea is to enter into a symbiotic relationship with it, conducting our life in a way that is mutually beneficial for the planet and ourselves.

These changing myths have a direct bearing on our topic of maintaining tranquillity while achieving full potential. The way of life these dying myths fostered prevented people from establishing a rapport with nature. This moving away from natural law led to the dichotomy of the paths leading to tranquillity and those leading to achievement. One very noticeable trend over the last several years has been the rise in the number of people suffering from Chronic Fatigue Syndrome. It seems quite evident that this is a symptom of burn-out; over-extending oneself beyond natural law. With the emergence of the Gaia myth, we can expect a return to the standard of living in harmony with natural law. This will lead to a time for activity and a time for rest in cyclic rhythm.

## To Do or To Be: Are They Mutually Inclusive?

Our culture has long placed a premium on doing. This encourages a produce/consume mentality which fuels ambition. You have to earn more to buy more. Ram Dass speaks of this philosophy of life as the "More is never enough" approach. Certainly it has been the driving force behind our economy. This takes the focus away from quality, as built-in obsolescence is desirable in an economy and way of life based on consumerism.

Our public education system feeds this mentality by teaching students how to develop skills for being in the world; yet very little emphasis is placed on how to be with oneself. This promotes a population that sees self-worth as based on performance. As a counselor, I see this cultural bias on doing, instead of being, in many ways. It is not uncommon for parents of those who have not bought into the American Dream to try to find out what is wrong with their children, who are just interested in getting by. The assumption is that there is something wrong with a person who does not want to join the race and try to get ahead.

We hear that primitive cultures would spend two to three days a week working on survival-related activities. The remainder of the week would be free for family, creativity and ritual. It makes us wonder how far we moderns have evolved when we consider that a current lifestyle often requires five to seven days a week of earning money to meet our needs. This leaves precious little time for family, creativity, and ritual. No wonder tranquillity seems so rare in the modern world. Who has time for it?

Different cultures around the world place greater importance on different aspects of life. Generally speaking, the Eastern cultures tend to place greater emphasis on inner development and spiritual issues. Western cultures tend to emphasize outer, goal-oriented issues. When these principles are taken to their extremes, we witness the shadow side of the behavior. The shadow side of achievement in the outer world is the addiction to power and control that so often consumes successful people. The shadow side of those cultivating tranquillity is the apathetic, lazy behavior that often characterizes those who have dropped out of the rat race.

Ideally, as we move toward a global community, we can take the best of both ideologies and combine them to create a whole-life approach to living.

### The Way Out: The Path of Effortless Action

The path of effortless action is described in Eastern literature in this way: "Without doing anything, leave nothing undone." This statement is puzzling to the Western way of thinking. How can you get anything done if you are not doing anything? The answer is to enter into the doing. Instead of imposing yourself on a project, you enter into a relationship with the task at hand. In this way you are not doing the task; instead, you are taking part in that which is being done.

This implies a philosophy of self-transcendence, which is not to be confused with self-denial. Self-denial is a martyr path and leads to the negation of the self. Self-transcendence is a shift of focus to a place in consciousness above the separate self. However, it is not through denial of the self that this state of consciousness is reached. Quite the contrary, self-transcendence leads to a unitive state of consciousness, where the self is seen connected to all reality. This allows one to enter into activity intimately connected to the task, instead of being separate from it.

## The Principles of Right Livelihood

During these times of powerful transits occurring in Capricorn, the question of right livelihood is a constant concern with most people. Since Capricorn is the sign that deals with career, vocation-related questions are always among the most pressing issues with clients seeking astrological guidance. What should I be when I grow up? What type of work will bring the greatest satisfaction? Many of those seeking career guidance have taken interest surveys, designed to show where they will meet with the greatest success. After testing, they are given lists of numerous jobs that would be possible. This cafeteria approach to the question of right livelihood leaves many people still in the quandary of facing too many options.

To simplify this process, I have come up with a test for right livelihood that has only three criteria:

- Do you love the work?
- Are you good at it?
- Does it meet a need that is in the world?

Why the first two criteria are so important is fairly straightforward. If you love the work, your heart will be involved and you will have plenty of energy to fulfill the job requirements. Of course, you also have to be good at it so people will seek out and reward your services. I may love to golf, but if I am not very good at it, no one will pay me for it.

The importance of the third requirement, of meeting a need that is in the world, is a little more subtle. First, it has the obvious quality of service, which in and of itself is a valid reason for pursuing an activity. Beyond this there is a metaphysical principle at work here as well. If you are attending to true needs that are in keeping with the well being of the collective society, then in a symbiotic relationship, the needs themselves create a vortex of energy that you can respond to. It is not just word play to say that responsibility is the ability to respond. By entering into a relationship with the task, the energy to complete the task is already existent within the task. You do not have to provide it yourself!

These three simple questions can effectively weed out all but the most relevant type of work for an individual. This could help overcome the attitude of "Oh, well, at least it is a job." This attitude is what I call occupational disease.

## Remaining Mindful

To maintain tranquillity while achieving, you must remain mindful in order to assess the quality of your energy. Most religions and spiritual paths encourage the development of that part of the character that can observe self while self is in action. Buddhists call it cultivating mindfulness; Christians call it the Witness; J. Khrishnamurti called it the detached observer; but by whatever name, it is the same point in consciousness. This is typically cultivated through meditation or contemplation, by withdrawing your attention from the activity at hand and observing it from within. In yoga, we talk about drawing our attention back into the cave of consciousness. Normally, our attention is pressed up against the eyes, but in this discipline you draw your attention back a few inches; not toward that point, but from that point. This is where self-observation can occur.

The importance of this can not be overstated. It is absolutely essential to be able to monitor the quality of your energy. Without this mindfulness, you would have no way of knowing if you were experiencing tranquillity or anxiety. The emotions of the experience would color your perceptions, justifying your experience as appropriate, regardless of how reactionary or centered it might be.

After one has cultivated mindfulness, the saying, "Being in the world, but not of the world" begins to make more sense. "Being in the world" refers to achieving and accomplishing. "But not of the world" refers to rooting your attention in the realms of consciousness, instead of in worldly affairs. This is what can allow an individual to maintain the tranquillity of consciousness while achieving in the world.

From the perspective of the *detached* observer, life takes on a whole new dimension. From this point in consciousness, there is no racing around, no being overwhelmed, no reactions to the pushing and shoving of life. There is a saying, "The measure of an individual's soul is in the ability to remain unruffled by the ups and downs of life." The soul is indescribable. It would be presumptuous to attempt to say exactly where it is within us. But if this saying has merit, perhaps the soul resides with the detached observer. This is where one can witness the play of life in a non-reactionary manner. From here, one can see the smiling face of the divine reflected back through all of creation.

## The Astrological Perspective:
## The 4th House/10th House Axis

The main tool that we utilize in astrology is the birthchart; the planetary map of how the planets were arranged around the time and place of birth. Fulfillment comes when an individual successfully integrates all of the many factors of the chart into daily life. This creates a whole life. It is important to understand that any given culture will have various biases that emphasize one aspect of life over others. To stress the point again, cultures have biases, astrology does not. To experience wholeness, each and every point in the chart is equally important.

This is the "to do or to be" axis. The 10th House relates to function in society, or the "doing" aspect of life. The 4th House relates to roots and where one can retreat within oneself, thus the "being" aspect of life. As mentioned earlier, our culture places a premium on the 10th House aspect of social function. This is reflected in astrology in many ways. Astrological computer programs often include aspects to the 10th House cusp, but never to the 4th. Considerable emphasis is often put on the Midheaven during interpretations, while the Nadir is often ignored. However, if one point in a chart is significant, its opposite is equally important. In our discussion, the 10th relates to achievements and accomplishments, while the 4th relates to the tranquillity that comes from entering in to a deep rapport with the self.

**The 4th House**

One of the most important themes connected to the 4th House is its physical locality. The 10th is that which is above you and the 4th is that which is directly beneath you. This is often portrayed in the literature as land and real estate. In the era of "Science will subdue nature," land is real-estate, something to be worked, improved, bought, and sold. As the Gaia hypothesis continues to emerge, the 4th House as one's relationship to Mother Earth surfaces as the core theme.

Forming a relationship with Mother Earth is not new. Primitive, noncivilized cultures always respected the earth and its creatures. Since the industrial era, however, there has been a steady decrease in lifestyles that are close to the land. We have lost connection to the physical source of our existence. An obvious manifestation of this is the ecological crisis that is upon us. A not so obvious manifestation is the alienation and lack of belonging that so many feel. Countless clients express the desire to know where their home is, where they belong, where their roots are. This sense of alienation comes directly from a lack of a meaningful connection to Gaia. Those who express this never have a garden, nor any type of direct connection to the food they eat, and generally would not know what I mean when I ask if they have found a power spot in nature, or how long has it been since they have walked barefoot on the earth? The earth sustains us and nurtures us. To experience a deep sense of peace and tranquillity, this earth-connection, one facet of the 4th House must be met.

The sign on the 4th House cusp describes more than our roots and origins; it is also our personal myth—a core theme that needs to be woven into the identity being acted out through the 10th house. The sign describes the fundamental psychological attitudes that we have about ourselves. These attitudes are formed so early in life that we cannot remember adopting them. They seemingly have always been there. Like the fish looking for the ocean everyone keeps talking about, we have been so inundated with the conditions of our early life, it is hard to see them as separate from self. For this reason the qualities of the 4th House remain largely nonconscious.

Although the qualities of the sign on the 4th House are largely unconscious, one way to activate these attributes is by getting in touch with the 4th House ruler. The house that the ruling planet is in, as well as its sign, are clues to the type of activities that can be cultivated to bring a sense of peace and personal identity to your life.

It is a fallacy to assume that tranquillity comes from inactivity and rest. Take, for example, Aries on the 4th House Cusp and Mars in Sagittarius in the 1st House. Would this person find peace through rest? Not likely! The natural state of Mars in Sagittarius is action. Hiking, bike-riding, being out of doors with plenty of space would be more likely ways of experiencing peace.

An example of a different type is Taurus in the 4th with Venus in Taurus also in the 4th. Here we would expect gardening, soaking in a hot tub, having an intimate dinner, listening to music, or painting as being preferred activities to cultivate a sense of tranquillity.

## The 10th House

The sign on the 10th House cusp describes how you go about carving out a niche for yourself in society. While the ideal of the 4th House is to be centered within oneself and to feel a personal and private connection to earth, the 10th is the opposite of the 4th, and is where you seek to contribute to the collective by developing a career or function in society. Since it is the highest point in the chart, it represents what you look up to, respect, and hold in high esteem. Thus it describes the nature of your aspirations.

Ideally, the 10th would be seen by the individual as his or her role in serving the collective best interest of society. The 4th House is an "I" house, and the 10th should be a "we" house. This is ultimately an important distinction, because if the "I" is seeking personal glory through its 10th House function, it begins to be at cross purpose with itself. The 10th is certainly not about personal sacrifice, nor is it about personal glory. Honor and dignity are the true rewards of the 10th. During the "more is never enough" phase of our cultural myth, prestige, power, and fame became the sought-after rewards connected to the 10th. However, these all celebrate the "I", and the person reaping these rewards still missed the satisfaction of the need to feel that one is doing something significant for the collective best interest of society.

Look to the ruling planet of the 10th as to how to go about achieving these aspirations. Its house indicates what type of activities to pursue for greatest success. The sign it is in describes the most natural attitude to develop to establish your position in society. Aspects from other planets to the ruling planet describe factors assisting or inhibiting the establishment of your social identity.

For example: Scorpio on the 10th House with Pluto in Leo in the 7th. With the Scorpio 10th, a career that creates change and transformation would be ideal. However, without tracking the ruling planet, we do not know what field of interest this individual would best pursue. Possible Scorpio-related careers include chemistry, waste disposal, recycling, dentistry, investment counseling, and being a therapist of some type. With the ruling planet Pluto in the 7th, it lets us know that this individual will excel in one-to-one interactions with others, perhaps as a counselor.

An example of a different sort is Cancer on the 10th with Moon in Taurus in the 8th. A career involving nurturing and caregiving would be ideal. This individual must feel emotionally connected to his or her work. It would be wrong to assume that one's aspirations are necessarily connected to making money. With the Cancer theme, school teacher, healer, or restaurant work could all satisfy the nurturing theme, but homemaker and parent are also valid Cancer nonpaying careers. Parenting is probably the least-paid and often least-respected profession, but in terms of contributing to society, is there anything more important? With the Moon in Taurus in the 8th, working directly with one's mate, or supporting the mate's career from behind the scenes, are likely paths.

As the current transit of Uranus and Neptune continues through Capricorn, we are witnessing the dissolution of the myth that a career is the *only* worthwhile aspiration. More and more you can see people changing their application of 10th House ambitions. Instead of pursuing the American Dream and measuring one's standard of living by the quantity of possessions, people are now beginning to hold the quality of life in greater esteem. As this shift continues, aspirations connected to the 10th will also continue to shift. For example, perfecting a yoga posture or creating a holistic lifestyle are valid aspirations that some may pursue.

This changing of the Capricorn myths that we are witnessing has certainly affected the global economy. Although the scenario is obviously more complex than any single issue, one contributing factor to the wind-down in the economy is that people are questioning the value of pursuing the American Dream, even when the work is available. Over and over again, I hear clients saying that they just can not push themselves in meaningless work, even if it leads to a reduction in their pay.

The 4th House/10th House axis ideally would be balanced in people's lives if they are to find satisfaction and fulfillment in both professional and personal arenas. This vertical axis is of critical importance to the theme of this essay. Without a deep connection to the earth and the feeling of being centered within oneself, the experience of tranquillity would be quite impossible. Without aspirations to look up to and a need to contribute to society, there would be no call to achievement. It can be seen then that the integration of this polarity is the essential first step towards the goal of maintaining an identity rooted in serenity while simultaneously performing a social function.

## Neptune and the Observer

Neptune represents the urge to transcend the everyday, mundane view of reality and to gain a spiritual perspective. Neptune, of course, also represents illusion and escapist activities that transcend reality in a less than healthy way. For most people, the experience of Neptune will be a random sampling of inspiration and disillusionment. A person can, however, cultivate the higher aspects of Neptune through prayer, meditation, contemplation, art, music, and nature mysticism. By cultivating the higher elements of any astrological theme, you utilize the energy available for that indicator and, thus, effectively diminish the potential for the lower manifestations of its expression.

Neptune has two important functions related to our topic. The first is the experience of bliss that accompanies the rising above the plane of duality that typically occupies consciousness. At the base level of reality, duality is the norm and everything presents itself in the polarities of good/bad, black/white, positive/negative, yin/yang etc. Here the battle rages. The successful application of Neptune energy allows one to ascend to a higher perspective that embraces *all* polarities. This is the state of "Unitive Consciousness" and the experience of nonseparateness. This, in and of itself, is a great reward and a major boon to the experience of tranquillity. However, the second function of attaining the highest level of Neptune, namely, developing the observer point of consciousness, is equally important.

It is essential to assess the quality of your energy field if you hope to experience tranquillity while achieving. This assessment is typically a retrospective process. We review an experience after it occurs and appraise its quality. This retrospective process is the only way this can be done until an individual learns to cultivate the observer part of the character. This is the point in consciousness that allows us to rise above an experience and *to see it while it is occurring.* From this vantage point, an individual can see self and self-in-action simultaneously. This gives the ability to monitor the quality of one's energy in the moment.

The house that Neptune occupies in the birthchart represents an area of life that you can get lost in or find your higher self in, depending on how successful you are at mastering its elusive nature. Neptune is famous for being the blind spot in the chart, where illusion and imagination can prevail over reason. When this is the case, the activities related to this house cause nothing but trouble. However, if you are able to employ the best of Neptune, then its house can become a refuge that provides a sanctuary for the finer sensibilities of consciousness.

## The Twelfth House and the Way of the Tao

There is no area of the chart that is shrouded in as much mystery as the 12th House. When you read the literature connected to this house you can see a tremendous evolution in our understanding of the workings of this important area of the chart. It was previously thought to be the house of self-undoing, hidden karma, asylums, prisons, and hospitals. Over the years the literature has changed and now the 12th House is seen as the area of the chart relating to spirituality. One may well wonder what is the connection between asylums and spirituality? The one point the earlier authors missed is that if you are spending time in an asylum, hospital, monastery, or prison, *you have plenty of time to contemplate.* This is the key to the 12th. It is where we need to detach ourselves from everyday reality to contemplate life and extract the spiritual meaning from our lives.

Without a spiritual perspective, there is not much about the 12th House that looks attractive. For those with an exclusive worldly focus, the 12th House is troublesome at best. However, for those who have developed the spiritual side of their character, the 12th House is a veritable gold mine. This is where one can learn about the Tao of life. The Tao can be described as the flow of life, like an invisible river supporting, guiding, and directing one's journey through life. Each of us has an original divine intent that brought us into this incarnation, and through 12th House activities we learn to reconnect with that original divine impulse.

Dreams and omens are particularly strong 12th House functions that reveal the hidden Tao of life. In youth, it is practically impossible to ascertain clearly the meaning of this hidden dimension. We are all so full of ourselves and are still guided by a willful need to make a major impact on the world. This willfulness masks the subtleties of the Tao. It is typically not until after the Saturn return that fires of youthful will begin to subside and one can start sensing another type of intelligence guiding life beyond will. That is when dreams become more than passionate remnants of unacted upon fantasies.

Dreams are involuntary. The understanding of dreams is not. Since dreams are symbolic, one needs to contemplate them in order to extract the message they reveal. The dream material often compensates for our experiences in the waking world, hinting at another layer of intelligence beyond the rational. Although many authors offer specific meanings to specific dream symbols, the ephemeral nature of the dream material resists this rational categorizing. To work with a dream, one must stay open to the mystery of life and allow the meaning to have a subjective quality that may shift and move as you contemplate its meaning. This is the nature of 12th House material: it is nonspecific by definition. The 6th House, opposite of the 12th, is where we can analyze and process information to gain specific insights. For the 12th, however, one must have an appreciation for the mystic path which seeks to know what can be known and then leaves the rest as a source of inspiration, wonder and awe.

There is a saying from Eastern religions, "The great way is easy for those who have no preference." To the Western way of thinking, this may sound like complacency and blind acceptance. The saying seems to fit right into our understanding of the 12th House and the way of the Tao. The saying could also have been put this way: "The invisible path of the Tao will reveal itself when one has quieted his will and watches the signs." It takes the subtlety of the 12th house perspective to see the omens or signs along the way. There are many magic tools one can become skilled in to facilitate this watching of the signs : the I Ching, Tarot, Runes, and Medicine cards to name a few. These are tools, however, and are not the actual source of the information. The source is the Tao. When you are in touch with it, it feels almost elastic. You can sense when you are with it and when you are not. This hidden guidance can be a source of deep peace when you realize that it is always there gently to direct the course of your life.

When you have developed your 12th house, your capacity to be "in the world, but not of the world" is greatly enhanced. From this vantage point, what begins to matter is not just what you are doing in the world; it is where you are within yourself as you are doing your worldly dance. The 12th House is where we transcend distinction and accept everything as a manifestation of the divine. This reverence for all life certainly aids in the experience of serenity.

The sign on the 12th House cusp describes how you approach your spirituality and what Karma you came to work on. The ruling planet by sign, house and aspect indicates where you need to incorporate activities that generate spiritual lessons.

For example: Virgo on the 12th, Mercury in Aquarius in the 5th. This individual attempts to approach spiritual issues in a precise and practical manner. The karmic pattern that needs to be overcome is being over-critical and dependent on the rational mind. In this life the individual needs to learn how to use the mind to get beyond the mind. Specific techniques such as yoga and breath control could be useful tools. This person needs to see the practical application of spirituality in order to be convinced of its worth. With Mercury in Aquarius in the 5th, unusual experiences with children, creativity, and love affairs provide the material for spiritual lessons.

Another example: Cancer on the 12th, Moon in Leo in the 1st. Cancer is well suited to explore the watery, subjective nature of the 12th. This is particularly strong for the dream material of the 12th, and this person would be well advised to keep a personal dream journal. This individual will have a highly personal approach to spirituality. The karmic test is to learn how not to take everything personally. With the Moon in the 1st, this situation is exacerbated. Personal pride and an over-dramatic emotional nature provide plenty of material for spiritual lessons.

# Aspects

The geometric aspects between planets provide a wealth of material for our discussion. Although each aspect is associated with its own separate, distinct energy, they can also be neatly divided into two groups for our benefit: dynamic and harmonious. The dynamic aspects include the conjunction, semi-square, square, sesquiquadrate, quincunx, and opposition. The harmonious aspects are the sextiles, trines, and quintiles. It can be seen that the dynamic aspects outnumber the harmonious aspects two to one; no wonder it is so easy to drift into a stressful life.

The dynamic aspects have the reputation for being troublesome, as they tend to create stress. The harmonious aspects have the reputation for being beneficial, because they facilitate an easy rapport between the planets involved. These initial categories are misleading, because the issues are not as cut and dried as it first appears. It is often seen in client's charts that the most harmonious are typically the laziest. Lack of tension often translates as lack of drive. Those whose charts show dominant dynamic aspects are typically the doers, but these are also the people who carry the greatest amount of anger and frustration.

This becomes most graphic when there is a major aspect pattern in the chart such as the T-square. This pattern is made up of two planets in opposition, and a third planet squaring both poles of the opposition. This pattern has the most latent energy in astrology. It is dynamic, passionate, intense, and very volatile. It is known for creating justifiable anger, and people with T-Squares in their charts often will say, "I have a right to be mad!" I call these people "adrenaline junkies," as they seem to become addicted to the rush of anger. The problem of the T-square is it needs to generate frustration or anger in order to produce the type of energy it is interested in. Those with this aspect pattern can typically get an incredible amount of work done with the energy available. The trick is somehow not to get caught up in all the negativity that accompanies anger, frustration, and irritation.

Khrisnamurti, in his book *Think on These Things*, describes a process he calls "Creative Frustration." He mentions that the energy of frustration is energy. It might not be the type of energy we wish it was, but at least it is energy. He puts forth a technique for transmuting the energy from its negative expression to free it for positive, creative expression. This would be ideal for all people with T-Squares in their charts to learn. Imagine having all of the energy that is typically locked up in negative frustration available to utilize in any way you choose!

The technique is basically to let go of the label of what is apparently creating the frustration. Instead of saying, "I am frustrated because _____", learn to let go of the "because" and whatever you say after that. The "because" becomes a screen upon which you are projecting the frustration. Know that if it weren't that screen, it could be one of a hundred others. *Simply claim the experience,* "I am frustrated." By owning the experience, you are free to alter the expression of the energy. When you use the word "because" and whatever you say next, you no longer own the energy. You attach it to whatever you labeled as the source, and it stays locked in the negative frustration mode.

Although this process is relatively easy to describe and visualize, it is very difficult actually to do. The main challenge to overcome is the attachment to the anger or frustration. While involved in anger/frustration, it is extremely difficult to rise above the experience to observe what is taking place. As was said earlier, the need to monitor one's energy via the detached observer is a prerequisite for this type of consciousness work. Herein lies the benefit of this work. It is not merely to become spiritually blissful; it is to liberate energy and make it available for creativity.

The ideal would be to develop elasticity, giving the ability to move from harmonious to dynamic energy and back again-at will! This is the alchemy of astrology. To learn the skills for transmuting energy frees one from the tyranny of a reactionary life. Then one can become a true co-creator of his or her life path; no longer simply reacting to energy, but being able to creatively direct its expression. Although the work has to be done within the consciousness of the individual, the astrologer should be able to direct the client toward areas within the chart that would be most productive for this transformation process.

When two planets are locked in dynamic tension, it is desirable to find an outlet for the energy. Is there a third planet that can act as a release valve for the tension? Activities related to the release planet will effectively relieve the tension in a creative manner. This is the ideal—the tension provides the energy and the third planet gives it a creative release. Look for mediating, alleviating, and dispositing planets into which to direct the dynamic energy.

A mediating planet is one that has a harmonious aspect to both planets involved in a tension producing aspect. For example, imagine Mars in Aries in the 1st House, in opposition to Saturn in Libra in the 7th. The opposition sets up the dynamic tension. Now imagine Jupiter in Leo in the 5th House, in trine to Mars and in sextile to Saturn. This is the best possible situation as *the mediating planet can effectively draw the tension away from both ends of the polarity in a creative, harmonious manner.* In this situation, we could direct the client toward, fun, creativity, activities with children, and romance to utilize the mediating planet in the best manner.

An alleviating planet is one that has a harmonious aspect to one or the other of the tension planets, but not both. To set the stage for this, imagine Mars in Aries in the 10th House, square Saturn in Cancer in the 1st. An alleviating planet in this situation could be Jupiter in Taurus in the 11th House, forming a sextile to Saturn and making no aspects to Mars. The alleviating planet is less ideal than a mediating planet, in that it only can draw from one end of the tension-producing planets, but it is still very effective for moving the stressful energy in a healthy direction. With this situation, we might direct a client toward group activities of a Taurean nature; a garden club, wine tasting group or a rock hound group are possible examples.

When there is no harmonious-release aspect for two planets in stressful relationship, then the astrologer is going to have to look deeper to find some way to help the client. One technique is to look for the dispositor of the planets in question. The dispositor is the planet that rules the sign the planet in question is in. The dispositor's position by house and sign are constructive activities the client can get involved in to relieve the tension.

During a session, if I point out a particular difficulty in the chart, I feel responsible to help the client find a solution. It will sometimes happen that two planets are in dynamic tension to each other and there are no harmonious aspects to either, and both planets are in signs they rule—thus they have no dispositors. In this situation, you would look for the houses the planets in question rule, and then direct your client to the activities of these houses to channel the energy in a healthy manner.

There are many tools available for cultivating tranquillity. A most helpful awareness that we can gain from astrology is that of the Octaves.

## Octaves

There are a few different approaches to this topic that we can take. First is the concept that the three outer planets, Uranus, Neptune, and Pluto, represent the higher octave of the personal planets: Mercury, Venus, and Mars respectively. Second, we can also utilize the concept of octaves in understanding the higher and lower potential for every astrological indicator.

We all have an ego, and it is the ego's job to maintain the self identity and to resist all information that is contrary to the existing set of beliefs. A healthy ego does this; therefore, blame is not being assigned, since it is the ego's job to help maintain the continuity of the self. However, many of the conflicts in which we find ourselves stem from this territoriality and seeing issues exclusively from the vantage point of the self. By utilizing the concept of the octaves, we can free ourselves from the tyranny of self-justification and find the liberation that a universal view offers.

Another reason for cultivating the energy of the higher octave planets deals with the issue of supply. The personal planets suffer the same fate as the lower chakras in the human energy system: their appetite is insatiable when we focus on them exclusively. A person can never get enough money, sex, or power, if that is all one is looking for. The ego perspective is isolated against the world, fears a lack of resources for its fulfillment, and thus pits itself against others to gain advantage. At the universal level of the outer planets, just as with the upper chakras, there is abundance of supply; thus from this level one never feels in competition with others for anything.

## Mercury/Uranus

Uranus is said to be the higher octave of Mercury. Mercury relates to the personal mind and the function of logical, rational thinking. Uranus, being one of the transpersonal planets, relates to the universal mind and the process of intuition within the individual. By utilizing the theory of the octave, one would be able to make the shift from the Mercury level of personal intelligence to the Uranus level of universal intelligence. By doing so, this would allow one to essentially depersonalize his or her perspective and get a glimpse of the larger picture.

Your ability to think is God's gift to you; what you choose to think about is your gift to God. This saying captures the essence of the principle of the higher octave of the mind. When you find yourself being consumed by petty thoughts, remember this saying and see if you feel good about your offering to the divine. The mind can get mired in the most inane, insignificant issues, or it can be raised to the sublime to consider the most lofty of human ideals. Remember that your mind is directly connected to the universal mind and that you have access to this collective intelligence through the octave principle.

## Venus/Neptune

Venus and Neptune are also considered to have a special connection that leads from the personal aspects of love and romance (Venus) to the universal and spiritual aspects of love (Neptune). At the Venus level, one becomes aware of the personal likes, dislikes, values and delights of the ego-encapsulated self. This level of love is very exclusive. It can be defined astrologically within the individual by the sign that holds Venus. Venus love, although delightful when circumstances allow for its experience, is also divisive in that it separates the world into that which is acceptable and that which is not.

One can transcend this separatist, personal love by raising one's vibration to the higher octave of love, Neptune. Where Venus has its filters—this it likes and this it doesn't. Neptune drops all filters to embrace the collective. Venus is personal and exclusive; Neptune is spiritual and inclusive. Through Neptune, one learns the love that transcends all differences. At this level, one is able to see the smiling face of the divine reflected back through all of creation.

It is important to understand that one level is not being judged as better than the other with the octaves. The ideal is to be elastic in consciousness, freeing oneself to move between the personal and collective at will. Some of life's sweetest rewards are certainly found at the Venus level of love: the delight of the senses, the appreciation of art and beauty, the sweet kiss of romance are all wonderful experiences to appreciate fully through Venus. The octave principle is helpful when the delights of Venus become limiting and isolating through attachment and the fear of not having enough. Then, we remember that personal love is only a reflection of the higher principle of divine love and at that level there is an abundance of love that can never be exhausted. With Neptune, we fill our cup with the ever-present divine love and share this nectar in the world, instead of looking ourselves to be filled in the world.

**Mars/Pluto**

Mars relates to one's personal power. Various expressions of this warrior part of your character include: how you initiate action, define your boundaries, and act on your passion and anger. The sign Mars is in at your birth describes the natural way that you assert yourself and take action. Pluto represents these same power issues at the collective level, and thus, it is one's relationship to the use of collective power. Collective power is easiest to understand in a formal sense when an individual is voted into office to represent the will of the people. The person in office then becomes a spokesperson for the collective power of the group. This also happens spontaneously when individuals defer or submit to another's will. Another nonofficial manifestation of collective power is when an individual pledges the expression of his or her will to the best interest of the collective.

Certainly both personal and collective power are important. Mars represents your ability to defend yourself, and there are many situations where it is important to define your boundaries and push back those that would invade or take advantage of you. However, the Mars energy can easily become overly defensive or assertive, setting up power struggles with others. Then it is wise to align with the higher octave of personal power, with Pluto and the "right" use of power.

The right use of power could be described as utilizing power in such a way that is a benefit to all involved and a detriment to none (including self). The misuse of power could be described as that which benefits someone while harming another. It should be stressed here that it is just as easy to abuse collective power as it is personal power, but abuse of either would not fit within our "no harm" definition of the right use. Many people fear their own power. Others have been taught that humility and obedience are the mark of the spiritual person, and thus have denied power in their lives as well.

True humility is not the denial of power. True humility is getting the ego to step out of the way so that the divine can become successful through you. To achieve this, the personal will (Mars) must align with the universal will (Pluto). It can be seen that the expression of the higher octave planet does not require the sacrifice or denial of the personal planet involved. Instead, it requires the alignment of the two to work in harmony.

Although, when we speak of the octave theory we are typically referring to the material just covered above, we could also expand this notion to *all* astrological indicators. An astrological indicator in and of itself simply represents potentiality. Until it is activated by the human will, the indicator has a range of possible higher and lower manifestations. This is true of all planets, signs, houses, and aspects. Take Saturn in Aries as an example: at the base level, it might represent the extremely defensive individual who asserts his will at inappropriate times with a pushy, insensitive temperament. At the higher level, this same indicator can manifest as the leader who knows the exact right time to be decisive and assertive and when to restrain the will to act.

It is important to remember that a chart does not show the level of evolution of the individual, or how much work this person has done in the arena of consciousness. Once an individual starts working on developing consciousness, issues of territoriality begin to disappear and the person begins to take on the attributes of a global citizen.

# Conclusion

There is an ancient Chinese curse: "May you live in interesting times!" That curse has landed on each of us, as we all certainly live in interesting times! The political maps of the earth are constantly changing as the entire world seems to be in revolution. There is stress, anxiety, and uncertainty everywhere. During times like these, it is certainly a test of skill to maintain tranquillity while achieving. It requires the integration of all that one has learned.

These are, indeed, interesting times, as the pace of cultural evolution has accelerated. Why is there a process of evolution? How do cultures evolve? Where does this new information come from? I see the outer planets as the agents of evolution, breathing new information into the zodiac through the signs they are transiting. When two of the three outer planets are in the same sign, particularly when conjunct, it is a time of tremendous evolution of that sign. With Uranus and Neptune dancing together in Capricorn, this sign becomes the major focus of planetary evolution.

I call this conjunction a time to evolve or dissolve. Scanning Rex Bills' *The Rulership Book*, we can see Capricorn rules (among other things): politics, time, skin cancer, business, crystals, the economy, government, Bosnia (Yugoslavia), credit, fields, lumber, old age and old people, and slums. We can certainly see the revolutionary activity of the outer planets with these items.

The key phrase connected to Capricorn is "I Use." This is the time to "use it, or lose it." We have all been given a tremendous amount of tools to utilize in times of need. We have all been through the self-development era where we have been exposed to hundreds of new age and ancient techniques for personal transformation. From Yoga to Holotropic breathing; from EST training to the 12-step programs; from past lives to disembodied entities; we have been given all of the tools we should ever need. If the flow of consciousness suddenly stopped and we were never given any more new information, it would likely take most of a lifetime just to integrate and utilize all that we have already been shown!

There is a shift of energy occurring as we are now in the last decade of this millennium. It is not enough to have awareness and to know. We are going to have to go beyond knowledge and on to action. When we take information out of the conceptual realm and apply it in our everyday lives, we find an amazing occurrence. Harmony begins to be the norm. When we live in a compartmentalized reality, knowing but not acting on the knowledge, the norm is chaos and conflict. We are either meditating and experiencing peace, or working and experiencing stress, or playing and having fun, each state experienced as separate and distinct from the others. When apply what we have learned, we can experience a multidimensional reality from a centered point.

When we look to the heavens, we see that harmony is the norm, and conflict is the illusion. This is not what the religions of the world have taught. The religions have conditioned people into believing the fall/redemption principle of life on earth. It is taught that we were in paradise with God, and somehow fell from grace into the earth plane. We are working at regaining divine favor so that we can rejoin God. This has been taught in a thousand different ways. The sad spin-off of this type of teaching is that it implies that here is not good. How can people ever experience the bliss of existence if they have been taught the doctrine of original sin?

Those who have learned the paths to tranquillity have traditionally renounced the world and its ways. The path of renunciation has been held in high esteem by spiritual seekers. Now, with the Capricorn conjunctions, we need to look at the themes of responsibility. It is the responsibility of those who are spiritually inclined to get involved with the schools, the cities, the children, and the environment. Otherwise, the people who have developed the morals, values, and ethics of the spiritual path are not contributing to the culture. Then the culture is left to those who have developed power and greed instead of the refined aspects of their character. If those who are aware of the profound gift of spirit that each and every life on this planet is, are also the ones who get involved with decisions impacting our lives, imagine how fast we could turn this planet around from its current tailspin.

People want to help. Astrologers are in a unique position of having the powerful tool of the horoscope available to help their clients connect with a meaningful existence. When we think about the conditions in the world and what can be done to change them, it is easy to drift into feelings of futility in the face of the enormous task. But change happens at the grass roots levels with individuals first, then follows to the collective. By helping our clients integrate the tools of consciousness into their daily lives, we will have performed a tremendous service to the planet.

**Errol Weiner**

Errol Weiner was born in Johannesburg, South Africa, on January 28, 1949. He relocated to the United Kingdom at the age of twenty-nine. From 1978 to 1980, he lived in the Findhorn Foundation in Scotland.

Over the past fifteen years, Errol has studied, lived, and taught transpersonal astro-psychology, and over the last twelve years has combined this with his work as a full-time networker and group facilitator. With his partner Imogen, he is the co-coordinator of the East Meets West Renaissance Network which is based in Brighton, England. The Network helps to link-up people and groups in the western world and in Eastern Europe and Russia.

Errol has worked in the United Kingdom, South Africa, California, and throughout Eastern Europe and Russia. In 1991, the Network organized an "East Meets West" gathering in Brighton, which brought together 120 people from East and West. He is the author of *Transpersonal Astrology—Discovering the Soul's Purpose* (Element Books) and is at present writing a new book on the relationship among the Rising Sign, Sun Sign, and Moon Sign.

# Transpersonal Values in the Birth Chart

Errol Weiner

## Introduction

In order to comprehend more fully the transpersonal dimension and values of the birth chart, it is necessary to gain a deeper understanding of the words "transpersonal" and "values." Many astrologers presuppose that transpersonal astrology simply implies a spiritual interpretation of the horoscope. From an over-all perspective this is true, but it is also an oversimplification of the science of transpersonal astro-psychology in its updated form. The foundations of this new science have to be understood before we can proceed to chart interpretation. "Values" are defined by the Oxford dictionary as "the worth of, and the ability of, a thing to serve a purpose." What therefore is the worth of the horoscope and what is its deeper purpose?

Traditional and humanistic astro-psychology have their own set of values, but it is necessary to reevaluate and update this ancient science in order to discover its transpersonal dimension. This requires the astrologer and psychologist to transform their own consciousness radically, so that they become attuned to the needs of 21st century humanity. In the classic book *Esoteric Astrology* by the Master DK and Alice Bailey, we are informed that there are two branches of astrology and psychology: one which is personality-based, and one which is soul-based. There are many differences between the two, including the interpretation of the Rising, Sun, and Moon signs. Because a large number of people are now entering into relationship with their higher selves (the soul) it is necessary to explore this transpersonal dimension quite consciously and energetically.

## Personal and Transpersonal

"Transpersonal" indicates that which is beyond (trans) the personal. "Personal" relates to the personality, lower self, lower ego or dweller on the threshold (see diagram 1). The soul, higher self, atman or angel of the shining presence is that transpersonal dimension of the self which overlights the personality (see diagram 2) and is a free consciousness or entity. The central quality of the soul is intelligent love because it is an integration of heart (the heart Chakra), higher mind (the brow Chakra), and higher creative action (the throat Chakra). The soul is also qualified by selfless service because it is a Master of the solar system and, as such, serves this system as an intelligent, loving, purposeful, and selfless agent. One aspect of this service is directed toward the human personality, its lower counterpart. So-called personalities reside on the planet, while souls reside in the solar system. The soul is the inner Master of each human personality.

The soul is a group consciousness and is integrally part of a collective whole, because it is a part of the 5th kingdom of souls, the human kingdom composing the 4th kingdom. The soul is consciously grouped under one of the seven great psycho-spiritual Rays (see page 105) which govern all life in

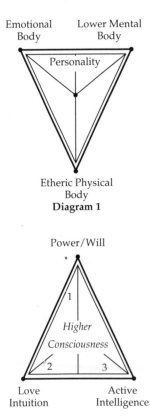

Emotional Body        Lower Mental Body

Personality

Etheric Physical Body

**Diagram 1**

Power/Will

1

*Higher*

*Consciousness*

2        3

Love Intuition        Active Intelligence

**Diagram 2**

our cosmic system. The group soul which serves our planetary system is said to originate from the planet Venus, Earth's sister or twin planetary system.

Venus in our solar system is the twin soul or alter ego of the Earth. Venus and the Earth compose a vertical polarity in transpersonal astro-psychology. The soul is referred to in the esoteric teachings as "the angel of the shining presence or the solar angel," and the personality is referred to as "the dweller on the threshold or the earth self." The soul and the 5th kingdom of souls form an integral part of the spiritual Hierarchy or inner government of our planetary system, who are the guides and custodians of the divine plan for the Earth. This understanding has to be integrated into the science of the new astrology and psychology.

## Soul and Personality Integration

The soul and the personality, on individual, group, and collective levels, are two interconnected entities and related to the Christ (Solar) and Luciferic (Earth) principles. It is only when true individuality begins to be developed; that is, when higher consciousness begins to awaken, that their interplay becomes a conscious accelerated process. The experience of this interplay between the polarities and their gradual but accelerated movement towards integration or fusion ("at-one-ment" in Christian terminology, or yoga or tao in Eastern terminology) underlie the very purpose of human evolution and govern spiritual initiation. Transpersonal astrology and psychology are directly concerned with this because *spiritual initiation underlies evolutionary experience.*

## Spiritual Initiation

The soul is the perfected human archetype of the human personality, and the 5th kingdom of souls is the perfected collective human archetype of the 4th kingdom of personalities. Personalities inhabit the physical, emotional, and lower mental planes of consciousness which correspond to the base, sacral, and solar plexus chakras; whereas souls inhabit the higher creative, higher mental, and intuitive planes of consciousness which correspond to the throat, heart, and brow chakras. These two triangles of energy eventually fuse into one interconnected, six-pointed star (the Star of David symbol; see diagram 3) when at-one-ment or yoga is

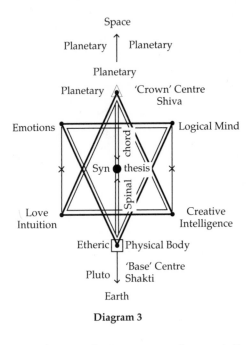

Diagram 3

achieved. This attainment brings to an end the wheel of death and re-birth and is referred to as the 3rd transfiguration initiation.

The sign and symbol of Capricorn hide the secret of this initiation. It is only after this initiation that one begins to enter the door of monadic or cosmic evolution, for the 7th initiation is the 1st cosmic initiation. The Christ and the Buddha have taken the 7th initiation which is why They are referred to as "Lords," the title of a 7th degree initiate. The words "master and cosmic" are often used by people in spiritual groupings without a real understanding of their meaning. The relationship among the monad, soul, and personality is the foundation of all esoteric wisdom (see diagram 4).

The Christ or Lord Maitreya is the head of the spiritual Hierarchy of our planet and Lucifer is the head of the material Hierarchy. Lucifer is also the doorkeeper to the world of the soul, and this is why the planet Saturn represents Lucifer and simultaneously the principle of testing and opportunity. Jupiter and Saturn are the two planets related to these dual principles. *The interpretation of the horoscope will differ when one sees things from this perspective.*

For example, let us take the Saturn and Jupiter conjunction that occurs approximately every 20 years. The last conjunction took place on December 31, 1980, in early Libra. The deeper meaning of this conjunction is that the soul and personality of Libra (the Spirit of peace, balance, and equilibrium) would be seeking integration and manifestation over the 20 years from 1981 to 2000. This is the underlying or "overlighting" factor behind the huge changes in the world over the past ten years. The end of the cold war signalled the cyclic fusion between these two Libran

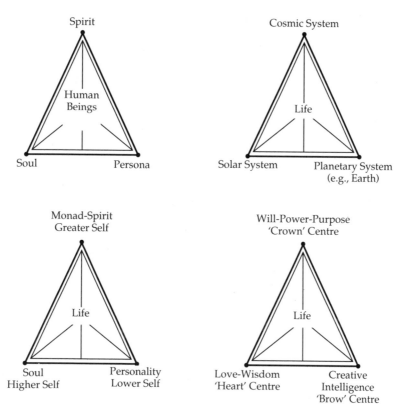

**Diagram 4**

principles, with peace and cooperation between the United States and the West (Jupiter) and the former U.S.S.R. and the East (Saturn) being the collective mirror of this conjunction. The first ten years of this conjunction (1981 to 1991) bring its energy into manifestation and the last ten years (1991 to 2000) result in its concrete conclusions. One might say that Jupiter rules the first cycle and Saturn the second cycle, and these cycles provide a good example of the inner and outer workings of both these planets.

These two polarized, yet interconnected, principles exist within the individual, within all partnerships and human relationships, in nature, within all nations, cultures and religions, within our planetary and solar system, and throughout the universe. Their fusion or synthesis is not a singular process but an ongoing evolutionary unfoldment that leads to greater and greater knowledge, understanding, love, wisdom, power (em-powerment), responsibility, creative action, and selfless service. There are many minor and five major initiations (in human evolution) along the Path that leads from darkness to light, from ignorance to truth, and from death to immortality. The task of Jesus was to demonstrate these initiations to humanity and they were symbolized through the birth, baptism, transfiguration, crucifixion, and resurrection. Soul and personality are finally fused at the 3rd initiation, and one becomes a Master of the Wisdom at the 5th initiation.

The vast majority of awakened humanity are in the process of taking the 1st and 2nd initiations which bring about a profound transformation in the material, emotional, sexual, mental, and spiritual life of the individual. It is these individuals who seek astrological and psychological guidance, and this is why the information we are discussing needs to become an integral part of the new astro-psychology.

## The Rising Sign and the Horoscope

As astrologers are aware, the Rising Sign is that sign rising on the eastern horizon of the Earth at the date, place, and time of birth. This could be the birth of an individual, a group, a nation, or an event, of course. If we are to understand the true significance of the Rising Sign, it is vital to comprehend just *what* is being born. Some would say it is *consciousness*, but what is consciousness? From the esoteric point of view it is a portion of the soul that is taking incarnation.

The Oxford dictionary defines incarnation as "the embodiment in flesh; the idea in concrete form; the living embodiment of quality." The soul is this "idea," for it is the perfected archetype taking concrete form. It is the immortal self that embodies the purpose, quality, and intelligence of any material form. The soul and the Ascendant are therefore directly connected, and it is this interconnection that the majority of astrologers fail to recognize. The Rising Sign is associated with the soul triangle and the Sun sign with the personality triangle.

*The purpose of the higher self and the path of its unfoldment, the Quest for the Holy Grail, are embodied in the Rising Sign,* and it is this understanding that, in many senses, is the greatest revelation of the horoscope. We say "First things first," and the Rising Sign is that starting point in the birth chart and therefore connected to the soul, *the causal factor behind the personality.*

The vast majority of astrologers, including those who call themselves transpersonal, still continue to interpret the Rising Sign in the traditional manner, and in so doing fail to interpret its true meaning. In other words, they miss out on the greatest revelation of the horoscope. The Rising Sign is the most important transpersonal factor in the horoscope, and its correct interpretation allows one to decipher the deeper purpose and the unique path of any incarnation.

The Sun can be found in any of the twelve houses of the chart, and it is the Sun sign and not the Rising Sign that represents the personality (persona = the mask). The Sun sign is a line of least resistance, but the Rising Sign has to be deciphered, clarified, worked upon, and unfolded in time and space if one is to fulfill one's higher spiritual purpose in life. Conscious alignment and relationship and cooperation with the higher self is the goal, and the Rising Sign holds the key to this accomplishment.

Each sign of the zodiac has a transpersonal keynote that is capable of revealing the soul-purpose of each sign. It is necessary to meditate on and contemplate these keynotes to decipher their inner meaning, and to to use this understanding in the attainment of our deeper spiritual goals. I have dealt with these keynotes in my book, *Transpersonal Astrology,* published by Element Books in 1991, and they can be found at the end of this article.

## The Science of Triangles

There is a triune dimension to every aspect of creation, and this, of course, includes the seven rays, the twelve zodiacal signs, the twelve planets of our solar system (which includes the Moon and Vulcan), and the human kingdom itself (see diagram 5 for examples of various interconnected triangles). Spirit or greater Self (the Monad), soul or higher self, and personality or lower self exist throughout creation, with "life" itself lying at the center of this trinity. A zodiacal sign, a planet, a solar system, and so on are "alive"; each is a dynamic living Entity, a spiritual life, integrally part of a greater dynamic whole which, in turn, is part of a greater whole. This science of wholism extends throughout all creation,

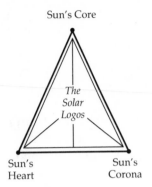

Sun's Core

*The Solar Logos*

Sun's Heart     Sun's Corona

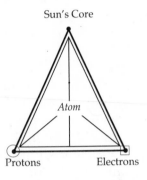

Sun's Core

*Atom*

Protons     Electrons

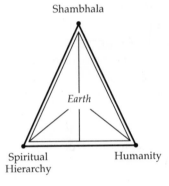

Shambhala

*Earth*

Spiritual Hierarchy     Humanity

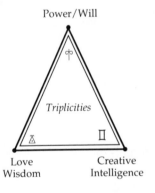

Power/Will

*Triplicities*

Love Wisdom     Creative Intelligence

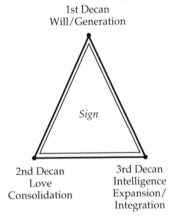

1st Decan Will/Generation

*Sign*

2nd Decan Love Consolidation     3rd Decan Intelligence Expansion/ Integration

**Diagram 5**

from the atom to the galaxies themselves.

Each sign of the zodiac has three facets, and each requires a different interpretation. For example Leo Rising, a Leo Sun sign, and a Leo Moon sign have different meanings because the first is related to the soul of Leo, the second to the conscious personality of Leo, and the third to the unconscious shadow of Leo. The same triangular science applies to the planets. For example, Mars is the personality ruler of Aries, Mercury rules its soul, and Uranus rules the monad of Aries (see diagram 6).

## Transpersonal Planetary Rulerships

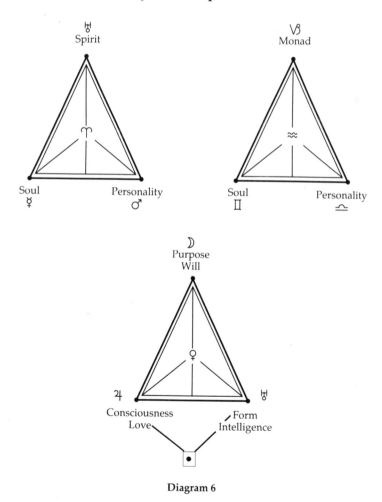

**Diagram 6**

From the perspective of horoscope interpretation, it is necessary to use the *transpersonal* planetary rulers in the case of the Rising Sign. It is also necessary to interpret the soul of this Sign and not simply its personality. In other words, Sagittarius Rising and Sagittarius Sun have *different* interpretations; additionally Jupiter is the ruler in the Sun's case whereas the *Earth* is the ruler in the case of Sagittarius as the Rising Sign.

The Earth in the horoscope is placed opposite the Sun (in traditional astrology the Earth is not included in the chart) because the Sun and Earth represent the polarities of male and female, father and mother, light and dark, consciousness and unconsciousness, and love-wisdom and intelligent action. The energies of the Sun sign have to be materialized through the Earth and its position in the chart.

The Earth also reveals much about the unrefined nature of the individual that requires purification and transformation. The Earth is a non-sacred planet and is unrefined and polluted, physically, emotionally, and mentally. The Earth, collectively and personally, ecological detoxification and transformation, has a dual interpretation: it is a planet of learning, growth, testing, and transformation; and a habitation where spirit needs to be anchored into intelligent action.

The above information will obviously result in major changes in chart interpretation because:

- The planet ruling the Ascendant is the most important planetary energy in the chart, the so-called lord of the chart, and, in the case of transpersonal astrology, this is *not* the same planet as in traditional astrology.

- This new ruling planet, is not only a different planet but it will be found in a different house (in the vast majority of cases) from the traditional ruler.

- The ruling Ray, the "Ray Lord"' of the chart, which is as important as the planet itself, will be different to the ray of the traditional ruler; in the case of Sagittarius, the 2nd Ray of love-wisdom (royal blue), a feminine Ray, rules Jupiter, whereas the 3rd Ray of active intelligence (nature green), a masculine objective Ray, rules the Earth.

## The Seven Psycho-Spiritual Rays

The seven Rays originate in the Great Bear constellation and sweep through and govern all life in our cosmic system, including the zodiacal constellations, the planets, humanity, and the individual. Each zodiacal sign and planet is ruled by one or other of these Rays (see Ray rulerships at the end of this article). The Rays ruling the Rising Sign and its transpersonal ruler and the Sun sign and its traditional ruler are the most important and play a major role in chart interpretation. The Ray governing the transpersonal ruling planet is the Ray Lord and plays a major role in the psycho-spiritual purpose, qualities, experiences, and spiritual work of the individual, group, or nation. If we again use the Sagittarian example, the Earth is the transpersonal ruler. Its Ray is the 3rd, the green Ray of creative intelligence and organization, adaptability, economics and business, material law and order (Saturn is also a 3rd Ray planet), and spirit manifesting through matter.

Those with Sagittarius Rising will be directly influenced by these 3rd Ray energies as they move toward fulfilling their deeper purpose, path, and goals in life. Green will be their soul color. Sagittarius is the major sign governing networks, the organizational infrastructures of the new Era, and networking, the activities related to the development of these networks. People and groupings with this sign Rising will pioneer these new organizations and will play a major role in the networking of information, people and nations. For example the USA, Mikhail Gorbachev, the Findhorn Foundation, and many global networkers *have Sagittarius Rising.**

The Sun sign and its personal ruler and ruling ray also play a major role in chart interpretation. The Sun sign represents the hero/heroine figure. This figure is defined by the Oxford dictionary as "the individual of superhuman qualities who is favored by the gods." In mythology, this individual goes on an adventurous quest in search of the Holy Grail, the Golden Fleece, and so on, *all of which are symbols of the immortal soul.* The journey includes many tests and battles with ogres, monsters, hydras, and other devilish figures, who symbolize aspects of the lower self such as greed, lust, fear, ignorance, attachment, glamour, guilt,

---

*   Readers should be aware that the Rising Sign of the United States is under debate. Most popularly it is Gemini; but research and arguments abound for further testing of Sagittarius, Scorpio, and other possibilities.—Editor

pride, and so on. The individual is "favored by the gods" and, at certain stages on the journey, is guided and protected by these higher powers. The soul, who has central responsibility for our evolution, is the true inner guiding Master in *all* these myths.

The particular "labor" that this figure has to enter into is represented by the Rising sign. The Sun sign represents the "individual" undertaking the journey and the particular qualities, characteristics, and creative gifts he or she embodies and can use on the journey. The sign and the Ray of the sign, and the planetary ruler and its Ray are directly related to this potential. For example the Sun in Aries has the 1st Ray of power and the 7th Ray of synthesis (Aries) and the 6th Ray of dynamic devotional idealism (Mars) at its disposal, and these ray energies and the energies of Aries and Mars need to be consciously used in fulfilling the labor or purpose and path of the person's higher self, represented by the Rising Sign. This is a different interpretation to that of traditional and humanistic astrology.

## The Seven-Year Cycles

The soul unfolds its purpose in seven-year cycles. There are not only individual seven-year cycles (birth to seven, seven to fourteen, and so on), but global seven-year cycles too. For example 1978 through 1984, 1985 through 1991, and 1992 through 1998 are planetary seven-year cycles. These global cycles were first revealed by the Master DK through Alice Bailey in the Arcane Teachings. At the beginning of each of these cycles, the spiritual Hierarchy releases new energies into the world. These energies unfold themselves over the seven years. For example, in 1978 President Sadat of Egypt initiated his peace process with Israel; in 1985 Gorbachev became General Secretary of the U.S.S.R., and in 1992 the Rio Summit took place in Brazil.

From the individual perspective, the soul releases new energy into the consciousness of its personality at the beginning of each seven-year cycle (the "seven year itch"). In fact, many people experience physical and emotional itching at 7, 14, 21, 28, 35, 42, 49, 56, 63, 70, 77, and 84 years of age. Each year of a seven-year cycle also has a specific significance that corresponds to the first seven signs of the zodiac (28 to 29 corresponds to Aries, 29 to 30 to Taurus, and so on). These cycles should be taken into consideration when interpreting the horoscope.

## The Horoscope of Mikhail Gorbachev

The example chart I am using in this chapter is that of Mikhail Gorbachev, the ex-President of the former USSR. There is no known time for Gorbachev's birth, and the time used in the chart was received in meditation by my wife, Imogen, who is a sensitive. The keynote of Sagittarius Rising is "I see a goal, I reach that goal, and than I see the next goal." Gorbachev's entire life history seems to have been dominated by this inner keynote and there are various books which reveal this Sagittarian aspect of his life (*The New Russians* by Hedrick Smith, Hutchingson Publications; *I Hope* by Raisa Gorbachev, Fontana; and *Perestroika* by Mikhail Gorbachev, Fontana). Gorbachev would see a goal, he would reach that goal and then he would see the next expanded goal and move toward achieving it with one-pointed aspiration.

In 1978, the first year of a global seven-year cycle, he was summoned to Moscow by the Communist Party bosses to take up his post in the Politburo. With the quick demise of Brezhnev, Chernenko, and Andropov over these seven years (1978 to 1985), Gorbachev finally took over the post of Secretary General of the Communist Party in 1985, the start of the new global-seven year cycle. Gorbachev was largely unknown to the western world up to this time, and his new status took everyone in the west by complete surprise.

Gorbachev was the first Soviet leader with real vision, and this vision was national and international in its scope. He travelled extensively in the pursuit of this vision and proved to be an inspirational and powerful communicator. In seven years, he completely transformed the socio-political climate of the world by pioneering the transformation of his country and initiating the end of the cold war. He resigned his Presidency on Christmas day, December 25, 1991, the final year of the seven-year cycle.

Gorbachev's visions, goals, and activities were all qualified by a step-by-step process (Sagittarius Rising). His critics often stated that he did not seem to have any clear long-term goal. To a large extent, this was true; Gorbachev's major purpose was to bring to an end the old Soviet system and plant the seeds for a new, and as yet undefined, system. Gorbachev stated during the earlier part of his leadership that "in order for there to be reconstruction there must first be demolition." Sagittarius is a fire sign and fire by its very nature is both a destroyer and recreator. Heat (fire) is necessary for transformation and transmutation. With Sagittarius rising, the major task is to destroy old crystallized forms while simultaneously revealing a new updated vision of the future. The task is *not* to concretize this vision (except in its initiatory form); this is the work of *Capricorn* rising.

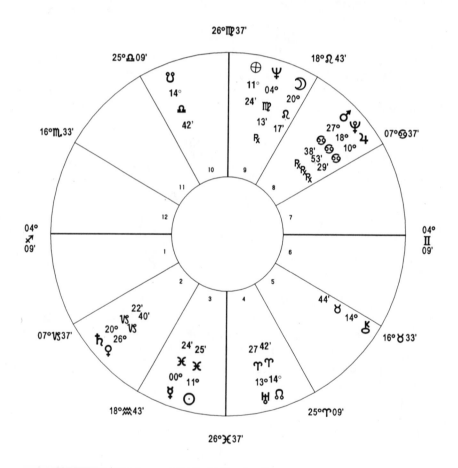

**Mikhail Gorbachev**
March 2, 1931, Privalnoye
10:59:24 PM GMT
47N29  32E17

Pluto and Mars in Gorbachev's 8th House (the co-rulers of Scorpio and in their own house) further accentuate this destroying role. Both planets are in Cancer, the sign ruling mass consciousness, the family, and home, and Gorbachev not only demolished the crystallized consciousness and forms of his own country but also those of the East-West divide and the world at large. By the time he resigned on Christmas day 1991, the old Soviet Union, the old East European block, and the old East-West order had all collapsed, and a new world order had been seeded.

## The Planetary and Ray Rulers

The Earth is in Virgo in the 9th House, the House of Sagittarius itself. Gorbachev's vision had a global context to it, and always included two keynotes: new thinking and a new soviet and world order. Sagittarius, the 3rd Ray, and the 9th House are all concerned with creative visionary thinking, and Virgo is concerned with clear, logical thought and communication, and structure, order, and efficient organization. In fact, the Earth (3rd Ray) in Virgo (2nd Ray of love-wisdom) in the 9th House of Sagittarius is a wonderful combination to integrate the higher abstract visionary mind and the lower concrete organizational mind. (See page 125 for Table of Rays.)

Here we have Mercury, ruler of Virgo, and Jupiter, ruler of the 9th House, working in cooperation. Mercury in Pisces just off the cusp of Aquarius in the 3rd House in opposition with Neptune, the ruler of Pisces in the 9th, is indicative of Gorbachev's open, inclusive, tolerant, highly idealistic, and globally orientated mind. The mutual reception of Neptune and Mercury is truly a divine gift in the above regard. Jupiter is exalted in Cancer, and this gave Gorbachev the graceful ability to bring about radical transformation (8th House) with a great degree of tolerance, understanding, and patience.

Gorbachev was also a great planetary networker. In fact he was more responsible than any national leader for bringing the leaders and the peoples of the world community together in the spirit of East West friendship and cooperation. He traveled extensively, a vital aspect of the spiritual work of Sagittarius Rising, and was able to adapt his consciousness to the varied national and cultural environments he found himself in, which is also a typical quality of Sagittarius Rising and the 3rd Ray. His smiling and humorous countenance and his positive outlook on life as a whole, another typical Sagittarian quality, made him by far the most popular leader in the world community. He gave hope to humanity and hope is a keyword of Sagittarius.

### The Sun Sign in the Transpersonal Chart

The Sun sign in traditional astrology is associated with one's identity and creative expression. From the transpersonal perspective, the Sun sign symbolizes one's personal and not one's higher (soul) identity, for the Sun is the *conscious channel* through which the energies of the zodiacal constellations, which represent the soul, enter our solar system. The soul is one's true identity, the silent watcher, the perfected archetype of who one truly is, and this self stands outside the chart although it reveals its purpose through the Rising Sign and its transpersonal ruler. It is important to distinguish the difference between these two aspects of the self because traditional astrology has often confused the two.

The Sun sign reveals the present life-stage of personal evolution that one has reached on the path of evolution. It is concerned with one's personality identity, integration, development, unfoldment, and fulfillment. It is a line of least resistance in relationship to the present life, for one is naturally one's Sun sign. It determines the overall way that one will express oneself spiritually, mentally, emotionally, and materially. The Sun sign obviously needs to be developed and matured as time goes on. All personal energies or the subpersonalities as symbolized by the other personal planets need to and will be integrated by the Sun sign, for the entire solar system lives by the grace of the Sun's rays. The Sun sign represents the causal factor of the personality, which is also the third quality (active intelligence) of the soul.

Gorbachev's Sun in Pisces (see page 108), the 12th and last sign of the planetary zodiac, indicates why he was such a selfless server of his nation and humanity. In Pisces, the ego has to give its all to the greater divine Plan; it has to release its ego desires, ambitions, and attachments and give, love, and serve unconditionally. The 2nd Ray of love-wisdom and the 6th Ray of devotional idealism govern Pisces and Gorbachev demonstrated these qualities abundantly: he was an extremely open, tolerant, inclusive, wise, forgiving, loving, and selfless human being, and communicated these qualities in writing and speech. He was also very diverse in his communication, and integrated politics, economics, social issues, international affairs, ecology, and spiritual matters in his work. He was a wonderful example of the Sun in mutable Pisces in the 3rd House of communication. Mercury in its own house enabled him to communicate in a very articulate fashion. He wrote his book *Perestroika* in one month, a fine example of mutual reception Mercury opposition Neptune inspiration.

The Sun in opposition to Neptune (its dispositor) is a very illuminating aspect: with this aspect, one could say that Gorbachev was a great archetype and initiate of Pisces and its Age, and thus his chosen destiny was to be the focal point for part of its completion and dissolution. Having power in his hands, he began to give it away, finally releasing it all to the spirit of the future. This is the crucifixion experience, which is directly related to Pisces, the final sign of the zodiac. Pluto and Neptune, the planets of death, dissolution, and mergence rule Pisces, as does Jupiter, the planet which reveals the future. Having crucified himself, Gorbachev is now in a period of rest (which corresponds to a similar rest period after physical death, before one continues one's journey) and will surely resurrect himself in due time.

### The Earth and the Sun

Sagittarius Rising has the unique disposition of having its transpersonal ruler, the Earth, always placed opposite the Sun. It is this placement that creates the opportunity for people to integrate and fuse their higher-self planet and Ray (the Earth and the 3rd Ray) and their lower-self planet and Ray (the Sun and the 2nd Ray). In Gorbachev's case, Virgo and Pisces are both ruled by the 2nd Ray of love, wisdom, inclusiveness, and service, and the 6th Ray of abstract devotional idealism, high aspiration, dedication, and selfless service. He is thus a great example of the individual who has fused soul and personality.

With the Sun in Pisces and its transpersonal ruler Pluto in the 8th House of Scorpio, it is obvious that Gorbachev's work was to dissolve and demolish the old Soviet and East West system and, in so doing, bring to a close the old age of Pisces. In the process, he would of course have to do the same to his own lower self. Self-destruction requires that one destroy one's crystallized self so that a transformed self can become a clearer instrument for the soul.

With Mars and Pluto in their own house forming a wide stellium with Jupiter, this destruction process, which is both psychological and material, was fated to succeed. Scorpio is not only the sign of death and rebirth but also of regeneration and *reorientation toward a new way of life,* because it comes after Libra, the sign of rest and equilibrium. Here we can see the vast implications of Gorbachev's greater work, namely the reorientation of humanity toward a new world order and new Era. Once Sun-in-Pisces Gorbachev had completed his purpose, he gave over power to Sun-in-Aquarius Yeltsin. Just before resigning, Gorbachev said "I have now completed my major life purpose." If ever collective humanity had experienced the personal pain of one individual in his crucifixion it was that of Gorbachev.

Just before Gorbachev's resignation, transiting Uranus was opposing natal Jupiter, so the planet ruling Aquarius and the planet ruling Pisces opposed one another. Neptune was about to oppose natal Pluto by transit (in 1992) and it was obvious that, with these two co-rulers of Pisces under siege, Gorbachev's time was up. According to the Master DK (Esoteric Astrology) Russia has Aquarius Rising and the Gorbachev Yeltsin swap-over was an archetypal transformation from an old to a new cycle which Russia was destined to fulfill. With Aquarius Rising and her ruling soul Ray the 7th (the Ray of "ceremonial order and synthesis" which rules the new Era) Russia was destined to play a major role in the dissolution of the old order and the birth of the new Era. In *The Destiny of the Nations* (by Master DK, Lucis Publications) it is stated that "out of Russia will emerge the new world religion," a religion that will demonstrate an inclusive spirituality that recognizes "one God, one humanity and one destiny."

## The Moon in the Chart

In transpersonal astrology, the Moon is a dead planet. According to the ancient wisdom (*Esoteric Astrology,* Lucis Publications) the Logos of the Moon left its body during the Lemurian Era and, since that time, the Moon has been in a state of disintegration. This planetary process corresponds to the soul leaving the human body at death. The Moon therefore symbolizes "that which is dead and gone; that which has no life and that which belongs to the bygone past." This "past" is related to one's upbringing and conditioning and is also linked to one's past life. The Moon is a line of least resistance in relationship to the past, because it symbolizes where and how one is chained to the past and how one clings instinctively to the habit patterns of childhood and bloodline upbringing. It is only when one has become conscious of these attachments and bonds (and this is a lifelong process) that one can begin to break them. It needs to be emphasized that it is the Earth and not the Moon as a feminine principle that is alive. The Moon reflects the energies of the Sun and other transpersonal planets to the Earth but this reflection is unconscious because the Moon has no life of its own.

The Moon in Leo in the 9th House with the house ruler Jupiter (royalty) in Cancer in Gorbachev's chart is a clear indication that he was in a position of royal leadership in a past life and that his present life upbringing was geared toward personal achievement and recognition. The Moon's quincunx to Saturn in Capricorn is related to the karmic link between the present life and this past life and the heavy responsibilities they both carried. Gorbachev's dilemma (quincunx) was to use the energies of this past life in a new, updated, decentralized, and democratic fashion. I would suspect that Gorbachev was a Russian Czar in a past life and that, with Venus (the partner) in Capricorn in its own house, Raisa Gorbachev had been his partner in that incarnation too.

The Moon in Leo linked Gorbachev to Russia's historical past. As someone with past-life memories and instinctive patterns of being a leader (Leo) his greatest problem was twofold. First, he always wanted to be in control and at the centre of things which is typical of Leo. Margaret Thatcher, another Moon in Leo, had the same problem, and both leaders were finally forced to abdicate and fully release their centralized power and control. Second, there were times when he refused to listen to any advice and made some catastrophic mistakes. The best examples are the warnings he received of an impending coup, which he refused to heed. He could not believe that anyone would attempt to overthrow him, which is rather typical of the ego of Leo! In the end result, it was this coup in August, 1991 (Leo), that led to his final demise. The paradox of this situation is that the coup resulted in the banning of the Communist Party and the end of Communism in the U.S.S.R. God does work in strange ways. The Moon in Leo clings to centralized power whereas Sun in Pisces knows that all power comes from above, and can be taken away at any time.

I do not feel that Gorbachev tried to control things in any power-hungry fashion but rather that he was responding instinctively to the Czarist habit patterns of his past life and to his present life conditioning. I suspect that there were two Gorbachev's at work: his Sagittarius *cum* Pisces side that inwardly knew the old Soviet system had to be completely dissolved and destroyed, and his Moon in Leo side that held on instinctively to the old system he knew so well. Pluto and Mars in the 8th in the Moon's own sign is sure proof that his lunar side would lose the battle and be annihilated in the burning ground ground of Scorpio.

My intuitive feeling is that Gorbachev was Czar Peter the Great in his past life, for both leaders were responsible for linking East and West and radically transforming the socio-political structures of Russia. In this regard I recommend the book *Peter the Great* by Robert Massie, Ballantine Books. Both were true pioneers, and the Moon trine the North Node in Aries links this past and present life-pioneering work. Although I have not as yet studied the interrelated charts of Gorbachev, Thatcher, and Reagan, I am bound to feel that they were "old friends" in a past life, and, in a strange and magical sense, they all played their vital roles in the seeding of a new world order in this life.

**The North and South Lunar Nodes**

The nodes play a very important role in transpersonal astro-psychology. The North Node acts as a focal point for the fulfillment of one's present life purpose, path, and work (or dharma). This is why this node has its link to Sagittarius, as does Chiron, for both placements are concerned with the synthesis of soul and personality and of the higher Sagittarius and lower Gemini minds. The Rising Sign, North Node, and Chiron are all placements of strong resistance; they all require focus, attention, energy, time, conscious intelligent development and struggle and effort if one is to fulfill one's true potential. All three of these indicators are ruled by their *transpersonal ruling planets*.

In Gorbachev's chart, Mercury in Pisces just off the cusp of Aquarius in the 3rd House is the inner ruler of the North Node in Aries, and Venus in Capricorn in the 2nd rules the South Node in

Libra. The North Node is in the 4th House, which indicates that his dharma was to initiate a new national and global order. Neptune is the transpersonal ruler of the 4th House and its placement in the 9th shows that Gorbachev was attuned to a high collective spiritual ideal.

It is of interest to note that Chiron in Taurus in the chart is ruled by Vulcan, which is conjunct Mercury, further accentuating the vital significance of Mercury and the 3rd House in Gorbachev's life. Vulcan is governed by the 1st Ray of power and Mercury by the 4th Ray of harmony through conflict, and both these Rays were strong in Gorbachev's thinking and communicating.

The South Node is related to past lives, that is, to a series of past incarnations in which one has developed certain qualities and characteristics that are of relevance to the present life and its purpose. This node is a line of least resistance, and like the subconscious influence of the Moon, tends to drag one instinctively back into past-life habit patterns. If the South Node energies are used in positive complement with those of the North Node, then the past can benefit the needs of the present and future, but this can only be accomplished by transforming the instinctive and habitual behavior patterns of the South lower-self Node.

Gorbachev's South Node is in the 10th House in Libra, ruled by Venus in Capricorn in the 2nd. One of Gorbachev's major problems was that he always tried to please everyone in the political spectrum, be it the old diehard Communists, the more liberal-minded Communists, or the new Democrats. This is typical of the Libra personality. In attempting to do this, he often missed opportunities to change the old Soviet system itself. I would also suspect that Raisa Gorbachev had some influence on Gorbachev in this area, since Venus represents the partner. Raisa has the Sun in Capricorn.

On the other hand, the Gorbachevs' partnership was an essential ingredient in the success of their leadership, and this node is further proof of their marriage connection in past lives. Venus in Capricorn makes for a very committed, loving, and co-working partnership. It is interesting to note that, from the beginning of Gorbachev's reign, I felt a very strong and unusual connection to him and Raisa. I have my nodes in the same position, my Venus is conjunct Gorbachev's Saturn, and my Moon is conjunct his Venus in the same house.

The ruler of Libra and the natural ruler of the 10th House are both in Capricorn in the 2nd, and this created an instinctive fear of losing control of the situation and of wanting everything to evolve in a harmonious fashion. Gorbachev was truly surprised and shocked when war broke out between the Armenians and Azeris, and when the coup took place in August, 1991. Transiting Neptune was T-squaring the North and South Nodes and Uranus was opposing natal Jupiter at this exact time (August 17 to 20). The third transit of Neptune and Uranus to these natal placements signaled Gorbachev's final fall from power and the simultaneous disintegration of the old Soviet Union and its rebirth into the CIS or Commonwealth of Independent States. This dissolution and new birth are typical of a combined Neptune-Uranus transit. The failed coup itself was responsible for bringing about this death and rebirth. It was the perfect situation at the perfect time: Uranus and Neptune are twin embodiments of the divine plan and are in tune with divine will.

Gorbachev always tried to walk the middle path between two extremes, which is typical of Libra and Venus. In a sense, this was the great Libran gift that he inherited from his South Node past lives. He was the grand mediator and had to walk a constant tightrope over the seven years that he was in power. He also tended to see the best in everyone, another Libran characteristic, and when he discovered that the coup members included many of his good friends (with friends like these, who needs enemies?) he was deeply shocked and hurt. To the Libran, honorable friendship is of great importance.

Gorbachev's North Node is conjunct Uranus in the 4th House and the opposition with the South node must have caused him much inner pain. He often acted on the spur of the moment, surprising everyone, typical of Uranus in Aries. He had a global outlook on life and often communicated his feelings, ideas, and thoughts on common, human, and planetary issues (Pisces IC). He initiated and pioneered the seeds (Aries) of a new national, European, and world order and era, which was his chosen task. Once again, Pluto and Mars, his 8th House planets, which are co-rulers of Aries, added the demolition aspect to this work.

Having accomplished his greater life purpose in seven remarkable years, Gorbachev still has much constructive work to contribute towards our planet. Pluto will square his natal Moon and Neptune will oppose his natal Pluto in 1992, and these two transits will force him finally to release his attachments to his past (including links to past lives). The fact that the Moon, ruler of Cancer, and Pluto in Cancer in the 8th are being activated by Pluto and Neptune, the co-rulers of Pisces, certainly indicates that 1992 will be a huge year of transformation for Gorbachev. It will free him from his links with Russia itself and enable him to move on to his greater planetary work.

Uranus will conjunct his natal Saturn-Pluto opposition throughout most of 1993. This suggests that the time to transcend one's personal karma has arrived, and Gorbachev can move on to greater and more freeing levels of thought, leadership, and responsibility. Also, Neptune will conjunct his Saturn in 1993 at the same time. All together, this will free Gorbachev from national karma and allow him to  proceed directly to his greater global work. It will also open him up to a great upsurge of illumination through his intuition, dreams, and life experiences, and will bring him into a far greater realization of his spiritual nature.

What needs to be understood is that Gorbachev's chart can not be interpreted *in a purely traditional sense.*  By his life example, Gorbachev has proved to be an initiate of a high degree. He has certainly taken the 3rd initiation and has thus fully integrated his soul and personality. As such, transits can not be interpreted in his chart as they would be in a normal chart. The stress factors he has integrated and the service he has selflessly undertaken throughout the past seven years and more have created quite a remarkable human being. For this reason alone, it should be fascinating to see how the 1992 and 1993 transits affect him and transform his life work. The world owes this great man a huge debt of thanks.

## The Uranus Neptune Conjunction of 1993

I have chosen this second chart example because this 1993 conjunction of Uranus–Neptune is of immense importance to the world. The conjunction takes place approximately every 170 years, and results in huge changes for humanity and the planet. The 1479 and 1650 conjunctions occurred in Sagittarius, and resulted in the fifteenth century Renaissance and the seventeenth century period of Enlightenment. Both planets had not yet been discovered. The 1821 conjunction was in Capricorn. It resulted in the liberation of a number of South American countries from colonial rule, major discoveries were made in the field of electromagnetism, and Babbage invented the first computer. Uranus had been discovered by that time, but not Neptune.

The 1993 conjunction will also be in Capricorn, but this is the first time this conjunction will occur since both planets were discovered and are in our consciousness together. The conjunction will be in 19 degrees 34 minutes of Capricorn in the 8th House, with Gemini Rising and the Sun in Aquarius in the 9th, in the chart drawn for London. The Moon is also in Gemini in the 12th. This means that Uranus, dispositor of the Aquarius Sun and MC, is one of the major conjunction planets, and Saturn, the dispositor of the conjunction itself, is in Aquarius conjunct Mercury and the MC. The 7th Ray (Uranus) and the 3rd Ray (Saturn) are directly interconnected, for the 7th disrupts and transforms the mental and etheric body of the planet and its lifeforms, and the 3rd brings about change in the corresponding physical structures.

### The Rising Sign and Its Ruler

The keynote of this conjunction's overall purpose is "I recognize the other self and in the waning of that self I grow and glow." This is the inner keynote of Gemini Rising. Gemini is the sign ruling all the dualities and their inter-relationship and integration. It is also the sign ruling human evolution, and it is the sign governing the soul of humanity. The Gemini full Moon cycle is called "the festival of humanity" because the Christ and the 5th kingdom of souls communicate Their knowledge to the human kingdom over this cycle. On this annual full Moon cycle, the Christ, the head of the spiritual Hierarchy, blesses humanity from His center in the Himalayas.

Gemini is the sign of the dualities at their extreme, so this conjunction is going to intensify the interplay of the polarities within the thoughts, feelings, and activities of humanity. The biblical statement, "the sheep shall be separated from the goats," seems most appropriate in this regard. Over the last seven years (1985 to 1991) we have witnessed the end of the cold war and many other positive political changes, but 1992, the first year of the new global seven-year cycle, has had a bloody start.

There is a statement in the Bible which says "there shall come a time of seeming peace but then, nation shall rise-up against nation, there shall be wars, earthquakes, famine . . . ." I feel that this conjunction in the 8th House with Gemini rising is going to produce this splitting of the ways as humanity is presented with the two alternatives of either becoming sheep (a lower symbol of Cancer) and returning to the past and its crystal-

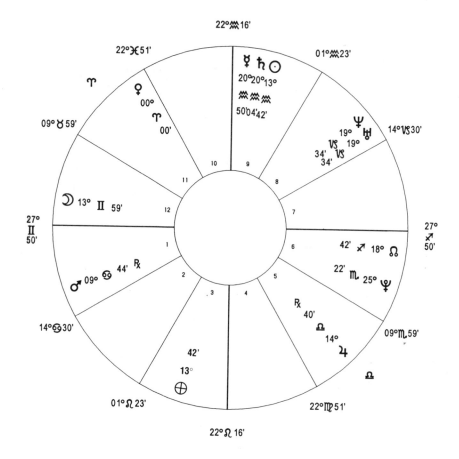

**Uranus–Neptune Conjunction**
**February 2, 1993**
*Gemini Rising Keynote: I recognize the other self*
*and in the waning of that self I grow and glow.*
Chart Ruler-Venus (Ray 5) in Pisces (11th House)

lized and self-destructive belief systems, or becoming goats (the symbol of Capricorn) and moving forward into a new, futuristic, cooperative, and constructive Era.

Gemini and Libra rule this factor of choice because both signs govern dualities and their interrelationship. The biblical statement that the Christ will return at humanity's darkest moment, symbolically "when the Sun and the Moon have been blotted out," seems to indicate that this return will occur when the dualities of the Sun and Moon, symbolizing the logical mind and its polarized thinking (Gemini), have been fused and thereby blotted out. What emerges from this fusion is the higher mind and life of the soul, and this produces "the third way" or the return of Christ-consciousness and all its repercussions. This is the deeper meaning behind this conjunction and its unfoldment over the new seven-year cycle of 1992 to 1998.

The soul of humanity will nevertheless be overlighting this conjunction and its repercussions. Why? Because of two factors:

1. The 2nd Ray of love and wisdom governs Gemini, especially when it is rising or in its transpersonal mode. This is the Ray of the Christ or Lord Maitreya and the overall spiritual Hierarchy, which includes the 5th kingdom of human souls. This Ray of soul love and wisdom will therefore overlight the conjunction. One could well say that the Christ Himself and the higher self of the individual will be overlighting this conjunction. With late Gemini Rising, we also have the Aquarian decanate, which makes Uranus a sub ruler. We thus have in co-rulership of Gemini Rising:

   – the 2nd Ray, the soul ray of the New Era

   – the 5th Ray, the Ray of Venus the soul ruler of Gemini, and the ruling Ray of the sign Aquarius

   – the 7th Ray of spirit/matter synthesis and organization, which rules Uranus, the personal ruler of Aquarius

2. Venus is the transpersonal ruling planet, and Venus is the alter ego of the Earth and represents the soul itself. The 5th Ray governs Venus, and this is the Ray of concrete knowledge. The central quality of Venus is intelligent love or pure reason, the integration of heart and mind (thus its

higher rulership of Gemini). Venus is on the cusp of Pisces and Aries in the 11th House, forming a quintile to the conjunction planets themselves. So the soul of humanity is overlighting and guiding the completion of the old Era (Pisces) and the birth of a new Era (Aquarius) in the house of Aquarius itself. The quintile is the most illuminating of the aspects for it is concerned with intuitive revelation, and it indicates that the soul of Gemini *cum* Aquarius (Venus in the 11th), namely the soul of humanity, will be guiding this dual process of death and rebirth.

## The Conjunction Placement

Uranus and Neptune are the rulers of Aquarius and Pisces, respectively, so this conjunction signals the fusion of these two Ages and the completion of the old Era and birth into a new Era. Uranus is in any case the dispositor of Aquarius-Sun, which will give revolutionary influence and great power to this conjunction. The fact that the conjunction occurs in the 8th House of Scorpio indicates that its influence will be extremely disruptive, and that a great deal of conflict between the old and the new is going to result. Capricorn rules politics and its infrastructures, international affairs, economics, financial institutions, and the infrastructures of world society, and we can expect immense disruptions and transformations in all these areas. If there is going to be an economic collapse (Neptune) and a rapid movement toward a new and decentralized (Uranus) socio-economic system, it will occur from February 2, 1993 on. The sub-rulership of Taurus/Venus through the second decanate of Capricorn, which is related directly to all economic values, issues, and institutions, and to food and agricultural production, points directly to such massive transformation.

A number of great natural catastrophies will also result from this conjunction, because Capricorn governs the earth elementals of the mineral kingdom, Uranus is related to earthquake activity, and Neptune to flooding activity. The 8th House placement will purge things that are out of alignment to the surface, and with its co-rulers Mars and Pluto both in water elemental signs, there will be powerful effects upon the emotions, feelings, and ideals of humanity.

The 6th Ray of dynamic devotional idealism governs Mars and this conflicting planet is in its own 1st House. The idealistic split between those who aspire to serve the future and those who fanatically cling to the crystallized past will be highly intensified. It is the repercussions of this battleground and burning ground that will create the emotional turmoil indicated by Cancer's ruler the Moon placed in the 12th House. Pluto is in the Cancerian (Moon) decanate of Scorpio and it is thus in its final purging phase since the Moon rules the past and attachment to form, and Pluto's work is to destroy these attachments so that humanity can free itself from the chains of the past and move into a new regenerative future. The fact that the co-ruler of Scorpio (Mars) is in Cancer itself (ruled by the Moon) is proof that these fiery Scorpionic gods will work together at purging and purifying the dross of the old and bygone era.

Therefore 1993 will be a unique year in planetary history. It will close down the 20th century and seed a 21st-century Renaissance in politics, economics, science, computer technology, energy, communications, the arts, education, psychology and, of course, in all interhuman relationships. But, like all Renaissance periods, it will also result in great conflict, confusion, fear, escapism, and separation between the old and the new. One thing can be guaranteed: it will be a year that will be like no other and will be remembered (like 1989) as a major turning point in human evolution.

The fact that, in the conjunction chart, the Sun is in Aquarius with Saturn (ruler of Capricorn) and with Mercury (exalted) in the 9th House indicates that the revelations of the new Era will be directly transmitted through the communications media. Television will play a major role in this. In *The Externalization of the Hierarchy* and *The Reappearance of the Christ* (Master DK and Alice Bailey, Lucis Press) we are told that television will be used by the Masters of the Wisdom to prepare the way for the return of the Christ toward the end of this century. Uranus and Neptune are directly connected to television communication: Uranus rules electricity and space technology, and Neptune rules color and sound. So the fact that Uranus is in Capricorn and Saturn is in Aquarius, and that Saturn, Mercury, and the MC are in stellium conjunction, seems to indicate that 1993 will see the media being used for this revelationary purpose. The Christ Himself will use TV to communicate His message to humanity when He appears to inaugurate the new Era.

With the Sun in Aquarius and the stellium of Aquarian placements, the message will of course be the interconnectedness of humanity and the world, and the need for all peoples and nations to work together in creating a new and enlightened world order. This is the highest goal and concrete work (MC) of this conjunction, and we witnessed the seed of this new order at the Rio Summit in Brazil in June, 1992. For the first time in human history, every world leader was talking about the planet. Whatever occurs in the first year of the global seven-year cycle (1992) is the seed for the whole seven years.

## The Moon and the Nodes

The Moon conjunct the South node in Gemini in the 12th of the conjunction chart indicates that there will be a great deal of mental and emotional confusion, fear, and trepidation within the mass consciousness. The Moon's influence on the lower response mechanisms of the masses, especially with its 12th House ruler Neptune in the 8th, is going to cause massive stress and disorientation.

Another result of this double lunar placement is that a great deal of glamour is going to ensue. Many false Messiahs will come into the limelight. These glamorized people will emerge out of their conventional and non-conventional religious groupings and make false claims to be the Christ, Jesus, the Iman, Mahdi, and so on. Many members of the general public, and this includes New Agers, will be drawn to these people and deceived by them because of a lack of real knowledge and understanding.

The Moon-Neptune combination has a very deceptive and self-deceptive influence, for the shadow of the 4th and 6th Rays is the naive and self-deceptive feminine mind and its corresponding emotional escapism. This is another aspect of Gemini rising, for the polar opposites will appear and choice will have to be made. The Moon and South Node are in the Libran decanate and the ego keynote of Libra is "Let choice be made." Saturn, in his Luciferic role of deceiver and tester, conjunct Mercury, ruler of the Geminian opposites, might well mean that the so-called anti-Christ and/or many anti-Christs will make an appearance in 1993.

The Moon exactly trine the Sun and Jupiter will open up the mass consciousness to realities and illusions of the new era. The grand trine in Air signs is a lovely mind-opening aspect, but the problem is that the masses might catch the idea and the abstract revelation *but not know what to do with it all.* On the other hand, many people will choose the line of least resistance (the trine aspect) and go for the easy way out by following those who present naive and simplistic solutions to this turning and crisis point in human evolution.

The North Node in Sagittarius in the 6th House requires people to put in some deep, pondering, and creative thought, combined with intuitive perception and day-to-day, corresponding service-orientated creative action to discover the way forward. The transpersonal ruler of this node is the Earth in Leo in the 3rd House, suggesting the need for individuals, groups and nations to discover the unique and co-creative contribution they can make to this new Era. The vision, ideals, knowledge, and understanding of the Age of Aquarius will be well-communicated through the 9th House Sun, but this knowledge has to be clarified, articulated, and creatively manifested through the Earth in Leo. It is the higher Sagittarian mind and the attunement to the soul through daily meditation and service-orientated action that hold the key to this individual, group, and national contribution.

The three conjunctions occur on February 2 at 12:48 GMT, August 19 at 20:26 GMT, and October 25 at 6:33 GMT. It will take nine months for the overall effect of this conjunction to unfold itself. Before there can be birth of a new life, there must first be conception, pregnancy (impregnation), and labor. The birth of the spiritual life (in the real sense of the word) of this great Uranus Neptune conjunction will conceive itself at the first conjunction, impregnate itself from February to October with a crisis point at the second conjunction in August (this corresponds to the sixth month Virgo-crisis cycle in human pregnancy), and birth will occur at the October conjunction.

The Rising Sign of the October birth conjunction is Libra 29 degrees 30 minutes. The final degree of any sign is the integrating "crisis degree" because it embodies *all of the sign within itself.* Libra is the sign of balance because its work is to balance or reconcile the opposites, and the final spiritual aim of this conjunction is to bring the opposites into balance which, by the way, also means to neutralize the karma from the past cycle of Pisces in order to open the door into the new cycle of Aquarius. Gemini Rising rules the conception, and Libra Rising, the birth, and Uranus and its 7th Ray, the transpersonal rulers of Libra, govern this birth.

# Transpersonal Keynotes

| Sign | Keynote |
|---|---|
| Aries | I come forth and from the plane of mind I rule |
| Taurus | I see and when the eye is open all is light |
| Gemini | I recognize the other self and in the waning of that self I grow and glow |
| Cancer | I build myself a lighted house and therein dwell |
| Leo | I am that and that I am |
| Virgo | I am the mother and the child, I, God I, matter am |
| Libra | I choose the path that leads between the two great lines of force |
| Scorpio | Warrior I am and from the battle I emerge triumphant |
| Sagittarius | I see a goal, I reach that goal, and then I see the next goal |
| Capricorn | Lost am I in light supernal yet on that light I turn my back |
| Aquarius | Waters of life am I poured forth for thirsty humanity |
| Pisces | I leave the father's house and turning back I save |

# Transpersonal Ruling Planets and Rays

| Sign | Planet | Ray | Keynote | Color |
|---|---|---|---|---|
| Aries | Mercury | 4th | Harmony through conflict | Yellow |
| Taurus | Vulcan | 1st | Power/Will | Red |
| Gemini | Venus | 5th | Knowledge | Orange |
| Cancer | Neptune | 6th | Idealism | Pink |
| Leo | Sun's Heart | 2nd | Love-Wisdom | Royal Blue |
| Virgo | Moon | 4th | Harmony through Conflict | Yellow |
| (the Moon channels Vulcan and the 1st ray) | | | | |
| Libra | Uranus | 7th | Synthesis and Order | Violet |
| Scorpio | Pluto/ Mars | 1st/ 6th | Power/Idealism | Red/Rose |
| Sagittarius | Earth | 3rd | Active Intelligence | Green |
| Capricorn | Saturn | 3rd | Active Intelligence | Green |
| Aquarius | Jupiter | 2nd | Love-Wisdom | Royal Blue |
| Pisces | Pluto | 1st | Power/Will | Red |
| | Neptune | 6th | Idealism | Pink |

**Diana Stone**

Diana Stone is actively involved in an astrology and counselling practice in Portland, Oregon, plus ongoing lecturing and writing projects. Her book, *The United States Wheel of Destiny*, was published in 1976. A health crisis in the 60s precipitated her studies in healing, psychology, and astrology. In the 70s, she trained as a psychodramatist and did postgraduate studies in Transactional Analysis and Gestalt therapy. A transpersonal crisis in 1980 preceded extensive involvement in shamanic practices, healing rituals, and rites of passage.

Diana currently specializes in work with teachers and healers coping with the psychophysiological transformation process. She is also an articulate teacher, translating her personal shamanic journeys into an eclectic model of healing and therapy.

# Beyond Your Wildest Imagination

## Diana Stone

Flight #240 heading for New York City from Boston, the plane on which I was a passenger, pitched about the midnight sky like a cork in an angry sea. Under a threat to life and limb, convention is quickly circumvented to establish intimacy with those with whom we share an uncertain fate. The passenger in the seat next to mine wrapped me in a bear hug and whispered, "Let's pretend we are vacationing on a big ocean liner." The plane touched down safely at Kennedy Airport. The man released me as we awkwardly returned to the typical demeanor of strangers passing in the night. I was shaking with relief when I disembarked and made for the baggage area. I did not suspect that my adventure was only just beginning.

I made my way down a noisy concourse, mentally reminding myself to retrieve the umbrella in my luggage before braving the storm still raging outside. By the time my familiar gray wardrobe bag negotiated the turn on the baggage conveyer belt, I was ready to put the frightening flight behind me and concentrate on getting checked into my hotel. With dismay, I hoisted my bag to my side only to discover that the zipper had somehow come apart. My red terrycloth robe spilled out. I leaned down and placed the luggage on the floor, fumbling with the bag and its contents. I stood up to signal a Red Cap and went numb with shock. Every single, solitary soul in Kennedy Airport had vanished. I was completely alone and it was deadly quiet.

Ignoring for the moment the turmoil in my mind, I spotted a luggage cart, loaded my wounded wardrobe bag onto it, and set out for an outside exit. As I walked along the empty corridors, the only sound was that of my own footsteps. I spied a large poster on the wall. It was a Holiday Inn advertisement describing a free shuttle service. The telephone numbers for several motels in the surrounding area were listed along one side. I silently paid tribute to my sense of organization as I produced a note from my flight bag listing the address of my particular motel. I called. I carefully explained to the man who answered that I wished to avail myself of their shuttle service. His reply revealed that whatever strange world in which I now found myself, I was still in it. He did not just refuse my request; he reacted as though I had asked him to donate one of his kidneys! He was indignant beyond reason. Still not to be deterred, I explained that I was standing beside a poster at that very moment which explicitly stated that Holiday Inn would send a shuttle from the motel to the airport. "It even lists your telephone number," I insisted. He hung up.

Considering the bizarre nature of my circumstances, I decided it was best to leave well enough alone as far as Holiday Inn's shuttle service was concerned. I smiled wryly as I walked past several more such posters, all clearly inviting passengers simply to telephone for service. "Posters from the Twilight Zone," I muttered only too obviously just to myself.

Finally I reached a cavernous lobby area with several doors leading outside to taxi stands. My flight from Boston had been delayed for several hours, so by now it was very late at night. I pushed and pulled my wardrobe bag into temporary order and lifted it off the cart. I leaned down and sat it on the floor. I raised myself up again, and there, as though appearing out of thin air, was a man in a brown uniform with a badge pinned to it which read, "Taxi." I was in the center of a very large open area. I could not have missed seeing this man. Nor could I have failed to hear him walking toward me. Yet *there he was.*

Tentatively, I inquired if he would get me a taxi. Just like the man at the motel, he reacted in utter shock, as though he could not believe his ears. He inquired if perhaps I had lost my mind, to expect taxis to be at the airport at that hour of the night.

"But, isn't this Kennedy Airport? Isn't this New York City?" I pleaded.

Further conversation became pointless. In resignation, I leaned down for my wardrobe bag and when I glanced up, the man was gone, vanishing as abruptly and noiselessly as he had appeared.

I glanced around at the benches expecting to sleep the night on one of them. I dragged my bag and sat down, aware for the first time how exhausted I was. I peered absently into the black night when a lone taxi, emerging like a phantom from the fog and rain, startled me back to my senses. Suddenly, the airport exploded with people and familiar sounds.

The uniformed taxi man yelled and gestured at me, this time in typical New York fashion. "C'mon lady, do ya want a taxi or don't cha?" Out from the approaching taxi leaped a big, handsome cab driver. He strode right for me, picked up my bag, and loaded me inside his cab. As we drove away, I could see a long line of other passengers waiting in the rain for a taxi. A man shook his fist at this woman who had commandeered one out of turn. I mumbled the address of my motel to the driver and shrank as far back into the seat as I could. When he asked if he could meet me after he got off work, I was more grateful than that guy will ever realize. Life was real again.

Most people will never confront the sudden disappearance of their fellow travelers from a major U.S. airport. Yet pollsters reveal in recent surveys that people in increasing numbers report some kind of paranormal experiences. Speculation is that this reflects not so much a growing phenomenon but rather a greater willingness to admit to it.

At this writing, the Kennedy Airport experience happened well over twenty years ago. Since then, I have sustained my career as a professional astrologer. However, the glitch that night in New York City, which baptized me into another reality, sent me off on a parallel track of powerful personal experiences. In this chapter, I will consider where the traditional boundary lines defining astrological symbolism interface with a world beyond our imagination.

The mutable signs of the zodiac represent mind and consciousness. Gemini, Virgo, Sagittarius, and Pisces rule the cadent houses in the horoscope, and, using both the old and new rulers, are governed by Mercury, Jupiter and Neptune. Mercury is associated with the logical, conscious mind, Jupiter with philosophy and belief systems, and Neptune with creativity, intuition and imagination. In my classes, I like to tell my students that on the way from Mercury to Neptune, don't forget to stop off at Jupiter.

Why Jupiter? Dealing directly with Neptune has an unnerving capacity to propel one into some pretty inexplicable realities, my Kennedy airport experience being a case in point. A belief system (Jupiter) that can accommodate nonordinary realities great and small is absolutely essential. Contrary to popular belief, it is much easier to access the Neptune realm than to change belief systems!

Perhaps some readers are familiar with the Silva Mind Control classes, now usually called The Silva Method. This is a program developed by Jose Silva in Laredo, Texas in the 60s. Teachers were trained and sent to many other cities, where, in week-end seminars, students were taught to access consciously the alpha state and do psychic readings. To most student's surprise, it worked.

When I attended the classes, there were about thirty others taking the course with me. I was the only person there with any kind of background in metaphysics. These were literally people off the street: a nun, an engineer, a beautician, and so on. During the closing hours on Sunday, everyone wrote on an index card the name of a person whom they knew to have a physical illness. Cards were exchanged.

I got the card of a boy twelve years old. His name and age were all I knew about him. I closed my eyes, went through the routine I had been taught, and saw in my mind's eye a large syringe entering the boy's arm with the symbol of Venus on the needle. I said he was diabetic. You can put that together, can't you? Syringe, Venus, sugar? What was more fascinating to me than correctly diagnosing the medical condition of a stranger was the impressions I had about the planet Venus as it related to the lad's life.

As it turned out, the man who submitted the name was the boy's grandfather. With eyes closed, I began to describe a need in the grandson's life for things Venusian. I suggested that he be exposed to art, to even hang a picture of Venus in his room. I could feel an excessive Mars influence in the life of this artistic child and also his hungering for the gentle beauty of Venus. When I opened my eyes, tears were streaming down the grandfather's face.

The father was a macho type who wanted a son with whom he could hunt and fish. He belittled the boy's disinterest and lack of skill in sports. The grandfather decided that he, himself, would strengthen the energy of Venus in the boy's life. The rest of the story? About a year later, the grandfather called me to describe the activities and symbolism of Venus that had been introduced into his grandson's life. And to tell me the young boy was no longer diabetic.

Everyone else in the class performed as I did. And before it was over, there wasn't a dry eye in the house. That was a powerful experience in itself, of course, but do you think I ever regarded Venus in quite the same way as before? And wasn't it interesting that I received the psychic information as it connected to astrological symbolism? The engineer I was paired with got his messages in engineering symbols.

I make two points with this story. First, it underscores what I said about *the ease with which the Neptune realm is accessed*. Thirty people essentially off the street did it in three days. The second issue is that after accessing the psychic information, the learning involves interpreting whatever form in which it comes. Just as I perceived in astrological symbols because I am an astrologer, so too will others receive this sort of information in their own uniquely subjective way. Dealing with Neptune is like the old joke about the dog chasing the car: what will he do with it after he catches it?

## Clark and Philip

So this brings us back to Jupiter and belief systems. Most people never suspect that a major shift in their belief system means *they* must change as well. I am reminded of two dramatic cases illustrative of what I am talking about. These are true stories of two men, Clark and Philip, whom I knew well for many years, and though their experiences seem extraordinary, there is a common denominator that is by no means atypical.

I met Clark at a theater party. He was tall, elegant, and a most amusing conversationalist. More than a year passed before we again crossed paths. He came in for an astrological consultation. Virgo was on the ascendant in his horoscope, with the Sun, Mars and Venus in Virgo in the 12th house and the Moon in Cancer. I was struck by the incredible potential for psychic ability, but when I asked about it, he brushed it aside as nonsense.

That would have been the end of the matter had it not been for the coincidence that we were both invited to a party of a mutual friend. At the party, friends exhorted Clark to play his guessing game. I was puzzled and interested to learn just what the guessing game was. This is how it went: Clark was given the name of someone whom he did not know. Then he proceeded to describe the person's dress and appearance and not only that, what he or she was doing at that moment. The unsuspecting subject was telephoned to confirm or deny the reading. The telephone call was only a formality. Clark was always accurate to the last detail. I turned to him and said, "I thought you told me you weren't psychic." He seemed taken aback. "Oh, is that what this is?"

Over the next couple of years, Clark developed a remarkable psychic ability. He did not involve himself in the stereotypical fare of psychic readings, predictions, and that sort of thing. He penetrated the core of the subject's life and essence. He had an uncanny sense of the appropriate material to access at any given time. His interpretations were deeply psychological. His insights were masterful. He seemed to pull the veil from the unconscious and view it with clear sight. He was possessed of inexhaustible patience. If there were traumatic or unresolved relationship problems, be it with parents or lovers, he named names and specific issues.

Clark and I worked together for many years. We also formed a deep friendship. I see clients in weekly therapy, and when progress stalled, I had not the slightest reservation about enlisting Clark's assistance. I knew I could trust him to perform brilliantly and sensitively. Eventually, Clark quit his job to devote full-time to his astonishing psychic work with a large clientele.

When I collaborated with Clark, I never doubted his ability to handle whatever was presented. However, you can understand that a certain amount of groundwork was necessary to prepare the client to work with a psychic. After my careful preparations, Clark joined me in the counseling room and without introduction or fanfare bluntly announced to the client his opinion that psychic work was all horsefeathers (censored). It became routine for me to warn the client that he was a bit eccentric and his obscene disclaimers were just his way of getting focused. Then we would proceed with such powerful, penetrating work that the client was soon distracted from any doubts he or she may have had.

Clark's puzzling attitude would have remained simply a humorous idiosyncrasy were it not for the fact that, as time went by, it became increasingly apparent that he really did have a grave conflict in his belief system. The apparent personality quirk ballooned into a stumbling block to the point where Clark completely disavowed his psychic ability and today will have nothing to do with it. He now lives in another city and I rarely hear from him. More about Clark later, but first let's look at Philip.

Philip consulted me as an astrologer to discover whether his long-standing, debilitating headaches were rooted in psychological or physical causes. I advised him that pursuing a physical cause would be the most rewarding course of action. I referred him to a holistic doctor who specialized in alternative therapies, an avenue new to Philip. His chart exhibited such extraordinary patterns of healing and psychic ability, I could not resist broaching the subject following our conversation about his health problems.

Philip was a big, handsome man in his late thirties, a former college football hero. By profession, he was in upper management with the largest bank in the city. You don't see much in that to suggest an interest in anything nontraditional! I could read from the quizzical expression on his face that he had no idea what I was talking about. However, he was interested and curious. Little wonder: his chart featured a Virgo ascendant, Sun, Mercury and Venus in Virgo in the 12th House, along with Neptune rising. The 12th House planets opposed a Pisces Moon on the 6th House. The Virgo-Pisces axis across the 12th and 6th Houses has become a classic signature for me, indicating powerful healing and psychic abilities. Sometimes the axis is reversed, placing Virgo on the 6th House, but, of course, the principle is the same. You will note that the planetary rulers involved in the configuration are Mercury, Jupiter, and Neptune.

Philip made a quantum leap in the three months following that initial consultation. During that time, he visited me at my office frequently. On one occasion, I introduced him to the pendulum and demonstrated how it can be used to diagnose what nutritional supplements one requires. In short order, that pendulum was standing at attention and whistling Dixie in Philip's hands. He joined my healing classes and was soon diagnosing illnesses and nutritional needs with the pendulum. This quickly gave way to diagnosing conditions psychically *without* the pendulum. When I asked what was the cause of various physical problems, Philip quickly branched out into the psychological patterns, traumatic events, and past-life influences at work.

One evening at class, a student brought her mother who was suffering from a long standing and painful back condition. I asked Philip to try his hand at healing. With no previous experience, he took command of the situation. He seemed to know just what to do. I wondered to myself in how many lifetimes he must have been a healer. After two or three "treatments," the mother was freed from her affliction.

After that, Philip and I worked closely together as healers. I had been a hands-on healer for many years before that, but I definitely was not in the same league as Philip. We saw people at my office several times a week. Many wonderful healings occurred. Philip's abilities to heal, as well as his skill in identifying and working with the underlying causes, were just phenomenal.

Philip found the cause of his headaches and, for the first time in seven years, was free of constant pain. However, his honeymoon period in the psychic world was showing signs that reality was setting in. Just as with many of those with whom he worked, pesky emotional material, apparently connected with his healing process, refused to be denied. When I tried to help him process his own issues, there was trouble in paradise.

During the two years that I was intimately involved in the healing work with Philip, he lost his job and was faced with marital problems. He endured a long siege of joblessness and financial uncertainty. Things came to a head one day at lunch. Philip had been willing to deal with his unfinished personal issues only up to a point. This was coupled with a growing inclination to complain bitterly that "they" owed it to him to straighten out his life in exchange for the powerful healing work he did. When I cynically inquired about just who "they" were supposed to be, that did it. It was the end of the line as far as Philip was concerned.

Philip probably has no obligation to devote himself to healing; I can't say one way or the other. Nor is it fair of me to judge that he has somehow failed if he does not continue with his psychic and healing activities. However, it is fair to point out some of his reasons: an exclusive egotism which I did not mention earlier, a refusal to deal with his emotional baggage, and his outrage that life did not smooth his path of all difficulties because he was a great healer.

Clark's reasons were different. He had potent unresolved traumas from his childhood. Whenever core issues surfaced, he ran in terror. This left him unable to trust or believe in anything, not even his own remarkable talents. From time to time, Clark suffered from terrible bouts of depression. They lasted weeks and months. I treated him with the Bach flower remedies on five separate occasions when nothing else worked. Each time they abruptly ended the black despair within hours. Yet, he cynically dismissed the flower essences as nothing more than "petunia gas."

As for Philip, today he is a successful businessman. His marriage is exactly as it was twelve years ago. He has a long-time mistress, a former client of mine. They are both alcoholics. Even though we can't really judge the journey of another, I mourn a little bit still the incredible magic both he and Clark wrought for awhile.

The relationship with Clark and Philip was fiercely painful and acutely disillusioning for me as we turned to follow separate paths. Personal feelings and judgments aside, however, I was still left dramatic evidence that encounters of the psychic kind are not the benign experiences I might once have been naive enough to believe they were.

### And now, Helen

Some years following the relationships with Clark and Philip, an event drove home yet another painful truth: whereas the two men personally developed their own mystical skills only to bolt from them later, my close friend, Helen, demonstrated in her life and premature death that dabbling with Neptune at arm's length is not only futile but potentially tragic.

Helen was my close friend for twenty years. At first, we shared an intellectual interest in astrology and other metaphysical subjects. In the last several years of her life, Helen awakened to things of the spirit. She embarked on what she called "consciousness raising." She read widely on the subject, went to weekend seminars, studied meditation, worked with crystals, and in general explored many aspects of the New Age movement. It was healing that really captured her interest, however. Eventually she became an accomplished healer in the Unity Church, primarily using hands-on healing and manipulation of the subject's energy field. All of this was quite a stretch for Helen in her development.

Helen channeled potent power and light through her hands. Yet other parts of her life remained in darkness. Even though she healed many others in supernormal ways, she herself clung to her belief in medicine and drugs. She regularly ingested a cocktail of prescription drugs, many highly suspect as carcinogens. When I and other healers suggested alternatives, she reacted with such hostility and defensiveness, we were loathe to broach the subject again.

Helen lived on junk food and Hershey bars. She was never without a glass of Coke. As her health problems worsened, we subtly urged a change in lifestyle. My husband is a holistic doctor and Helen was intimately familiar with his work in nutritional therapy. Yet, we quickly learned that any reference to a change in her diet was absolutely taboo. So vehement was her resistance that to pursue the subject was to jeopardize the relationship.

The part of this story that is the most shocking to me was her refusal in the end to deal with her inner life. Shocking because Helen lived through the relationships with Clark and Philip from beginning to end. She was aware of everything that happened, blow by blow. More than that, she was aware of my work with several other very powerful people who went off track after several years because of deep inner conflicts with which they refused to come to terms. There were many nights that we talked until dawn about these matters.

About four years ago, I was suddenly gripped by the inescapable realization that my friend was going to die of cancer. I blurted out my fearful premonition to my husband and begged him to work with her somehow on her healing. He managed to convince her to participate in some fabricated research, and paying for all her supplements out of his own pocket, conned her into a therapy program. Many of her symptoms fell away. Helen suffered debilitating migraine headaches weekly for most of her adult life. Mercifully, those ceased. After a year, she decided that she no longer wanted to continue the regimen. My husband was troubled. Indications were that she was stopping too soon. Her medications and diet seriously countered his healing effort. We felt helpless to do more, so I changed tactics.

I was hoping that I could engage Helen in some deep inner work that would get at some of the root causes for her destructive course. This way she might come around to making changes of her own accord. Fortunately, she was willing to do some rebirthing sessions with me. One evening, she reached a very deep level and reexperienced her prenatal life. Helen came in with a twin brother. There was great animosity between them all their lives. She got in touch with a deep hatred for her twin brother while still in the womb.

She stood up and looked at me. "I've projected hatred for my brother onto all men." This had been another taboo subject that no one dare broach with Helen, yet it was apparent to all who were close to her that she was a man-hater. I thought, "Now we are really starting to get someplace." I was jolted out of my thoughts when she exclaimed "And if you think I am ever going to let go of it, you are very much mistaken!" And with that she stormed off to my guest bedroom, slammed the door and this subject was never mentioned again. I felt the hatred that gnawed her guts and remember still a sickening sense of foreboding.

A few months later, Helen called with the sad news. She had undergone surgery for breast cancer. Not long after, tests indicated that the cancer had spread to the liver. I decided to make one last desperate attempt to get her on a therapeutic regime and also to drain off the poisonous emotions. I drove to Seattle where she lived (I live in Portland, Oregon) on my eleventh-hour mission. Helen felt well until then. I arrived on a Thursday evening, and she had prepared a nice dinner. Early the next morning she called to me. I ran to her bedside. She collapsed into my arms, dead from a heart attack.

Here was a woman who invited the higher consciousness into her life and into her body. This was a woman who was a tireless healer, who went out of her way many times to help a sick person without ever asking for payment of any kind. Those potent energies amplify everything we are; the good, the bad, the ugly. We can't have it both ways. Not all the good works in the world can save us from the powerful energies that not only heal but can just as easily potentize hatred and destroy us.

## Creating Reality

Helen's experience brings up another idea that is widely popular in New Age thinking: *the possibility that we can create our own reality.* When Helen first telephoned me about the cancer, she asked my advice as to what course she should follow. I outlined a specific course of action, a very intense regimen. I reminded her of three other women with whom I had worked. Each one was dismissed as a terminal cancer patient by traditional doctors. They accommodated their belief systems to a new way of thinking and each one is still alive today, years later.

Helen alluded to the heavy Pluto transits in her chart and told me on many occasions that she must transform or die. What she ultimately decided to do in a desperate effort to save herself was to enlist the aid of a hypnotherapist. Essentially she floated in an altered state while he repeated affirmations of healing and the like. Do you see how this perfectly conformed to her agenda of refusing to deal with her inner life? She talked to me a lot about creating her own reality. She replayed the tapes from hypnosis sessions while propped in bed downing tranquilizers, Coke, and chocolate bars. It is obvious what the actual reality was.

I do believe we can and *do* create our own reality. And if you want to know what your own reality is, look at your life. That is it. This philosophy is the basis of my astrological counseling, and that of a good many psychotherapists, I might add. The problem with this idea is that so many people believe reality is so easily manipulated that chanting affirmations or visualizing a new car is all there is to it. The stumbling block is that the universe creates reality out of the whole piece, both the conscious *and* the unconscious parts. Our lives are the outtakes of the jumble of fragments composing our hopes and fears. Heavily entrenched systems outside conscious awareness are not turned aside by a litany of affirmations to the contrary. If your intention is to explore the world of the imagination, don't be surprised if that world turns out to be your own inner self.

No matter from which direction an individual opens the door to non-ordinary reality, the unresolved contents of the inner life will spill out sooner or later. No one is spared the consequences of avoiding the inner work. Perhaps Clark and Philip were responding to some wise inner guidance in closing that door, given the impasse they both had reached. At least they are going on with their lives, and there is always tomorrow.

My intention in sharing the dramatic stories about Clark, Philip, and Helen is to underscore the true force and potency of things Neptunian. The Neptunian nature, the imaginational sphere, is regarded as hazy, vague, unclear. Our estimation of its power and force has become so blunted that we deceive ourselves as to its ability to have any real impact on our lives or circumstances. Frequently it is only begrudgingly acknowledged by default: the disempowerment of the drunk tank and psychiatric ward. Compare that to the blunt edge we feel from Saturn. No one has a problem recognizing the power there!

It is we, in our left-brain intensive culture, who *underestimate* and *disregard* the non-ordinary aspects of consciousness;it is *not* the consciousness itself that is inherently ill-defined. The only access to the personal or collective world of non-physical reality is through the personal unconscious. The personal unconscious is, among other things, *the playground of the unresolved issues in our lives.* If we want to play there, treachery lurks until we clear out our personal demons.

Maybe we need a closer look. Clark, Philip, and Helen went head to head with Neptune on his turf. They were powerful in Neptune's playground. But they disregarded the rules of the game. Not one of them is aware of the true reasons why they turned away. They made choices which they absolutely believed were authentic, never suspecting the taint of their own unconscious motives. The view from here is that "Neptune Power" can bring down the mightiest ego as it resists the stripped down realities of the inner world. So whence come vagueness and delusion?

In light of the previous discussion, crossing the cusp into 12th House territory may seem perilous. We cannot lose sight of the fact, however, that many other denizens of that dark house are not demons, but rather the gods themselves, singing to us about an astonishing world of creation and adventure beyond our wildest imaginations, a world that we would not miss for anything *in* the world!

To prove that the gods are as good as their promise of adventure, let me share an episode they cooked up for me. More than adventure for adventure's sake, this scenario reveals how the workings of the inner worlds not only intersect with ordinary reality, but can radically alter it on the strength of only a wish or a prayer. Those of us who shared this experience have come to call it "The Larch Mountain Caper."

The Larch Mountain Caper began on a gray, misty Saturday typical of late fall in western Oregon. My son, David, was driving to his office when an inner voice prompted him to drive to Larch Mountain. No explanation was given. Larch Mountain is a popular vantage point for viewing the high peaks of the Cascade Range, from Mt. Rainier in Washington State to Mt. Jefferson in southern Oregon. David was puzzled, but complied with the inner instructions.

The road leading to the top of Larch Mountain is a twenty-mile stretch of snaking curves continuously rising in elevation. Seven miles from the summit, the road that day was barricaded by the Forestry Service. The road is so treacherous in winter, it is routinely closed for the season. David's assumption that he had imagined the whole thing was quickly dispelled when "the voice" commanded, "Walk the rest of the way."

This was a distasteful prospect, to say the least. It was already mid-afternoon and a chilly wind was coming up. David had not dressed for hiking, especially in such weather. Fortunately, he was an experienced hiker. He set out on foot resolving to cover the seven miles to the top and to return before dark, meanwhile puzzling over what he was doing there in the first place. Arriving at last at the Larch Mountain visitor's parking area, he was startled to encounter a woman there alone. She explained that she had come by way of one of the hiking trails from Multnomah Falls Lodge below, a hiking trail David had used many times himself. Her husband was to pick her up in the car. Obviously, she did not realize that the road was barricaded.

Knowing the return trail to be much too treacherous in the dark, David brought the woman down the road to his car and drove her to the lodge himself. There was never any sign of the woman's husband. David drove away congratulating himself on following his intuitive guidance system and grateful that the woman was spared a very cold and unpleasant night on Larch Mountain. He excitedly shared the story with me, and we both agreed that indeed he had had an excellent adventure.

Several nights later, we had a good time retelling the whole story again. Great adventures are worth repeated tellings!

This time I remarked that a young man had fallen to his death once when I visited Larch Mountain. David answered that he, too, was there when someone was killed. We recalled that David's father had also been on Larch Mountain when someone fell to his death. We looked at each other aghast. A close family friend took his parents to the mountain on a sight-seeing trip and, yes, they were horrified when still another visitor fell to his death from the viewing area while they were there. The hapless victim in that case dropped his binoculars over the railing of the viewing platform. He climbed over the side to retrieve them and lost his balance. A pall fell over my living room.

David looked horrified. "What's the matter?" I asked. "There is something I left out when I told you about going to Larch Mountain. When I walked up that road, I was terrified out of my mind. My heart pounded, and I could hardly put one foot ahead of the other. I wished I had my pistol with me. I tried to argue myself out of it. I have hiked many times and never felt terror like that. I did not know what I was afraid of. I really didn't believe there was anyone threatening there. I wasn't afraid that a bear or wild animal would come out on the road. But I couldn't talk myself out my fear. I had to talk to myself the entire trip to keep from running to my car and getting the hell out of there. Believe me, I wanted to. Later, I explained away the fear by telling myself that I was just intuitively picking up on the woman's predicament at the top of the mountain."

We both knew that we were touching into something more ominous. The strange coincidence whereby everyone in our circle bore witness to tragic accidents on the mountain stirred the suspicion that there was more to this whole incident than we first thought, especially in light of David's inexplicable terror. "You had better take a look at this psychically, Mom," David said. His tone of voice belied his words. He dreaded what I might see.

I closed my eyes. I put myself back in time on the road to Larch Mountain and retraced David's steps. I shuddered with a sudden chill. Stalking my son along the opposite side of the road was a huge shambling thing, hairy and menacing. I easily empathized with David's terror!

A monstrous "elemental" was ranging across a wide area surrounding Larch Mountain. I saw no sign of the usual nature spirits. This thing was straight from a nightmare. I sensed that this monster was responsible somehow for the inordinate number of tragedies on the mountain over the years. We felt the horrible certainty that David's presence on the mountain that day aborted the woman's rendezvous with death.

Four members of the group with whom I work on such business, assembled to try our hands at elemental bashing. We looked at the situation with inner sight and witnessed a long-past scenario involving two men in bloody combat on Larch Mountain. Their dispute over a woman left one man dead on the ground. We observed his shade remaining in the area, consumed with hate and thoughts of revenge. Can such violent incidents eventually spin themselves into creatures like the one we had stumbled onto here?

Inexperienced in matters elemental, we followed our inner guidance the best we could until we sensed that the mountain monster was no more. We summoned the deva and nature spirits back to the area. The ritual concluded, we wondered whether or not we would ever know if our effort had changed anything.

I chose this story because it illustrates several important considerations that come into play when encountering non-ordinary realities. And I deliberately chose the story-telling format throughout this piece as a way to stir the imagination concerning things that sometimes lie just beyond words. It is very hard to nail Neptune down to particulars.

Staying open enough to investigate intelligently anything completely alien to present reality is a mindset that must be consciously cultivated. Beyond that, it is tempting to dismiss phenomenal circumstances, even ones perhaps enjoying validity as a singular event, as nonetheless beside the point to most people's experience. To do so, however, is to overlook a process relevant to even the most mundane encounter with the inner consciousness.

Let's look at the sequence of events from another perspective. The Larch Mountain Caper is neither the unpredictable adventure nor the isolated incident that it may appear to be. Had it not been for many years of highly structured inner work, intensely focused mental discipline, and a devotion to complex group interaction, the Larch Mountain Caper never would have happened at all. That is the story behind the story.

First question: Isn't it curious that anyone would so readily abandon his or her plans to some wild goose chase in the wilderness on the strength of an inner voice? It is even more baffling given that the person persisted in the face of barricaded roads, a fourteen-mile hike in inclement weather, and an overwhelming terror. That was some inner voice!

It is unlikely for many people to trust an inner voice to this extent. I can honestly say that everyone in my little group has followed the inner voice on other occasions with as much conviction (The rest of us could never have made the fourteen-mile hike, however.) All of us in the group can rely on our inner guidance because we have done the work and paid the dues. This faculty is available to everyone, but more about that later.

You may question the usefulness of a voice that sends people off on wild adventures, the true purpose of which may never be known for certain. I ask you to consider that this is the same intuition Helen could have used to make life-saving choices. Helen was convinced that she was being guided by a true inner sense, never ever realizing how skewed the unconscious was toward her own personal agenda of avoidance. Clark also would be well-served by an intuition powerful enough to blast a belief system out of absolute paralysis. His fear and disbelief could be dispelled, clearing the way to utilize the proven healing of flower remedies to resolve the depression that plagues him still.

We needn't single out Clark and Helen as exceptional examples of people who refuse to isolate and resolve problem patterns in their lives. Perhaps the consequences are not normally so dramatic as in the cases I have described. With most people, though, it is business as usual. But who of us can know that we may someday find ourselves in a situation where *the intuition gives us our only edge* in a judgment call involving critical, even life and death, issues.

Another decisive element in the Larch Mountain story, if you think about it, is the emotion of fear. It was the fear that tipped us off to the presence of the elemental. A powerful dynamic comes into play between the intuition and the emotions. A complex process of establishing intimate familiarity with the unique inner workings of one's emotional life must be cultivated before any such interaction can be trusted to function reliably. From previous experience, David and I do know how to navigate our own emotional signals and trace them to their proper source. It didn't "just happen."

In many ordinary life situations, the intuition sends us information. The signals are often sent via emotional reactions. There is usually a physical reaction along with the emotion. We all have experienced chills, a knot in the stomach, or a dry throat associated with strong emotions. If we turn a deaf ear, the intensity of *the emotional response is increased.*

Most people walk around every day oblivious to personal motifs inimical to optimum functioning. The play of these unresolved inner contents around incoming information distorts what the intuitive signals really mean. It may not mean that you are stalked by an elemental, but it could be the early warning system of a disease. Helen was told in her dreams as far back as eight years before her death that she had cancer. She gave me her journals before she died. In her own handwriting were six separate dream entries literally telling her so. It isn't necessary to be a master or a mystic. *We must simply decide to listen.*

The third ingredient in the Larch Mountain soup mix concerns belief systems. Battling nasty elementals is going to strain most belief systems, that's for sure. Just how many of my fellow citizens would I realistically expect to transcend existing beliefs to run around Larch Mountain in the rain battling an invisible elemental with murder on its mind? I think I would anticipate great difficulty in rallying a posse for that.

## Is Seeing Believing?

There is a saying that "seeing is believing." Don't believe it. Seeing is not necessarily believing. Clark "saw" the Bach remedies heal him. He even acknowledged it at the time. Yet his belief system did not permit that to be true, so he doesn't believe it. Helen did not believe her own dreams, yet she acknowledged the importance of dreams and kept a dream journal. The evening before she died, she told me she had never had the slightest inkling she would ever have cancer. I could give you hundreds more examples.

One outstanding example hits very close to home for all astrologers. We have a hard time understanding why the general public does not "believe in" astrology. It is so obvious that it works and handily holds its own alongside other great sciences. I have long been completely disinterested in any effort to prove astrology to skeptics. It makes little difference how high the mountain of proof. Seeing is not believing. The doubting

Thomases believe they are acting out of intellectual integrity. What they don't realize is that a biased belief system, not objectivity, dictates absolutely what they will see.

One of my lectures is, "When you believe it, you will see it." In this lecture, I expound on the idea that when it comes to seeing and believing, the whole idea is reversed as reflected in the lecture title. Left unexamined, individuals may unwittingly find themselves locked inside belief systems featuring glitches as irrational as the public's confounded blind spot toward astrology. The lecture material goes on to include an analysis of the 9th House to encourage astrologers to consider the extent to which emotional issues bias clients' belief systems.

So just how does any self-respecting, straight-thinking soul make the leap of faith about things that go bump in the night without some proof? On the other hand, how can anyone possibly prove conclusively that there *are* things that go bump in the night? This is only an apparent impasse. It is not necessarily a contradiction in terms to require some corroborative testimony concerning extrasensory perceptions. On the contrary, learning to coordinate intuitive awareness skillfully with intellectual evaluation forms the basis of a powerful system of checks and balances.

I most emphatically want to say that I have never yet abandoned my insistence on validation simply because an experience lies outside five-sense reality. I was surprised to find the universe outright indulgent in its willingness to answer my requests for signs and confirmation. Of course, that takes into consideration the fact that I am willing to meet the universe half-way by communicating in the language unique to it.

The issue of proof, then, closes the chapter on Larch Mountain. First, however, what passes for proof may require some serious reconsideration. Proof of nonphysical reality does not exist in the dimension that the rational mind seeks it. How it worked in this case clearly illustrates the dynamics involved. After the dust settled and we had enjoyed several retellings of our adventure, David and I seriously requested a sign indicating beyond any doubt whether or not we had really done something of substance in the vicinity of Larch Mountain. The answer was not long in coming.

First came evidence that there was indeed an extraordinarily malevolent influence at work. We already were aware of the inordinate number of tragedies in the area, and there was the strange coincidence that all in our group bore witness to one at various times. David's destiny, it seems, was tied to the mountain long preceding our later involvement. He had hiked to the summit of Larch Mountain each 4th of July for seven years. He later admitted to an unexplained fear each time, yet the mountain held a weird fascination for him.

On one of his annual treks, a peculiar set of circumstances revealed that David was being stalked by an actual person. He listened to his intuition, immediately hastened to his car via a shortcut, and drove to another trailhead to continue his ascent. Once there is a feel for such things, just this much confirming evidence is really enough. But, since the universe is willing to be indulgent, why stop there.

This is what clinched it: a woman called my office to ask me to donate an astrological consultation to an auction. I wasn't really too clear what the organization was, but I agreed. That is how I got on the mailing list for their obscure little newsletter. I never received their newsletter before and strangely enough, I have never received one since, either. The universe likes to add tricky little touches like this.

The organization is an environmental group. As I casually flipped the pages of their newsletter, a headline fairly jumped out at me. "The Guardians of Larch Mountain," it read. The article told of the disgraceful destruction marring the spectacular scenic beauty of Larch Mountain. It had become a dump site for paint cans, batteries, and other toxic waste materials which, it was feared, was contaminating water supplies below. Not only that, shooters had leveled a two-mile area of every living tree. In fact, the National Rifle Association had asked the Forestry Service to designate the area as an official shooting range.

David had observed first hand on his hikes the shocking destruction there. It seemed impossibly bizarre that the violated landscape could vomit this hellish anomaly in the midst of such pristine beauty. That sort of ugly litter and devastation is extremely atypical of Oregon, which enjoys a well-deserved reputation for aggressive environmental responsibility, far exceeding that of other regions. Also, the Forestry Service behaved with uncharacteristic apathy in this case.

My environmentalist friends turned out to be the heroes in this story. They generated support from nearby city councils, state representatives and other government agencies. The old road to the shooting and dumping sites was closed by the Forestry Service. The area was cleaned up and water contamination is now regularly monitored. The article in the newsletter concluded with a solemn oath of vigilance by the Guardians of Larch Mountain "who will never sleep."

That was proof enough for us that, all told, an atypical malevolent presence had existed on Larch Mountain and, also, that our elimination proceedings cleared the way for a return to normal. The added presence of permanent watchdogs on our mountain was an elegant touch that we relished no end. Within my frame of reference, information alone is never the most compelling validation. Always the most striking testimony is the uncanny timing and synchronicity of events.

There have been many Larch Mountains, great and small. Some were merely anthills by comparison. Yet, *if the intention is held in consciousness, an unmistakable force enters the equation.* After dozens of experiences with altered states, it is overwhelmingly evident that there are guiding signs aplenty for anyone who is willing to transcend rigid skepticism and poorly-reasoned personal biases.

Many experiences cannot be explained within the common frame of reference. At that point, we all have a choice. One choice is simply to dismiss the matter as nonsensical. The alternative is to expand the consciousness to embrace a frame of reference from which there is an explanation. The first option is the easy way out. The true seeker will confront the hard questions. To choose consciously shapes our personal experiences around the intention to move forward in the evolutionary process, and whatever advances the individual contributes to the group evolutionary processes as well.

Considering some of the frightening pitfalls inherent in unknown territory, why is anyone motivated to forsake his or her familiar five-sense world to explore other dimensions of consciousness? Or, questioning things from the opposite perspective, it is also fair to ask why must we fiddle while Rome burns? The earth is undergoing transition, a rite of passage, and if humanity is unable to align itself with this cycle, its very survival is at risk. Our five-sense world is deteriorating and the decision to extend our vision seems a moot point by now.

At this writing, Pluto and Neptune are traveling in their long sextile aspect. The two planets conjoin every 500 years. In the 60-degree phase of the cycle, there emerges the first indicators of the new vision, *a radical conceptual shift*. In the 16th century, Pluto and Neptune danced together in this same phase relationship. That is when Copernicus advanced the heretical notion that the earth is not the center of the universe. Astrologers, in particular, can appreciate the shift from a heliocentric to a geocentric focus. That shift in perspective extended far beyond the boundaries of mere astronomy. I can imagine the identity crisis of those times running parallel to our present survival crisis.

It seems that the time may be rapidly approaching when the refusal to access other realities is as foolish as clinging to the pre-Copernican 16th century mentality. The dissolution of the old order is further underscored by the disruptive cycles in Capricorn throughout the last years of the 20th century. The language of astrology speaks to the forces moving us into closer alignment with nature and nature's cycles. Understanding the changing relationships in the zodiac empowers us to transcend purely personal concerns in order to align ourselves with the needs of the collective. To do that, we must be willing to merge with our intuitive faculties more fully, to recover and actualize the new vision.

Pluto relinquishes its outermost orbit during these times. It is closer to the earth and Neptune. Its transit through Scorpio awakens us to our deepest primal roots. Pluto demands transformation. Nothing can be left under the rock. We must clean house beginning with the cells of our bodies. The mythology of Pluto opens to the deepest levels of dysfunction and healing. It bespeaks the ultimate purge.

What role is there for the astrologer during these transition times? Many astrologers have already articulated the Plutonian descent into the underworld, the journey into personal and collective darkness. This recognizes one aspect of a well-known process encountered in numerous mythologies that ultimately leads to rebirth into the light of a new vision. Ultimately, however, it is the dedication of the astrologers themselves to do the work personally in their own lives that is the most powerful agent of change, both for the collective and for individual clients.

There is a philosophy that says counselors can not help others past the point at which they, the counselors, are willing to go in growth themselves. I believe that is generally true. For that reason, any suggestions I outline here are considered to apply as equally to the astrologer as they do to the clients whom they may wish to serve. Working to develop the client's intuitive sense, while the counselor observes from the sidelines, is an exercise in the abstract at best.

The case histories I have shared emphasize how absolutely necessary it is to recognize the repeating themes and patterns in our lives. That, of course, we recognize as a familiar goal of any good therapy. But I remind you afresh that I am addressing a process that extends well *beyond* psychotherapy, the development of the intuitive sense and penetration into formerly invisible realms. The personal work is just one step along the way, albeit one to be skipped only with disastrous consequences.

I must say that I am absolutely appalled at what most people are apparently willing to live with, without so much as a cursory glance at their lives. That, of course, is a feature of Western cultures. It is a mindset oriented almost exclusively toward outer life affairs. We are confronted with the dual task of challenging the state of cultural hypnosis alongside the demands of a personal awakening. That is one of the reasons becoming conscious is so difficult. It requires the cultivation of an unflagging attention to every aspect of one's life. The enormous power of consensus reality constantly threatens even the slightest lapse in a carefully crafted personal individuation.

While on the subject of people's choices, it is important to censor any judgmental attitude. Stories about Clark, Philip, Helen and others are not intended as judgment. It is not our place to judge anyone. In no case can we know all the reasons why any soul calls forth certain experiences. It is equally important to understand that there is also no reason we should blind ourselves to negativity when we see it. Negative choices are made by people who are hurting. Discernment is not judgment. It helps us to learn to behave appropriately to circumstances ourselves, and also to address realistic solutions for others who need our compassion and help.

**Specific Practices to Develop Intuition**

Assessing the model I have presented so far perhaps dispels somewhat the notion that it's impossible to chart the reputedly unfathomable mysteries of Neptune. When it speaks through the inner voice, we must listen. If it challenges our beliefs, we must expand our consciousness. When it signals through our feelings, we must distinguish them from our own emotional issues. When it encounters emotional blocks, we must honor them. When it activates physical reactions, we must detoxify the body. When it promises confirmation, we must acknowledge the synchronicity of events.

Now let's consider specific practices that develop the intuition. Our dream life suspends the outer consciousness and reveals the inner landscape uncensored. Lucid dreaming is a state of consciousness in which we are awake in the dream world. One powerful exercise to develop this faculty is to hold your arms out straight and focus on your hands. Repeat several times, "When I see my hands in my dream, I will be awake in my dream." Do that before you go to sleep. It works!

The power to remain completely conscious and the ability to alter dream material while one is actually dreaming is the ultimate goal. Even lucid dreaming that falls far short of this has enormous impact on waking life. I have trained myself in lucid dreaming to a point where I am always two people in the dream. I am the dreamer acting in the drama and simultaneously my conscious self observing the dream. My consciousness now always stays with the observer self. In that role, I comment about the dream material, even to the extent of commanding that some parts be repeated. Rarely, a third Self appears who interprets dreams and gives guidance of a high order.

Humor and playfulness are primary characteristics of the imaginary kingdom. Astrologically, these traits are key patterns in the signs Gemini and Sagittarius, and their ruling planets Mercury and Jupiter. Activating the child within aligns the psyche with the spontaneity and creativity of the imagination. It is important for parents to participate in their child's world of magical thinking. This is invaluable in encouraging the children's development as well as reinforcing it in the parents.

My young stepson came to live with me. To make him feel more at home, I confided in him about the herd of unicorn in the yard. We visited the unicorn stables where he was allowed to choose one for his special pet. In the spring, we very quietly observed the birth of the baby unicorns. One year, we even had twins. Once in a while, we had a sad day when one of the old unicorns had to cross over to the other side. We sang hymns and had a nice funeral. One day the boy was climbing the nut tree in my yard, and took a bad fall. I cleaned him up and rebuked him for being so reckless. He looked at me in all seriousness and said, "One of the unicorns butted me."

When my own son was a little boy, much of the discipline and training was accomplished with fantasy. One fantastic tale concerned eating inordinate quantities of lettuce and turning invisible. We had a large closet in which my husband could hide himself. When David came walking by, my husband spoke from the closet so that it sounded really spooky. "I'm invisible, David. I can see you. Can't you see me?" With that, David came streaking to tell me that his father had once again eaten too much lettuce and had turned invisible (the lettuce consumption in the house rose considerably for a time after such episodes.) Today my son is a powerful shaman, refuting, I might add, my mother's predictions that he would be a mental case with all my nonsense.

One of the very best techniques for accessing the inner life was put together by one of my chapter mates in this volume, Edwin Steinbrecher, in his book *The Inner Guide Meditation*. If you read only one book on the subject, make it this one. I have helped my clients get started using the guidelines laid down in the book. Still, one eye must be peeled for personal blocks. One client, Carol, worked with someone trained by Steinbrecher in his methods. It was a very positive experience for her. At one point, she got stuck and was going nowhere, no matter how hard she tried.

Rather than guide her in her meditation, I took a look at her horoscope. Her chart had Capricorn rising, a sign on the Ascendant which may have trouble with anything other than the straight, rational-mind world. The Ascendant also describes the early life influences. I asked a simple question, "What did your mother think about psychic ability?" Her answer? "Mother thought it was a sure sign of insanity."

The inner self accepted that without question and was acting to prevent her sure descent into madness. These kinds of things will surface with any inner work, and the counselor must watch for them. The horoscope can be invaluable in spotting the trouble. Once Carol worked through Mom's curse on all psychics, she was able to contact the inner guidance. It was just as important, though, that I make her aware that she is enhancing her intuitive ability just as much by learning to identify and work through her personal issues as she does with her meditation practices.

There is one aspect of intuitive work that has received very little attention. That is the fact that consciousness reaches a stage with some people *wherein the body is very powerfully affected and changed*. The changes are directed at the cellular level, mutating the DNA itself. Those changes are invisible. Yet the symptoms may be profoundly distressing as the physical body struggles to accommodate itself to the higher energies. It is becoming increasingly commonplace for individuals in Western cultures to encounter this particular phase of development. Profound physical difficulties are typical of the journey into shamanic consciousness and are well-documented in other cultures. Since this has figured heavily in my own growth experience, I recognize it more readily in others.

It is good to be on the alert for any clients suffering physical symptoms as a feature of an otherwise committed spiritual life. In these cases, folks must be encouraged to see their physical problems as *an aspect of transformation*, the wounded healer pattern perhaps. Obviously, the physical level itself must be addressed in any case. Common sense must be strongly encouraged. Proper nutrition is essential. Continuous detoxification of the body is required. In most cases, natural therapies are most effective. If symptoms persist, all spiritual practices such as meditation, yoga, or martial arts should be suspended for a time. The body already has all it can handle of the new consciousness.

The trip from Mercury to Neptune with a lay-over on Jupiter is one that probably requires many lifetimes in which to achieve excellence. It is not realistic to consider all possibilities in the space of a single chapter. At least I hope it is clear that the objective in all of this is not just disappearing airports or mountain climbing in the twilight zone. Nor is the experience of non-ordinary realities something divorced from any relevance to mundane life.

Humanity has reached a point in the evolutionary scheme of things where exploring alternate realities is not just another choice among a smorgasbord of hobbies which we have the luxury of picking up and putting down like knitting. We face the crisis of transition times. People are dispirited because the prevailing institutions seem so ill-equipped to negotiate the quantum leap to a global consciousness. Bold, new creative solutions await us just at the edge of our imagination. Those who dare to venture there will co-create with their playmates a new vision and a new world.

**Lucy Pond**

Lucy Pond has practiced astrology actively for twenty years, with clientele both in Seattle, where she resides, and throughout the United States. She has spoken on astrology at conferences and workshops, and has written articles for *The Mountain Astrologer.*

Lucy is co-author of *The Metaphysical Handbook* (with her brother, David) and has a B.A. in humanities from the University of Washington. Lucy's commitment to astrology, she admits, was perhaps best described by her brother David, when he said of her: "She's just doing what she's been doing all her life—minding other people's business!"

# Spiritual Outreach, Wayward Journey, and Neptune's Dance

**Lucy Pond**

With 20 years of astrological study and practice behind me, I admit to being enchanted still with the pure study of astrology and with the unquenchable impulse clients show in searching for answers to the riddle of their lives. But much as I have been in awe of the power astrology has to heal, I'm also frequently confronted with its power for self-deception. Here are some examples of using astrology for these ends.

*Consider this client's story:* "I just can't seem to exercise any discipline right now. I started going out dancing once a week and then began drinking again, after being off alcohol for over two years. I think it's because transiting Mars is going through my 5th House and conjuncting my natal Venus. But I'm really having fun and I sure wasn't before. I can clean up my act when Mars moves into my 6th House."

*Or this:* "Transiting Saturn is going through my 4th House, and I have been overwhelmed with feelings of sadness. I'm in therapy because I need to process my past, but I wasn't prepared for how bad I would feel. So when my doctor prescribed antidepressants, I used them. Now I don't want to give them up. I can't tolerate this pain for the next two years."

*Or this:* "My progressed Moon is moving through my 6th House and all I can think about is cleaning up my diet and getting going on everything I have been learning about these past few years. I am studying with a new yoga teacher and finally quitting the job that's been holding me back for many years. I also have transiting Mars in my 6th House right now, so I am using that energy to kick-start these new beginnings."

Clearly, astrology can be used in a variety of ways. It can be used to heal and bring enlightenment or keep one stuck in self-delusion. Its potential to help personal growth is profound. Many of our clients learn to move past the barriers in their lives and grow, using the powerful gift astrology offers. But as with all tools, the skill and awareness from which it is used makes all the difference.

I believe that it's essential to bring along a truly inquiring mind on the spiritual journey, and that doing so is essential to a conscious journey. Sometimes, in addressing clients' issues or even our own, we fall into the trap of not asking the right question. It's easy to trick ourselves; it's easy to avoid looking at what's really going on. It may seem that we're truly seeking counsel when we've looked at transits and progressions and compared horoscopes. But if deeper questions go unasked—if we delude ourselves about alcohol, drugs, money, or inappropriate relationships—whom are we kidding?

The art of learning to ask the right question takes practice. Using astrological techniques alone is not enough to achieve personal clarity. That's why, in practicing this rich, complex art, it's sometimes necessary to look into our clients'—and our own—motivation.

In this chapter, we will look at a number of horoscopes, mostly of people we all know about. They represent a small but interesting group of life-journeys, of individuals who have followed an earnest but erratic spiritual path, of others who have preached purity while practicing worldliness, of still others who had a special gift for telling us about ourselves, then succumbed to their own weakness, and of some who have simply been wise and humane teachers.

Some of these people were also astrologers, so perhaps we can assume they tried to use astrology to guide their lives. Most are not astrologers, but I believe there is something about the spiritual journey we can learn from their lives and horoscopes as well. Along the way, I will share some aspects of my own spiritual journey, where there is something useful to share.

# Astrologers and Spiritual Seekers

When I began studying astrology in 1970, I was taken with the great opportunity for consciousness it offered. I was literally pulled into astrology by the opportunity to expand my own consciousness and perhaps be a part of a journey of awakening in others. I can't imagine another career.

I thought that to study astrology and one day to be an astrologer would lead to something Confucius said about living in accordance with the I Ching. Near his death, he observed that if he had another 50 years in which to practice the I Ching he could live a life "without fault."

For me, the spiritual journey—and especially the study of astrology—has been a process of aligning ideals with reality. At first, I believed, my study would lead to a life of wholeness— maybe, eventually, one "without fault"—just as the serious study of yoga was necessary to become a yogi and studying the Bhagavad Gita was a step towards a life of "purity and investigation." Now that I see that none of this is so easily accomplished, I wonder: was I ever really so innocent?

## Dane Rudhyar

My first astrology book was *The Astrology of Personality* by Dane Rudhyar. Rudhyar is perhaps the most elevated and remote of all astrologers. Through his writings, one gets a sense of the exalted position an astrologer may hope to hold within the community of man. When I read his book *The Practice of Astrology*, I was deeply moved by the ethical and moral positions he attributed to practice of this art.

While studying the first book, I realized what a feat it would be to become an astrologer. I hadn't even focused on that goal; my expectations were more modest. I hoped simply that I could finish Rudhyar's book and understand some of what I was reading.[1] Rudhyar is a complex thinker who doesn't slow down at all for the reader. When you read his books you have the sense of the author saying subliminally: "Either you will understand exactly

---

1   This being my first book, it is a wonder that I continued my study. Those who have read it know it is pretty thick going.

what I am saying, or you are stupid and should not bother with the study at all." Not wanting to be counted among the stupid, I persisted. If only Steven Forrest had been writing then—so much time could have been saved.

When I learned that Rudhyar was going to be speaking at the American Federation of Astrologers convention in San Francisco, it was late summer of 1974. My friend and teacher, Joanne Wickenburg, and I made plans to go to the conference. We were

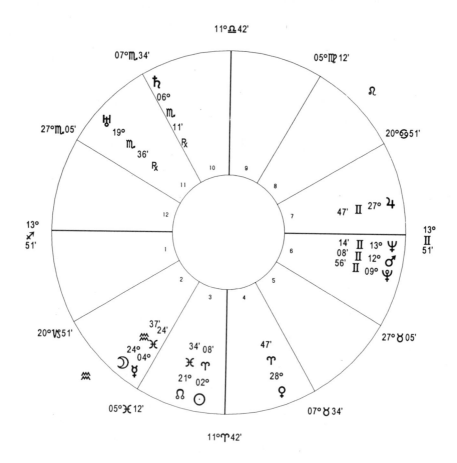

**Dane Rudhyar**
March 23, 1895
12:42 AM LMT, Paris, France
02E20 48N52

both very excited. I think that for both of us it was our first national convention, though Joanne had already gained recognition as an astrologer of considerable talent.

Finally, it was time to hear Rudhyar speak. The assembly hall was filled with many eager students. There was a wonderful air of respect as he began to speak. Unfortunately, Rudhyar spoke as he wrote; it was difficult to follow what he was saying. People started raising their hands, asking him to clarify different points, which irritated him. Finally one person asked, "It seems that you think that none of us are intelligent enough to understand what you're saying. If that's the case, what do you suggest we do to ready ourselves for understanding you?" Rudhyar paused thoughtfully, then said that what we all needed was to stretch our minds. The only way that he knew to do that, he said, was to "listen to music you have never heard before. Then your minds will be stretched enough to understand what I am saying. Then come back to my books."

This was my first astrological experience with a Sun sign Aries in action. They will surprise you more often than not, as their spiritual business is continually to transform into a more perfect example of themselves. His talk was not what I had expected, and I left the talk with my mind swirling. Rudhyar was exciting, certainly a pioneer in the field. Whether I understood him or not, he inspired me.

The key to understanding the astrology of Dane Rudhyar is the Gemini stellium in the 6th House. It involves Pluto, Mars, and Neptune, all within three degrees of one another. This is the mark of a truly inspired and unique individual. They make a loose square to his Mercury in Pisces, which suggests also that he could be a combative communicator, as indeed he was. It also suggests a visionary being of profound scope. There is no questioning the spiritual intention of Rudhyar's work.

That Rudhyar was prolific as a writer might be assumed from the Gemini stellium and his Sun located in the 3rd House, and the rulership of Neptune conjunct Mars. His books are a must for anyone seriously contemplating a career in astrology. Even if you don't understand everything, you will encounter one of the great astrological thinkers of our time and some of it *will* rub off on you. As far as I know, Rudhyar never lost his enthusiasm for the position he believed astrology could play in the life of modern humankind. He wrote on diverse astrological topics of broad scope and always forced his reader to think.

Rudhyar was so difficult to understand. He was acerbic, iconoclastic, and, somehow, idealistic. Now I see his horoscope, which is mostly Fire and Air, and define him simplistically as a man of spirit and ideas who lacked the practical connection with everyday life. An astrologer studies the rhythms and cycles of human life; yet, in true Aries style, Rudhyar wanted to remain forever youthful and was dismayed at his own aging process. As well, most astrologers exhibit a curiosity about people that I found missing in Rudhyar. He was irritable when dealing with people. Nonetheless, he was a true visionary.

Another clue to Rudhyar's horoscope is the position of his Lunar Nodes. He was born with the South Node in the 9th House. This is the mark of an individual who is a natural philosopher, one who sees the big picture. But with his North Node located in his 3rd House, he has difficulty formulating these concepts into everyday language.

## Marcia Moore

Marcia Moore was another outstanding personality at that same AFA convention. At the time, she was causing quite a stir with her outspoken ideas on reincarnation. She was not allowed to speak at the convention itself because her ideas were declared to be outside the interest of the AFA, which only allows talks on astrology. So Marcia would sit on the lawn across from the convention and give talks on reincarnation to many of the conference attendees. Often there were more people around her than attending the lectures inside. I thought she should have been allowed to speak inside. This was my first introduction to the political element of astrology, and I found it disturbing.

Marcia Moore's Gemini Sun sign, combined with a Cancer Moon in the New Phase, made her appear an innocent seeker. Her curiosity about past lives was engaging. Perhaps it was her Moon conjunct Pluto in the sign of Cancer located in the 12th House that gave her such a powerful attraction toward a life outside the here-and-now.

When I next heard Moore speak in 1977, her ideas had only become more radical, but this is what we come to expect from an individual with Mars conjunct Uranus in Aries at the Midheaven. By then, she was married to an anesthesiologist, and they were experimenting with past-life regressions with the aid of a drug, ketamine. Her talk on this at the convention made the "journey into the bright world" (the title of her talk and later a book) appear exciting and harmless. I later discovered otherwise.

Again I found Marcia engaging. When I returned to my home in Hawaii, I looked into obtaining the drug. I had married a

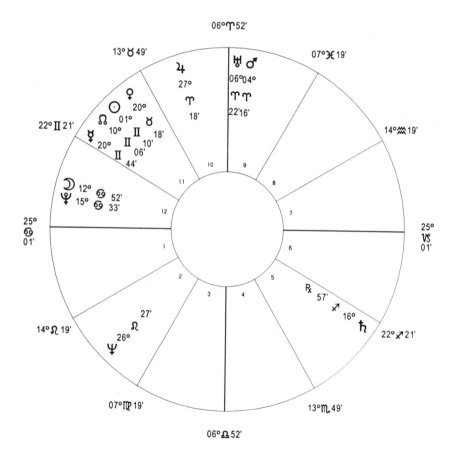

**Marcia Moore**
May 22, 1928
9:00 AM EDT, Cambridge, MA
71W06  42N22

psychiatrist who was interested in what Marcia had to say and in her experiments. I corresponded with her and we set up a time to meet in Seattle to share what we had been exploring. My husband and I flew to Seattle with great expectation.

But the night before we were to meet, just as we were flying into Seattle, Marcia was making news headlines as a missing person. Later, sadly, it was discovered that she had died under mysterious circumstances. This was a period when transiting Neptune was conjuncting her South Lunar Node and Saturn. I believe she was confused and disoriented because of the influence of the powerful and somewhat experimental drug that she was involved with. It seems she had lost control.

It would be difficult to call Marcia Moore anything other than a true spiritual seeker with a good astrological mind for correlating experiences. She was exciting, accessible, and naive. She wrote a book on the Kennedy family that is both entertaining and a good astrological study of how families work. She wrote on yoga and proper diet. She wrote an excellent book on general astrology.

In true Gemini fashion, Marcia could not be typecast as one kind of astrologer or writer. She could not even be categorized as any one type of spiritual seeker. What we can say is that she was an astrologer and that her spiritual search appeared always to be her first concern.

Perhaps her journey with drugs was part of a wayward journey that ultimately cost her her life. We will never know. She was born with Neptune square Venus, and it seemed likely that the drugs confused her values. With her loaded 11th House, she was not willing to live a conventional life; she wanted more. Her investigative mind was intact as she wrote and openly shared her journey with her public. But her perception of where she was heading was clouded. Through her lectures she was encouraging astrological students to embark on a journey similar to hers and I believe that is where she began exhibiting self-deception.

There are many interpretations of Neptune in the horoscope, ranging from association with drugs, delusion, deception to the highest and most spiritual center of selfhood. Marcia was under strong Neptune aspects while she was experimenting with drug-induced past-life recall. As I think of her now, it appears that her role was to remind all of us that there are no short cuts on the spiritual journey, especially with drugs.

In the early 1970s, the search for expanded consciousness was strong. I remember fondly the beach in Mexico where I was living at the time, studying astrology and tarot. I was involved with a daily meditation practice that involved the I Ching; I practiced yoga twice daily and was also experimenting with fasting. In other words, I was deeply into "the journey." I had been living there for six months, and there was quite a community of us, sharing our ideas and our lives. We didn't come to this spot knowing each other; we simply learned with time that we were on the same quest of consciousness raising.

## Ram Dass

One day I sat with a friend from California as he opened his mail. It contained a copy of *Be Here Now* by Baba Ram Dass, a/k/a Richard Alpert. It was a simplified version of what I was struggling with in my spiritual studies with astrology and yoga.

Ram Dass's book addressed what it meant to live a life of investigation and purity. With this book, he introduced a new way of thinking about money itself and deeper issues about the spirituality of daily living. Though the book was profound, Ram Dass made everything accessible. He was a visionary like Rudhyar, but his approach was so much clearer.

Why was Rudhyar so difficult and Ram Dass so clear?[2] They are both Aries Sun sign personalities, but there the similarities stop. Ram Dass's horoscope is a window into his life's work. He has an exact Sun/Uranus conjunction in Aries in the 10th House. The Sabian symbol for that degree is "Brownies dancing in the setting sun." His message is about the celebration of life. One degree away we find his North Node, in Aries.

Baba Ram Dass believed that something was missing in the lives most people were living, yet he was a voice of the people. He spoke of his journey as "our journey"; his trials were "our trials," his disillusionment, "our disillusionment." Perhaps he wrote much about "us" and "we" because he was truly searching for "I" and "me." (Intercepted Sun in Aries with Pisces on the 10th.) In

---

2  When compiling charts for this chapter, I looked through my extensive astrological library and was amazed at how many people had used his horoscope in their books. For this reason I almost chose to leave him out of this chapter, but decided not to because he was an important part of my own journey.

any case, his 10th House influence allowed him to be an example for all of us.

For many years now Ram Dass' ideas and development have been closely watched by many. He is a natural leader, with a Jupiter/Pluto conjunction on his Ascendant squaring his Sun/Uranus conjunction. His has been a life of upheaval and drastic change. He doesn't look for easy answers and he is quite willing to share his personal trials as an opportunity to increase common

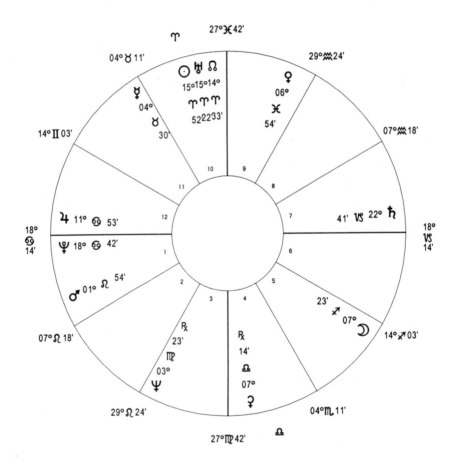

**Baba Ram Dass (Richard Alpert)**
April 6, 1931
10:40 AM EST, Boston, MA
71W04 42N22

understanding. Had he been trying only to be famous or present the face of a saint he would not have been so willing to share such a diverse self.

Ram Dass is also a clear writer. Perhaps his Mercury in Taurus helps ground his fire. He writes about his own spiritual awakening process in a way that invites a similar journey in the reader. While his life has not been easy—nor does he pretend it has been—he appears thankful for the opportunity his experiences have offered. I have especially appreciated his honesty in sharing even the parts of himself that he wished weren't there; for instance, his homosexuality. Yet we expect disturbance when there is a Mars inconjunct Venus in the horoscope. Ram Dass is a good example of someone who has remained crystal clear about his spiritual journey even when that course has appeared, even to him, wayward. Ram Dass is an example of the notion that, with consciousness, "there is no wayward journey."

After reading the Ram Dass stories about the clairvoyance of his guru, I secretly wanted the nationally famous astrologers back at the San Francisco convention to be able to look at me and tell me how many people I ate lunch with that afternoon and about the disturbing dream I had last night but had mentioned to no one. Maybe I wanted astrology to be so spiritually correct that there would be no flaws, only a practice of pure consciousness. I still hold that as an ideal.

## Timothy Leary

The philosopher Timothy Leary, an early and close associate of Ram Dass at Harvard University, is another example of a Sagittarius rising individual. Leary is engaging, charismatic, and evangelical. He is a prolific writer and a fascinating human being. In 1979, I heard him do a show rather in the manner of a stand-up comic. He talked about personal freedom and observed that his greatest freedom came as the result of people defining him as crazy. "At first I wanted to convince people that I was not crazy until I realized it lowered peoples' expectation of me, which meant that I could do almost anything I wanted. That's real freedom: lowered expectations," he said.

As I was listening to Leary, I suspected a strong Uranus. He was born with Uranus conjunct his Aquarian Moon. These are trine his 11th House Libra Sun (another Uranian association.) People with Sagittarius rising usually have Cancer on their 8th House. This combination suggests people who do not want to be responsible for someone else. Not surprisingly, it is the Sagittarius rising individual who preaches the value of a life of adventure and personal freedom, and these can indeed contribute to a life of spiritual integrity.

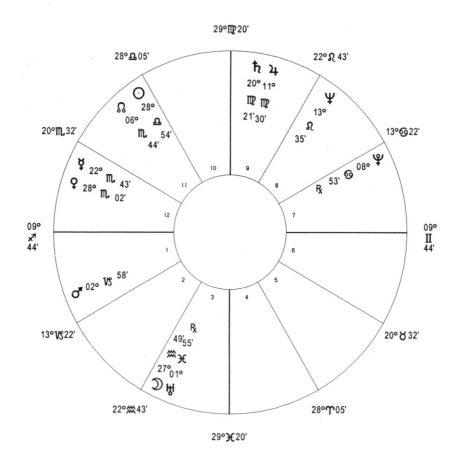

**Timothy Leary**
October 22, 1920
10:45 AM EDT, Springfield, MA
72W35 42N06

In 1985 I heard Leary speak at a computer software convention. Again, he was fascinating. He had written some interactive software that was designed to make the user "think"—something he said people didn't do enough of. He shared his familiar message from the 1960s: "Tune in, turn on, drop out." (His other familiar messages are: "Think for yourself" and "Question authority." He uses these injunctions as a frame of reference for most situations.)

Though Leary was the drug guru of the 1960s, he said he would not take drugs today unless he knew who made them and what their effect would be. "Question authority." It is interesting to note that someone who is so against authority, has Saturn—the planet of authority and discipline—as his most elevated planet. For many people, ironically, Timothy Leary continues to *be* a voice of authority.

Astrologically, Leary fits the Uranian/Aquarian stereotype. He might even be the ideal example. He has Neptune in the 8th House, which surprisingly often appears to be a mark of the drug abuser. I find it interesting that he is the grand drug *experimenter,* but he is not usually labeled as "alcoholic" or "addictive."

From his early days with LSD onward, Leary has been an eccentric pioneer who was willing to break the rules. But he never stayed on any one path too long. Being born with Saturn and Jupiter in his 9th House, it's safe to say that his destiny (spiritual and otherwise) revolves around teaching. These planets are in the Balsamic phase, which assumes that he is ahead of his time in society's eyes. True to that form, his greatest teaching is the life he leads. The question could be asked, "is there a way to get off the journey of your life?" It would appear that the answer is "no."

Leary was meant to be an unusual individual who would search for unusual ways to live a life of value. He was meant to be provocative. Whether through the words he writes and utters or his life, Leary has lived in harmony with his vision. He investigates—or "questions," as he calls it—his own self and his choices. His horoscope fits into the locomotive pattern which again emphasizes his nature as that of a hard-driving individual. The leading planet is Uranus. Whether people appreciate Timothy Leary or not, he always seems to be what they least expect him to be.

With both Mercury and Venus in his 12th House, it is not surprising that Leary should have spent time in prison. He told an interesting story about life on the inside. Being the friendly type (Libra, Aquarius, and Sagittarius) he quickly made friends with other inmates. They started talking about rebelling against conditions in the joint. They asked if he wanted to join their revolution and this strong Uranian type said, "Yes!" At their first meeting to map out what they would rebel against, they decided they wanted better televisions and more of them. They wanted better food and sleeping facilities, more control over their visitations.

Leary walked out in disgust, saying he wanted nothing to do with them or their revolution. He was appalled because they wanted to be more comfortable on the inside, while he wanted freedom from incarceration. "The last thing I want is to be more comfortable in prison and perhaps sedated into thinking life was okay on the inside."

## Errant Journeys

In the Capricorn 1991 issue of *Planet Earth*, Kim Rogers-Gallagher discusses the horoscope of Jimmy Swaggart. What a prime example of someone who supposedly is on the "spiritual path," yet has clearly fallen off it into a ditch. His episodes outside the church with prostitutes and a life quite unlike the one he publicly professes are well documented.

### Jimmy Swaggart

For the millions involved with tele-evangelism, Jimmy Swaggart has been the pinnacle of spiritual leadership. He has a strong horoscope for charisma and magnetism. Sagittarius rising is the mark of the enthusiast. With Sun conjunct Saturn in the sign of Pisces it is likely that he believes life is a struggle.

Swaggart has a Pisces Sun exactly trine his Jupiter in Scorpio. (Sun in the 3rd House and Jupiter in the 11th). He *is* a talker. His words are powerful; people believe in him. He has a highlighted Mars, close to the Midheaven in his 10th House. He was destined to be a man of authority. Sagittarius rising often shows up in evangelical types—not only religious types, but anyone who proselytizes for a viewpoint. His Mars in Libra is retrograde and exactly inconjunct his Sun. He has desires that conflict with his purpose.

In astrology we call the Sun sign the life purpose, but I would imagine that Jimmy has not studied astrology. As a funny aside, in the movie "The Jerk," the title character, played by Steve Martin, is told that "special purpose" is the name for his male organ. Throughout the movie, Martin refers to this organ as his "special purpose." I kept thinking of Jimmy Swaggart as I watched that movie again recently. Perhaps Swaggart had the same advice. His search for another "special purpose" in his for-

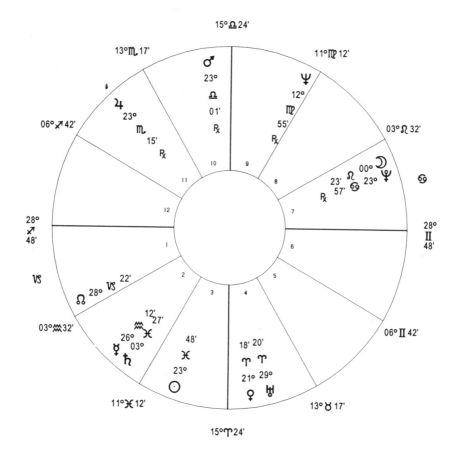

**Jimmy Swaggart**
March 15, 1935
1:35 AM CST, Ferriday, LA
91W33  31N38

ays with women suggest that he was not fulfilling all sides of his nature with his public life in the church.

Mars retrograde indicates a self-driven individual who is ruled more by his passions than logic. Being inconjunct his Sun, there are times Swaggart is at crossed purposes with his passions and basic life intention. When transiting Neptune moved into his 1st House, his self-deceptions became public. With natal Mars opposing his Venus/Uranus conjunction in Aries in his 4th House, we can assume that this is a complex man with confused passions that he may not have fully understood. His Mars projects sexuality and power, so I imagine it is women who give his ministry most of its money.

I don't think Jimmy Swaggart is less on his "journey" because of his transgressions. I do think that he is less spiritual because of his lack of inquiry into his own actions and his willingness to accept answers that are too easy. I wonder what he tells himself now about his fall from grace. Does he really believe that the "devil" gets inside of him and makes him do bad things? As the Church Lady from "Saturday Night Live" says, "How conveeeenient!" What about investigation and personal responsibility? There would be more room for growth and development of character if he were to ask himself why he behaves the way he does. Easy answers, like "the devil made me do it," stunt growth. They stop the inquiring mind and cast an uninteresting light on the character involved.

## Tammy Bakker

Tammy Bakker is another public example of being on a journey that could be described as "wayward." I am more inclined to say that she is on a journey that is difficult to define. Like Swaggart, she is also a Pisces 3rd House Sun with Sagittarius rising. Both are charismatic (if you like that sort of thing) and both are convincing, atavistic types. Together with her former husband, Jim Bakker, and Swaggart, this threesome changed the face of tele-spiritualism. (Each of them has a strong Pisces orientation)

To look at Tammy's cosmetic make-up is to know that she is not in touch with herself. How could she cry on television and never have that eye make-up run? Perhaps God *is* on her side, but I still imagine that she does not know herself very well. She was born with natal Neptune opposing her Sun, which can signal confusion about the self. From looking at that make-up, I think she wishes she *were* someone else.

Her fall from grace began when Neptune crossed her Ascendant. She is still trying to find her footing in the world of mega-religion. It is interesting to note that she and her ex-husband both have the South Lunar Node in the natal 2nd House. It appears that money is a root cause of confusion for both of them.

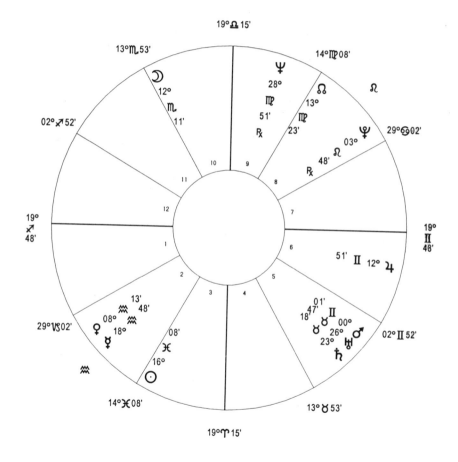

**Tammy Bakker**
March 7, 1942
3:27AM CWT, International Falls, MN
93W25 48N36

Her Pisces Sun is conjunct the South Node. She has a tendency to be her own worst enemy. To find happiness and to grow she needs to spend more time following her Virgo North Node. She needs to be critical of her choices and follow techniques that have worked for others. This placement demands that the individual be analytical and practical about life choices. That approach does not appear to be operating in her life.

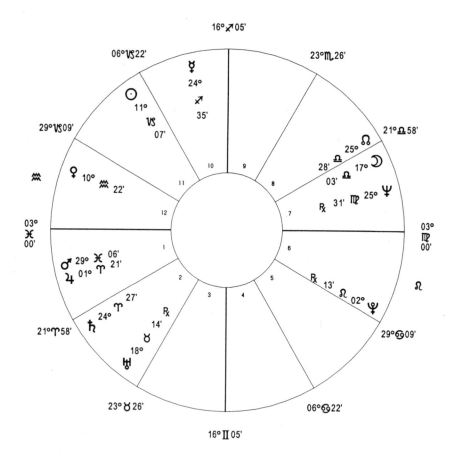

**Jim Bakker**
January 2, 1940
11:00 AM EST, Muskegon, MI
86W16 43N14

## Jim Bakker

In Jim Bakker's horoscope we find Pisces rising with Mars conjunct Jupiter in the 1st House. It appears he believes in the power of the individual: he was riding a wave and wanted to see how far he could take it. His 1st House emphasis made him narcissistic in ways he might not have been aware of. His 11th House Capricorn Sun made him want to deal with large groups of people, which he was good at. He craves an adoring audience, which he was able to have most of the time. With a Saturn/South Node conjunction in the 2nd House he also wanted the power that money brings.

It is likely that Bakker's spiritual journey began exhibiting definite aberrations long before his indiscretions were brought to the public eye. When transiting Saturn, Uranus, and Neptune moved into his Sun sign of Capricorn, in 1988, he began his public fall from grace.

Any astrologer is excited to study horoscopes and watch patterns emerge. Something that became apparent as I was correlating horoscopes for this chapter is that the *mutable signs show up with pronounced frequency as you study themes of spirituality.* Neptune and the sign of Pisces show up with prominence in the horoscopes of spiritual leaders. Transiting Neptune shows up when you talk about self-deception and falling from grace.

## J. Z. Knight

A final example of spiritual self-deception appears in the horoscope of the channeler J. Z. Knight. Once again we see familiar themes. She has a Pisces Sun with Sagittarius Rising. Her Sun is conjunct the 4th House cusp, but very close to the 3rd. This makes her horoscope greatly similar to that of Swaggart and Tammy Bakker.

The 1980s were J. Z. Knight's decade. People flocked to her channelings and spiritual retreats. She became a spiritual phenomenon and, through her spiritual channeling of Ramtha, made national headlines and a lot of money. Then she fell from grace in the eyes of the media. What was it that pulled her from her tremendous position of power? Perhaps it was all of the money and power that she attracted, perhaps she lost objectivity.

From astrologer Lois Rodden, I learned that J. Z. was molested as a child, which was sure to have had far-reaching effects concerning trust and capacity for intimacy. Having all the "heavies" (Mars, Pluto, and Saturn) in her natal 8th House would make her wary about surrendering power. She could be a watchdog about making sure that people are who they say they are. These planet placements could make her a good spiritual teacher, but probably a difficult personal mate. (She is in the midst of a messy divorce.)

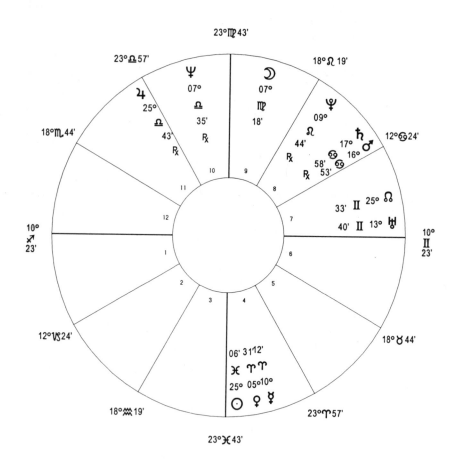

**J. Z. Knight**
March 16, 1946
00:02:00 AM MST, Roswell, NM
104W32 33N24

Her strong 8th House intensifies her desire for not wanting anyone controlling her, yet that is the relationship she developed with Ramtha, who through her gives advice as to what she and others should be doing with their money and their lives. This combination of planets in the 8th House might explain her five marriages and divorces. Most likely she pushes people to their limits.

Knight grew up in poverty, which was likely to have been its own powerful teaching about the importance of having money. It seems she learned that lesson well, as she continues to accumulate a personal fortune in the business of spirituality.

With Neptune located in her natal 10th House, it was likely that she would become a spiritualist of some sort. Opposing her natal Venus/Mercury conjunction, it may have opened the door to tremendous perceptions. The being she channels has a voice and accent quite different from her own. For some, this validated her authenticity and for others it signalled a deeper deception.

Neptune moved into her 1st House in 1975, when she began attracting a more powerful following. By 1981, she had entered the world of mega-spiritual business. She was making a lot of money. This was when Neptune started squaring her Sun and conjuncting her natal South Node. This is when a good astrologer could have warned her that trials in self-deception were present. By 1989, when transiting Neptune was squaring its natal position, her integrity was questioned and her popularity faltered. In 1992, with transiting Uranus and Neptune opposing her natal Mars/Saturn conjunction, she is still a source of inspiration for many people, yet her reputation has been compromised. With a Gibbous Sun/Moon phase in her natal chart she is a perfectionist who is continually learning to be a better human being. It is likely that she is learning from this part of her journey as she has learned from other opportunities for growth that life has presented her.

## Literary Voyagers

### F. Scott Fitzgerald

A well-known personality from quite a different world is the novelist F. Scott Fitzgerald, chronicler of the lives and values of the wealthy and wealthy wannabees in the Jazz Age of the 1920s.

Fitzgerald has an 8th House Sun widely conjuncting Venus and Mercury. They are located in the sign of Libra, intercepted in his 8th House. It is the strong Libra influence which accounts for the years Fitzgerald lived a charmed life and was richly acclaimed. His was a romantic vision in a romantic time. We expect this idealization of love with the Sun sign Libra. Though ruled by the Scales, the Libran personality is often looking for balance through very extreme behavior, perhaps more so when found intercepted.

Fitzgerald was born with an exact Mars/Neptune conjunction in the sign of Gemini, located in his 5th House. How much more classically creative can you get? This placement is the mark of a great writer. These planets are conjuncting Pluto, which would suggest notoriety. His 8th House Sun is inconjunct his 3rd House Taurus Moon, indicating that he was often in a state of inner turmoil. This was reflected in his close but difficult relationship with his wife Zelda.

Scott and Zelda married in April 1920, with transiting Jupiter and Neptune conjunct in his 7th House. He then entered into a life of extremes and intense romance, punctuated by a great deal of social drinking. Their high-living lifestyle (Taurus Moon), imposed a constant need for more money. Money problems may have impelled him to write as a source of releasing tension, but no doubt pushed him to drinking to numb the pain, in turn making the writing more difficult. (Neptune problems: ruler of the 2nd conjunct Mars.)

As is usual with writers of fiction, much of his work drew on his life. In *The Great Gatsby, Tender is the Night,* and in fact all his writing, Fitzgerald was highly romantic about love, women, and money. Jay Gatsby, the embodiment of a man's uncritical love for an attractive, stylish woman, is the extreme statement of Fitzgerald's idealization of *the* woman. Gatsby's love for Daisy Buchanan was ideal, untarnished by the reality of who she really was. A true Libran, Fitzgerald found the ideal stronger than the truth. Sadly, the fall from grace that befell Gatsby and Dick Diver in *Tender is the Night* is eerily similar to Fitzgerald's own decline.

Fitzgerald's writing glamorizes life and people. He might have been so widely read because he spoke so glowingly to an audience that had forgotten about love. He wrote in a style that was charming and poetic. We expect nothing less from a writer with three planets in Libra and 60 percent of his horoscope in Air.

If the wayward part of Fitzgerald's journey began with his too-high lifestyle and loss of his own vision, it certainly arrived when his need for money (accelerated by Zelda's mental illness) drove him to Hollywood, where he was a studio pet, totally out of his element. The world of money and society that he and his protagonists had so desperately wanted as young men rapidly become a great source of disillusionment.

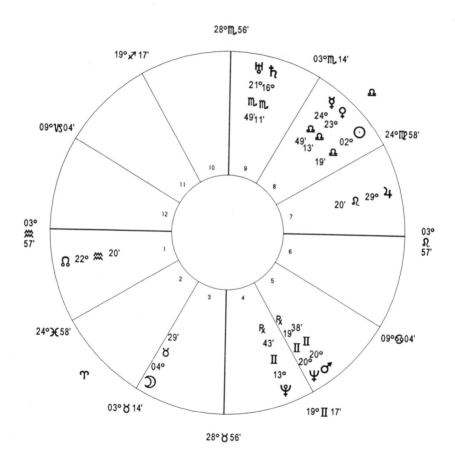

**F. Scott Fitzgerald**
September 24, 1896
3:30 PM LMT, St. Paul, MN
93W06  44N57

Fitzgerald's romantic vision of women also set him up for disillusion. His Mars/Neptune conjunction makes an exact trine to his Venus/Mercury conjunction in Libra. He was an idealist who got into negative Neptune problems when alcohol started taking over his life. With his highly aspected natal Neptune he should have developed more of a spiritual foundation to help ground his creativity. Instead he built a life around alcohol, and it probably cost him his life.

He died in 1940 at the age of forty-four after a heart attack. Transiting Saturn was conjuncting his natal Moon, and transiting Uranus was opposing its natal position and natal Saturn. Both suggested the need for change. To live, he needed to curb his excesses and restructure outdated habit patterns, but he was unable to do so.

By the time of his death, though he was still relatively young, his work was no longer popular (in the 1930s, the rich he had lionized had become class villains) and Zelda was institutionalized. This was not the sort of ending he had had in mind.

For those who followed his dramatic life with Zelda and peered into the giddy glitter-world through his novels, Fitzgerald gave voice to the longing for one's heart's desire. He offered a look at the romance in each of us and a painfully real glimpse of the "good life," 1920s style. As Fitzgerald himself did, the reader could puzzle over where true value might lie.

### Truman Capote

Another writer whose life seemed as rich and public as his writings is Truman Capote. Like Fitzgerald, Capote has a Libran 8th House Sun. Here the astrological similarities stop. He has a Moon/Saturn conjunction in Scorpio in his 9th House. They are in the New Phase, which explains astrologically a kind of radiant charm that expressed itself through him. He seemed to have an honesty that drew people to him. As a writer, he had popularity and acceptance right from the beginning.

Capote's life may best be seen as an example of the adage, "Be careful what you wish for, for you may get it." He grew up in poverty and, like Fitzgerald, wanted very much to experience the high life his rich imagination saw the wealthy living. He had the usual high ideals that can so deeply distract the Libran personality. To be born with your Sun in the 8th House means that you will go to great extremes to find yourself; the height and depth of experience will be yours.

Also like Fitzgerald, Capote was perhaps the best American writer of his age. His writings are perceptive and provocative. His eloquent writing was in sharp contrast to his personal life, which was often wild: he was openly gay when few men were.

For most Librans, friendship is of the utmost importance. The moment of truth in Capote's life came when he published the

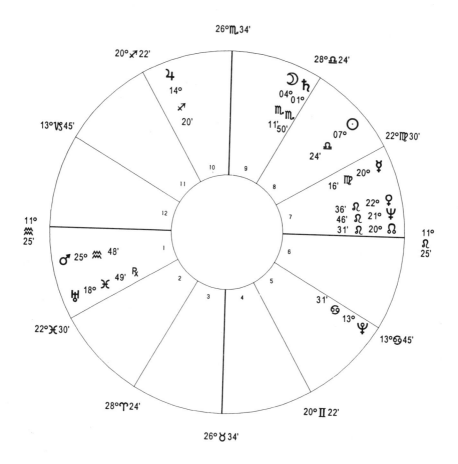

**Truman Capote**
September 30, 1924
3:00 PM CST, New Orleans, LA
90W04  29N58

story "La Cote Basque." The story recounts a lunch between two women at the fashionable restaurant that gave the story its title, in the course of which they air choice bits of gossip and dirty linen about their New York glitterati pals. The story cost Capote all his society friends when it was published. They never imagined their buddy and confidant Truman would get it all so right, so bitchily, and in black and white too.

When "La Cote Basque" appeared in the October 1975 *Esquire*, it changed the course of Capote's life more than any book—even more than *In Cold Blood*, which had made him wealthy, though it had not brought him the critical praise he had wanted.[3] "La Cote Basque" was to have been just a chapter of Capote's great and long anticipated novel, *Answered Prayers*, which was being published in serial form in the magazine.

The upshot of the story and Capote's exile from his life as society pet was that he never finished the book as it was intended to be; it was published posthumously in a form much diminished from what he had imagined, though it was still a remarkable book.

As you might expect, at this time transiting Neptune was lurking around, transiting his 10th House and coming within four degrees of his natal Jupiter. Before his fall from grace, Capote was just regaining some of the literary ground that had been lost with his long inactivity after *In Cold Blood*. Looking back at his transits for that time should remind all of us that astrology does work. It was a powerful time for him. Transiting Pluto was conjuncting his 8th House Sun: a once-in-a-lifetime aspect. With the articles he was sending to *Esquire*, he was fighting for his literary life.

Transiting Uranus was conjuncting his natal Moon/Saturn conjunction. Whatever he did at this time, it would have far-reaching effects. When he was ostracized by his rich friends (Uranus), he never regained control of himself and his gifts. The alcohol and pills (Neptune) took over. Capote never understood it. "I'm a *writer*, for God's sake," he was heard to say. "What did they *think* I was going to do?"

With Neptune we expect anything from deception to spiritual inspiration. With "La Cote Basque," Capote had both. History proved that his perception was faulty at this time. He had no idea

---

3   Its form was so unusual it gave rise to a new name for the genre: "faction."

of the far-ranging negative effects this would create in his personal life. Creatively, the story was a stunning success, but at what price?

A good astrologer could have told Capote, if asked, to slow down and use control (transiting Pluto) as he executed his next move. A good astrologer would have gone over all the options, good and bad, that could occur at this time. With the power of transiting Uranus, he should have expected that things might not turn out as he imagined. But then his would have been a different life.

A wayward journey? That's difficult to say. Capote's dance with death through extended, excessive drug and alcohol use doubtless shortened his life. He was a brilliant writer who (like Fitzgerald) got tangled in the trappings of success. He was born with Venus/Neptune conjunction opposite his Mars in Aquarius in his 1st House. He was no stranger to inner turmoil. The sedation through drugs and alcohol were a salve he couldn't resist. For those of us who have never known great success, wealth or fame it's difficult to comprehend fully the sort of challenges that go along with these high stakes goals.

In an interview that rock genius Jimi Hendrix had with Dick Cavett at the height of his career, Cavett asked Hendrix what it was like to sing the "blues" when you are the number one recording artist in the United States and maybe the world? He asked if Hendrix was embarrassed about singing the "blues" when he was experiencing such phenomenal financial success? Hendrix answered that he never really knew the blues until he made it to the top. *Now*, he said, he was *really* singing the blues.

When you are on your way up, you are sure that money and fame will give you all that you desire. Then you see more clearly: "I have everything I wanted and I still feel bad. Now what do I reach for?"

## Humans, Not Gods

### Bhagwan Shree Rajneesh

To close this magical mystery tour of life journeys, errant and otherwise, I want to use the horoscope of Bhagwan Shree Rajneesh. He was born with a Sagittarian Sun and five planets in the sign of Capricorn. He was a wise man who understood much about the practicalities of the spiritual life.

I heard a tape of his once in which he was talking about the axiom, "It is easier for a camel to walk through the eye of a needle than it is for a rich man to enter the gates of heaven." With that teaching, it is usually assumed that a rich man is so insulated from God and the search for truth that he could never enter the spiritual life. He would first have to leave behind the comforts that his wealth has given to him.

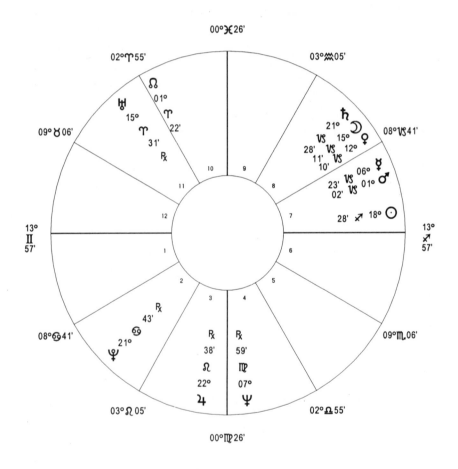

**Bhagwan Shree Rajneesh**
December 11, 1931
5:08 PM INT, Gadarwara, India
78W47 22N55

Rajneesh saw it differently. He believed that *only* a rich man could enter the gates of heaven. He claimed that if you have never known wealth you will always secretly covet it, and that this powerful desire will take precedence over your spiritual quest. It might be the grand illusion of life, but most of us are stuck in it.

We can't know what Rajneesh was trying to accomplish with his own life. Was he becoming a "rich man" to test the Gods and see if he could also become a spiritual master? Rajneesh is a New Moon personality and a Life Path No. 1, which meant that he was not following anyone else's guidance: he was charting his own course. He was an effervescent individual who had a unique plan to find inner peace. With all of his Capricorn emphasis, he knew how life worked. He had a good feeling for "the journey." He was excellent at expressing the "hows" and "whys" of spirituality. I never doubted him as one of the true masters and teachers of our day, but many people did.

His life was enigmatic. He spoke often of this life being "either Heaven or Hell—you decide yourself." He was clear about his appreciation of the luxuries of life. He was not a suffering saint, nor did he suggest this as a path others should take. He talked of life as a celebration, and for most of his life he was a living example of this teaching. But when he moved to the United States there was a definite downward turn. At this point, transiting Neptune conjuncted his natal Sun and in many ways his life went awry. His problems with the Indian government were coming to a head and I'm not sure if the United States was ever really a home for him. It seemed that he just had too *much* money, too *much* power, and too many Rolls Royces.

## Deception Versus Disillusionment

In many of the lives presented here we see deception and disillusionment. There is also creativity, achievement and spiritual vision. It is not within the scope of this article to delve into the "right" role that money and fame play in defining personal happiness. I don't pretend to know where money fits into larger questions of spirituality. However, I do know that there is a connection.

All of these people, at one time or another, could have used the services of a good astrologer. Their destiny may not have been altered, but they would have been more prepared for the drastic changes their lives were taking. As astrologers we know that you can study your horoscope daily and still never be fully prepared for what life will offer. Part of the journey is dealing with the unexpected.

The last time I heard Marc Edmund Jones speak was thirteen days after his wife had died. He was very shaken, yet he chose to keep his speaking engagement with the Seattle Astrological Association. He told the group that he had known for many months that his wife would die soon and that he was doing transits and progressions on both of their charts as a form of readying himself for the experience. She died approximately when he thought she would.

But he found that the loss was more profound than he could have ever imagined and that neither his astrological preparations nor anything else had readied him for the grief he was experiencing. With or without astrology, he said, life is going to throw you curve balls that will shake you to your core. He found this disillusioning.

Marc Edmund Jones knew something profound was going to happen to him, but his preparations proved to be simply a distraction from dealing with the pain of her dying. Perhaps his experience shows that when you think you know all the answers you have shut the door to spiritual growth.

## Affairs and "Easy Answers"

Keeping in mind the diverse wayward journeys above, I want to look at an issue that shows up frequently in an astrology practice: extramarital affairs.

There are no formulas to tell you what to do when counseling a client in this situation. Suppose you have a married client who is attracted to another man, someone she works with. It's never happened before and she feels confused. Being adept at astrology, she looks there first. Perhaps she sees his Venus conjunct her Moon and his Mars conjunct her Venus. This would certainly signal attraction.

How do you help her? You might suggest that rather than focusing on the man she is attracted to, or on their compatibility—

rather than asking, "What is it *about him* that I want?"—that she ask another question: "What is it that I want?"

She may see herself as stuck between the obvious polar alternatives—go for the passion of the moment, or bury the feeling ("I don't *have* affairs"). But if she is seeking wholeness and integrity, she might do better to see the situation as a window through which to look *at what's missing in her own life*. Focusing on the *subject* of the feeling, rather than the *object* of it, will more likely lead to a fruitful outcome. While this observation borders on the obvious, it's surprising how often it's overlooked in the drama of attraction.

Attraction can be compelling when we feel one-down in day to day life, regardless of whether anyone is at fault. Suppose your client is a married man who feels unappreciated at home because he has lost his job, yet inexplicably finds himself the object of an attractive woman's attention. Going for that thrill could be temporarily therapeutic, but it could also stress his marriage and lead to a far more devastating loss.

Focusing on what is missing in one's life could, of course, implicate the relationship and lead to its end. That may be desirable. But focusing on the client's own journey first, rather than on technical aspects of chart compatibility, will offer deeper insight into the client's issues and reveal a promising course of action. Even if the marriage is too far gone to fix, at least your client may avoid the trap of looking to a new relationship to fill a void. The real problem may be deeper and more profound.

Another outcome is also possible. If the client faces the root cause of the dissatisfaction, this could begin a movement toward greater intimacy and honesty in the existing relationship. Yes, the awkward excitement of a potential affair could actually end up saving a marriage, when the cause of the unhappiness is better understood.

To have an inquiring mind will not take temptation away, nor should it. To be flirtatious and fully alive is a birthright to fight for. To be married does not mean a death of spirit, nor is it necessary that every marriage last forever. But for the thinking individual, there is a lot of middle ground between these two poles.

Affairs are not the only area where we come in contact with questions of integrity. One of my clients is HIV positive and ashamed of it, and of being gay. For the most part, he believes, people in his life do not know that he is gay and he feels that it is no one's business. We spent several of our last few sessions discussing when such information should be shared. Push came to shove when he insisted that he need not tell his dentist of his situation because his sex life is private. That, of course, is true; he has a right to his privacy. But when someone else's safety is involved, the inquiry must go deeper.

## Ushering in the New Age

Astrology, like other tools, is only as useful as the astrologer is conscious. It is also a tool that is more than the sum total of its parts.

You can memorize meanings of planets, signs and houses. You can learn about the correct timing of transits and several kinds of progressions. You can learn to read a solar return chart. All of this is possible through studying good books and the assistance of good teachers. But without an understanding of life itself and of people, something will always be missing. These two elements cannot be taught. They are the results of your own personal journey and your own work on yourself.

During this past year I sat in with a committee that was discussing certification of astrologers. While we are still trying to define just what it is that makes one an astrologer—something I am greatly curious about—I admit that in the meeting I was put off by some definitions.

Are you a better astrologer if you can set up a chart and do the necessary mathematics? Are you a still better astrologer if you can do more complex mathematics? The computer has changed the face of astrology. We no longer need to spend all of the time that was once necessary to hand-calculate horoscopes. I believe it's an unnecessary drill, at least for most of us.

Meaningful testing, I believe, would have to find a way to measure integrity, objectivity and the understanding of the human journey. And, of course, skill with the mechanics of astrology is absolutely essential. But wouldn't it be exciting to have a test that could measure the individual's understanding of life itself?

It is easy to deceive oneself (and others) with impressive astrological tools and jargon—like the Beatles' "nowhere man." But this does not mean one is a wise seeker. Perhaps now more than ever we need spiritual foundation for our lives. My hope is that astrologers can step up to this need and play a more significant role in the spiritual regrouping of the collective unconscious.

The Uranus/Neptune conjunction we are experiencing now is profound. Since 1988, when Saturn, Uranus, and Neptune all conjoined in the sign of Capricorn, there has been a movement back to the conventional churches. It is a powerful reminder of the vast emptiness in most peoples' lives and their need to fill their lives with spiritual meaning.

In typical Capricorn fashion, we are still seeking authority figures. The old figures will probably work until both Uranus and Neptune move out of Capricorn and into the sign of Aquarius. But soon these planets will move into a new phase of spontaneous expression. What an exciting time to be alive! The kind of spirituality we need for this new time has never been on this planet before; the past will be truly past.

Those who are already feeling the impact of the Balsamic Uranus/Neptune know well that the old ways are crumbling and that a new age—with new challenges about what it means to be human and conscious—awaits.

**Sandy Hughes**

An Aquarian born in Neptune, New Jersey, Sandy Hughes was probably always an astrologer at heart. Growing up and raising a family in and around Hollywood, California exposed her to many faces of reality which piqued her interest in psychology and metaphysics.

Sandy stepped onto the astrological path in 1976, just prior to moving to Vancouver, B.C., Canada. She turned professional in 1979, and has been an astrological teacher, counselor, and lecturer ever since. She co-founded Universal Search, a chapter of the Fraternity for Canadian Astrologers, in 1982, was president for three years, and coordinated the second national FCA Conference.

Sandy strives to help people become more aware of the symbolic nature of life in order to apply most effectively its "hidden" messages. Her insights are drawn from years of working with the I Ching, Jungian psychology and mythology, past-life therapy, meditation, Tarot, and various other avenues of metaphysical study.

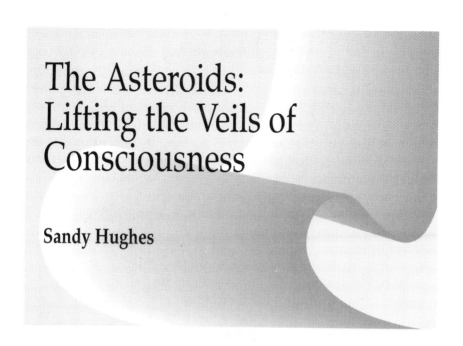

# The Asteroids: Lifting the Veils of Consciousness

**Sandy Hughes**

## Introduction

When the outraged voice of feminism resounded in our ears back in the 1970s and women began to rethink their position in contemporary society, we all suddenly realized that there was far more to "Woman" than any of us had dared think! We know now, of course, that this re-emergence of the feminine principle into life is relevant for all of us, male and female alike.

Following the consciousness explosion of the 1960s, we were all primed for a new window to open, providing further clues to self-realization. It was time to acknowledge the shocking price we had all paid for our accelerated technological development and rampant capitalistic greed, where the value of Mother Earth and her children had been sadly ignored.

Is it any surprise, then, that astrologers suddenly had an ephemeris available for four major asteroids that *just happened* to represent the four primary roles women play in society: Ceres/Mother, Pallas Athena/Daughter, Juno/Wife and Vesta/Sister? Was this not a signal of some kind that we were ready to begin exploring the depths of the inner world, the realm of the Feminine, with greater insight and understanding?

Most of us have not been immediately receptive to the idea of putting four extra symbols into the chart, but neither have we, as a people, been very receptive, period! That is the whole point. I, too, was reluctant, yet found myself compelled by something inside to take the extra time to look. The subtleties in life are often where the fine points are hidden. The asteroids may appear to be inconsequential at first glance, too small to consider, but upon deeper contemplation, as with most things sacred, their implicit value becomes astonishingly clear.

This discussion on the asteroids will focus primarily on the four feminine archetypes mentioned above. There is one other fig- ure, however, which also appeared in the 1970s. Though not an asteroid at all, its message is equally vital. The discovery of the "planetoid" Chiron in 1977, orbiting between Saturn and Uranus, revealed a much needed male archetype, providing a new role model for the masculine side of humanity. In addition, he sym- bolizes the wounded child in all of us, as well as the holistic con- sciousness of Self, once healed and redeemed. A harbinger of the Aquarian Age, the astrological Chiron points the way for our full realization of Self.

If we choose to ignore these new "windows" into our horo- scopes, it seems to me that we are foolishly refusing a helping hand in times of great need. There is no sense trying to spin a stick to start a fire if you have matches in your pocket! Perhaps the next pages will help you open the door to these late arrivals on the astrological scene. The more we allow ourselves to open up and listen, the closer we come to the Truth. Ceres, Pallas Athena, Juno, Vesta, and Chiron are waiting to be discovered inside you, their hands outstretched with bountiful gifts. Are you ready?

## Veils

Before we embark on our journey to discover the asteroids, it may be helpful to look at them as a group. Most scientific theories about their origin seem to agree that all (several thousand) of them are remnants of an ancient planet whose orbit ran between Mars and Jupiter. Some immense heavenly calamity shattered that planet into thousands of pieces, but those pieces still main- tain their pre-programmed orbit as if they were one.

This fierce persistence toward continuity reveals the feminine core of the asteroids. Just as the consciousness of the value of the Feminine was shattered by patriarchy, so these planetary bits display that fragmentation. We may also note the current state of disarray that has been reached by the Virgo archetype. The tendency of many Virgoans to dissect and split apart, often not knowing how to reassemble the pieces of any puzzle, is another clue that secrets have been hidden within the asteroids.

According to H. P. Blavatsky in *Isis Unveiled* (vol. II, p. 456), the 6th sign of the zodiac was originally Virgo-Scorpio, there being then only 10 signs. The insertion of the patriarchal Libra (the only inanimate symbol of the zodiac, the Scales) and the simultaneous ripping asunder of the Virgo-Scorpio oneness may have been the original "rape," from which we are all still trying to recover.

These three signs (and all of us) have carried the scars of this huge injustice ever since. Virgo, the Virgin, became the pure white innocent Madonna, while Scorpio took the rap for all the sleeze and whoredom (Mary Magdalene). And dear sweet Libra has been trying to keep the peace ever since. Or so the story goes.

Is it any wonder that lifting the veils of consciousness to reveal the hidden Feminine within us all has evoked such radical resistance? It takes a great deal of humility and a willingness to take responsibility for what is found behind those veils. Most of us seem to prefer to stay where it's "safe," burrowed in our ruts, hopelessly lashed to our addictions, blaming all those evil folks "out there" for ruining our lives.

The asteroids have been treated as nonessentials by many traditional astrologers, but, in my mind, this is akin to killing a female child because it is of no significant value and represents nothing more than an extra burden on an already exhausted family. Could this be our family of planets? The Greek/Roman pantheon astrology we've inherited gives us only two feminine deities, the Moon and Venus. Especially when considered from a predominately male point of view, these two goddesses represent only the most basic principles of femininity. Many of the more definitive characteristics of the yin experience were seen as irrelevant and allowed to fall into the darkness, unconscious and out-of-sight. Until the asteroids made themselves known, that is.

The message seems to be quite clear: that the dark and the light must dance together as one. Perhaps the most significant attribute of Libra is its function as our own reflection (opposite Aries, "I Am"), to provide the mirror with which to see both sides of ourselves: the innocent, unsuspecting Virgin and the conniving villain. Could this be the role the asteroids have come to play, to illuminate the subtleties of the dance?

As I write this, the High Priestess of the Tarot is reminding me of her role as the veiled Isis, keeping her secrets. She sits between the black and white pillars, guarding the gate into the realm of the Feminine, offering a choice: *accept the opposites or suffer ignorance of the mysteries.* Her veil can be compared to the veil embodied by the asteroid belt, just recently lifted.

Attaching affinities between the asteroids and the zodiacal signs is extremely helpful in understanding their functions and energies, but I do not think it is necessary, nor even desirable, to assign rulerships as we have with the planets. Seeking them as a group consciousness to reveal further the intricacies of the feminine Soul (in men and in women) seems to me to be more helpful in comprehending their purpose.

Chiron, of course, is a category all its own. Barbara Hand Clow has made an impressive case for Chiron ruling Virgo in her book, *Chiron: Rainbow Bridge Between the Inner and Outer Planets.* This may be true if we can see Virgo in her fully blossomed holistic state, which is surely what Chiron is asking of us. My personal feeling, however, is one of a multiple rulership. I see Chiron as governing the mutable cross: Gemini, Virgo, Sagittarius, and Pisces. This may sound like I am afraid to commit, but Chiron is an energy of the Aquarian Age, and perhaps its role is unique in this way. I invite you to ponder this possibility.

## Ceres: The Beginning

Ceres was the first asteroid to be discovered, in 1801, and is the largest. It is fitting, therefore, that Ceres (the Greek Demeter) is the fertile Earth Mother from whom all life springs. The Goddess of Agriculture naturally symbolizes the richness and fertility inherent within us. She is goddess of the corn and cereal grain, all the seeds of life and fruitfulness.

Thinking of her as a Virgo Moon may help give you an accurate picture of her character.

She can easily be perceived as another Moon in the chart, in that she is a mother figure, nurturer, and protectress. Ceres fosters growth in all she contacts, and she is our doorway into the cycles of Birth, Life, Death, and Rebirth. She asks us to follow her lead into our own cauldron of creative juices. The sign and house placement of your natal Ceres will show you the most likely approaches or places in which to find yourself stimulated into creative activity.

When her daughter, Persephone, the innocent maiden, was abducted by Pluto/Hades and taken captive in the Underworld, Ceres was outraged and totally bereft. Consequently, all the vegetation on Earth began to wither and die. Death to all living things was inevitable. She adamantly refused to come out of her black mourning until Zeus/Jupiter, King of the Gods, intervened. Finally, an agreement was reached that allowed Persephone to come back above ground for part of the year, so her mother would stop the Death Curse and get back to the business of fertility.

Ceres' emotional reaction to Persephone's fate brought forth the antithesis of the mothering instinct, the shadow side allowed to run rampant. Due to her personal attachment to her daughter (sound like the Moon?), she refused to acknowledge her own universal role as Goddess of Fertility, as well as Persephone's profound destiny to become Queen of the Underworld.

The loss of our innocence, regardless of the nature of the situation, is always a bit hard to swallow, especially when the status quo is completely upset. We tend to feel safe when things stay the same; the familiar terrain usually seems preferable to unknown territory, regardless of how incomplete or destructive the present circumstances might be. The static condition of an eternal virgin is symbolic of stagnancy and nonproductivity, loaded with potential, but sadly unrealized.

If we are confronted with the loss of something dear to us under a transit to or progression of Ceres, we will often find ourselves flung into a mourning period or a refusal to accept the conditions of life as the river continues to flow. Moving *through* the process is the key, allowing the pain to release itself in a renewed impetus to *grow* with life, instead of the initial reaction to withdraw from it.

Seeing our inner Persephone through the Ceres in our charts can further illuminate our path of self-realization. If we choose to remain the "raped virgin," we will never become the "ravished bride." Resenting our initiation into life's experiential realm is spitting in the face of Divinity. Once we open our eyes and begin to look around and wonder what we are doing here, then the sacrifice can be honored with dignity. Then our Queenship can be claimed. Otherwise, we are always at the disposal of the evil god who holds us prisoner.

One of my clients, an RCMP officer, wasn't the least bit surprised when I told him his chart was almost identical to that of another of my clients, who is a drug dealer. He said, "In order to be a good cop, you have to have a criminal mind." Persephone, too, must learn the language of the Underworld, if she is, in fact, to reign there. Real-life experience gives credibility in a way nothing else can. Will any of us listen to advice from someone who has "never been there"? This is Persephone's lesson. There are no innocent victims.

To truly acknowledge our birthright to be creative, self-supportive individuals, we must somehow find a way to make the passage from adolescent to adult, from naivete to wisdom. The dance of life, the natural balance of opposites, can only manifest itself completely if we are willing to accept the darkness with the light. The highest peaks are only made possible by the deepest valleys. Denying our own inner shadows simply results in the outer ones looming larger than ever. Accepting our *whole* selves and taking responsibility for them gives us back control of our lives, rather than keeping us dangling at the end of somebody else's yo-yo string.

Relinquishing the ego's conscious control of the situation will usually allow an inner voice to rise above the din of confusion and offer insight unavailable from any other source. Knowing that we have at least attracted, if not consciously invited, everything we have in our lives, receptivity to inner patterns can bring astounding revelations. Ceres contacts, even in synastry, will often facilitate this kind of inner vision.

In *The Pregnant Virgin*, Marion Woodman spoke of the need to be ever "virginlike"; in this case meaning to stay open and vulnerable to new experiences in order to release the inherent creativity with which we are all "pregnant." Refusing to allow unexpected change into our complacent lives insults the Goddess, Mother Nature, who knows far better than we do how the cycles of life and death and life and death keep the wheels of the universe ever-spinning. Presuming that we have a superior plan is a very dangerous aberration. John Lennon's words keep ringing in my ears: "Life is what happens while you're busy making other plans." Ceres and Persephone can teach us a lot about that if we will give them a chance.

All four asteroids are keys to inner doorways through which we can access our own inherent rhythms, the ebb and flow of life. Ceres is the one most closely attuned to our biological cycles and, therefore, is a clear indicator of fertility. A few years ago, I mentioned to a client that her progressed Moon had been within a degree of her natal Ceres in the 5th House for about two weeks, and that if she wanted to get pregnant this would be a perfect time. She phoned a few weeks later to tell me she had been exactly two weeks pregnant on the day of our appointment. Dreaming of pregnant women, babies, eggs, etc., may also indicate a fertility cycle of a different sort.

Other physical symptoms often display her messages, too. If our Moon Lodge (New Moon down-time) is not respected, we may manifest the flu or allergies or menstrual cramps or PMS, in order for our Ceres to get her just due. This applies to men as well as women. If a fertile space is not provided for our creative juices to begin to flow, it may be necessary for us to sprain an ankle or wrench our back, just to get some time off work.

Ceres is directly connected to Virgo in her role as Goddess of Agriculture and the harvest, but Virgo's dedication to the Work is also implicit here. Thinking of work as simply the job you go to every day is a dangerous mistake where Ceres is concerned. In her case, the "work" is the Life's Work, which must include, if not revolve around, new growth. Tilling the fields, weeding the garden, and reaping the harvest are all favorite roles of Ceres.

Because of her affinity with the Moon, the Great Mother, our personal Ceres placement points in the direction of our natural nurturing instincts, not only to see the project completed (*a la* Virgo), but also to see the people involved being taken care of as well (Cancer). She is just as much a symbol of familial patterns and social relationships as is our Moon. Aspects to Ceres will reveal deeper levels of the interaction among family members. Stressful aspects, especially to the Moon itself, will show double agendas and inner conflicts within our mother, our inner "mother," and even in the domestic atmosphere in which we have been raised.

**Elvis Presley**

Elvis Presley's natal Ceres/Pluto conjunction in the 8th House, directly opposing his Capricorn stellium in the 2nd, seems to have locked him into a consuming pattern of attachment and symbiosis with his mother. He was totally devoted to her and even predicted his own death at 42, based on his mother's death at 42. His Ceres/Pluto conjunction trined his IC in Pisces and his 11th House Jupiter in Scorpio. While he undoubtedly lived an increasingly overindulgent lifestyle, he also never lost his downhome

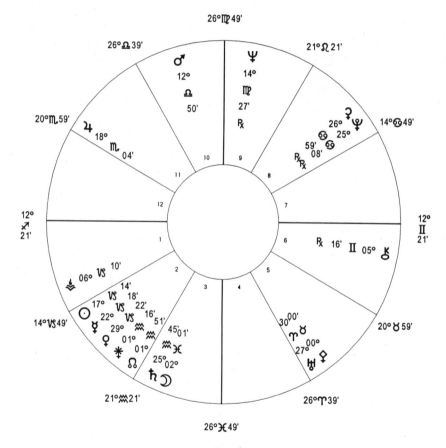

**Elvis Presley**
January 8, 1935
4:35 AM CST, Tupelo, MS
34N16  88W43
Source: *American Book of Charts*, by Lois Rodden

appreciation for his blessings and remained ever generous to his friends and fans, one way he could successfully nurture others.

## ⚵ Pallas Athena: The Wise Warrior

This lady (Minerva, in Rome) holds a most unique position in the Greek pantheon. Since her father, Zeus/Jupiter, had "swallowed" his pregnant wife in order to dispel a prophecy that his progeny would claim his throne, she was born instead from his forehead (3rd Eye). She was fully armed for battle, a feminine warrior, yet her battlefield was one of the mind. She is our inner chess player, the strategist of the zodiac. When pitted against Mars, the God of War, she knew better than to fight him on his own turf, physical combat. Instead, she observed his behavior and determined that he predictably charged at lightning speed in a straight line. Logically, she wove a net across his path, and he ran right into it.

In times of duress, thinking rationally is not always easy. Calling on Pallas Athena means using our ability to detach from the personal involvement of a situation and see it from a more collective point of view. An Aquarian goddess by nature, she always kept the welfare of the people a top priority. Personal preferences were relegated to the back burner.

The ability to listen to one's intuition (3rd Eye) and stay unattached to the outcome is Athena's gift to us. Your personal Pallas Athena will show you how to best access this inner wisdom. If it is in a fire sign, you may need to do something physical like chopping wood or pumping iron in order to activate that part of your consciousness. In earth, she may prefer digging in the garden or finishing a task, whereas an air sign Athena is more likely to phone a friend and talk it out. Athena in water withdraws into meditation or a bubble bath to call up the inner voice.

Wherever you find Pallas Athena in your chart, you will find an aspect of yourself that is particularly individualistic, the "Aquarian" in you, even if you don't have any Aquarius emphasis. She is the voice who will speak your truth, without distortion of emotion or circumstance. She may symbolize where you feel like the odd man out, but don't let that deter you. Pallas Athena was always on the winning side of her battles; she can lead you to victory.

If prominently placed, especially conjunct an Angle, or the Sun or Moon, she often denotes a very special birth position in the family. Bizarre circumstances may have surrounded the birth, as well as being the "only one"' in the family to live out certain patterns. One of my Pallas Athena/MC clients was actually the 7th son of a 7th son; another was direct heir to a kingdom. A lady with Pallas Athena conjunct her ASC was the first girl after 6 boys! (I suspect she needed her "armor.")

Pallas Athena is quite familiar with her role as the "black sheep in the family." That may mean you are the only one who goes to university, or the only one who doesn't. Athena in the 9th House is likely to be the non-Christian in a Baptist family; in the 5th she might adopt a cultural assortment of children, or take on the world as her "child."

Perhaps the most relevant *difference* between Athena and Aquarius is that she is feminine, a goddess. Associated in many ways with Libra (ruled by Venus), justice and harmonious relations are her forte, and her feminine touch is not lost on those who come in contact with her. She has been painted as quite an Amazon by many astrologers, but I heartily disagree. That may be her extreme expression, if placed in Aries conjunct Mars and Jupiter in the 1st House, but her title, remember, is Goddess of Wisdom. Universal balance is her mindset, and this may sometimes offend personal friends. It does not mean, however, that she is a cold, hard woman.

Her love is spread over a wider terrain than most, and it may take some adjusting to integrate her ways into your life. Pallas Athena in the 7th House is often confusing because she *does* want relationship, but she also wants lots of space and needs to reach out to a large number of people. Her energies cannot be confined to a cloistered home life without immense frustration resulting. This asteroid can be just as disruptive as Uranus if need be. She is the little bird in our heads who whispers the answers to us, but sometimes she has to become a woodpecker rapping loudly on our thick skulls.

Psychological problems connected to Athena revolve around an over-identification with father and an absent or distant (Uranian?) mother. I have several clients with Pallas Athena conjunct the ASC (or Anti-Vertex) whose childhoods were filled with males, or with an intellectual atmosphere devoid of art and feeling. A lack of emphasis on the feminine was a major theme. Re-integration of the opposites is often required in adulthood, through various experiences with vulnerability and dependency.

Since she invented weaving, she has often been associated with the art itself. I obtained birth data for all the members of a weaving co-op to see if Pallas Athena would show up strongly in their charts. To my surprise she did not. Neptune was the most obvious significator, by far. Symbolically, however, it is a weaving together of the patterns of life with all its alternative choices that make up her tapestry. Perhaps the fact that she *invented* it is more to the point. Necessity being the mother of invention may have originated with her.

Progressive and forthright, she is not intimidated by the fact that "it has never been done before." She simply aims her camera in a slightly different direction and comes up with an innovative angle of approach. It was Athena's shield that Perseus used to view the Medusa only by *reflection*, so as not to be paralyzed by her stare. Becoming too absorbed in our problems, we often forget to step back and have a fresh look. Athena's shield can be likened to Libra/Venus's mirror, providing us with the reflections in life that are truly our own.

When I first began using asteroids, their most obvious role for me was that of signal flags to already existing patterns in the horoscope that were simply accentuated by the asteroids' positions. It was as if someone had highlighted parts of the chart for me to make sure I didn't miss the significant themes.

## Jane Fonda

One that comes to mind is Jane Fonda's chart. Her Sun at 29 Sagittarius quincunx Pluto at 29 Cancer and square Saturn at 29 Pisces sets a powerful stage for identity crises to do with her father. To add confirmation to the root of the issue, Pallas Athena is conjunct her Jupiter in Aquarius and square Uranus in the 10th House (the awesome public persona of Henry Fonda, father). Jupiter and Athena are father and daughter, carved from the same block, as it were. Yet, with that conjunction square Uranus in Taurus (carved in stone), how was she to know where he stopped and she began, unless she rebelled by taking up one unconventional stance after another?

Luckily, her Leo ASC trines her Venus in Sagittarius and her Leo Moon trines her Sun. Jane may have been stripping herself bare in front of an international audience, while most of us were exposing ourselves only to our therapists, but she did stumble through it, and in typical Sagittarius/Leo fashion, came out shining. Anyone who followed her life also learned many lessons through her display. She was always outspoken in political affairs, believing her interests to be for the good of all. Agree or

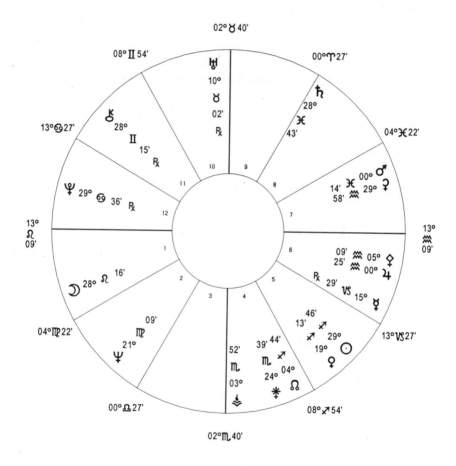

**Jane Fonda**
December 21, 1937
7:57 PM EST, New York NY
40N45 73W57
Source: *Profiles of Women*, by Lois Rodden

disagree, we must at least give her credit for daring to speak out. She has often been the brunt of mass criticism, unpopular, and ridiculed, but she continues to bounce back, insisting on her truth being known.

Pallas Athena in a strong career position can make for an excellent lawyer, mediator, counselor, ambassador, or strategist of any kind. The impersonal side of Libra is her domain. If your own Pallas Athena is not particularly deemphasized, call on a friend whose Athena is, whenever you need to maintain an objective vantage point, to see how it is done. Athena learns easily through observation. Allowing yourself to use her energy will facilitate your own bird's-eye view of the situation. Check your lawyer's natal Pallas Athena. Does he have what it takes?

If you start out thinking of Pallas Athena as being like Venus in Aquarius, or sometimes like Uranus in Libra, then add the influence of the sign and house it occupies in the chart, you will begin to grasp her essence. Allow the air to move around and through your head. Hear the call of the owl, Athena's totem, become one with his energy, and let his night-time vision reveal its secrets to you. Can you remember these illuminations in the daytime? Can wisdom accompany us wherever we go?

The active principle in Athena-ruled activities is choice. One of the virgin goddesses, she may exemplify that status better than most. To be a mythological virgin did not mean being chaste. It meant their bodies were their own. Never entering a spousal relationship left Athena free to perform her duties as a goddess without restriction, including mating with a god if she deemed it advisable. Pro-Choice activists may want to check their charts for Pallas Athena's influence. It is likely to have undergone a significant transit about the time they became personally involved in the issues, as well as being strongly aspected natally.

### Juno: Magnetic Mate

Known as Hera to the Greeks, Juno is the famous wife of Zeus/Jupiter, who repeatedly dragged him back from his escapades and reminded him of their marriage contract. Her nature is much like that of Venus in Scorpio. Honoring the commitment is Juno's primary concern. Obsessed with balance and fairness (Venus), she can be absolutely vindictive when scorned (Scorpio).

Her position in our charts says a lot about our view of personal relationships. In Capricorn or aspecting Saturn, she might insist on a traditional marriage, while in Sagittarius she might feel that her greatest commitment is to life itself, and being a wife might slow her down. If she doesn't acknowledge her own instincts, however, Juno in an earth sign might marry a staunch, older, conservative spouse and resent it, or the fiery Juno could link up with a series of gigolos and hitchhikers, wondering why she can't find true love.

My biggest personal revelation about Juno came when I realized she was not only a significator for personal relationships, but also our "relationship" with the matters governed by the house and sign she occupies in our charts. With Juno in Libra, for example, we might expect personal relationships to be a top priority, but if she were in the 12th House, we might choose to "marry Christ" and become a nun or, at least, consider our number one relationship to be with God, or our spiritual path, or our art. In Juno's case, a human partner would have to fill the bill as soulmate in order to be given a place of honor in her life.

Juno in Cancer in the 6th House might not even miss having a family of her own if she loves her work and feels embraced by her co-workers. I know a potter with Juno in Virgo in the 2nd House who puts so much of her personal passion into caressing and manipulating each lump of clay, that she feels like she has an intimate relationship with each creation.

### Elizabeth Taylor

A more complex example is Elizabeth Taylor. Her natal Juno is conjunct Pluto in Cancer in the 10th House, opposing Ceres in the 4th. Her constant struggle between home life and career is evident here, but also how deeply rooted her security needs are in both places. Squaring her Libra ASC (believing she needs a spouse in order to exist) and her Venus/Uranus conjunction in the 7th ("You don't own me; I belong to the world"), her Juno has bounced back and forth like a billiard ball from marriage to divorce; how many times now?

The "committed partner," Juno, in Ms. Taylor's chart links into a Grand Trine in water from Pluto in Cancer to the North Node in Pisces to the Moon in Scorpio. Need we ask if this woman cares, if she is filled with passion, or if she believes in what she is doing?

Juno holds the culminating position in her chart, conjoining the Midheaven. The traditional flavor of the 10th House surely contributes to her belief in the institution of marriage. Additionally, Juno's trine from the Sun, Mercury, and Mars (ruler of her 7th) in Pisces, themselves opposed by Neptune, helps keep the fantasy alive. She has completely devoted herself to each of her husbands, believing each one to be "the love that will last forever."

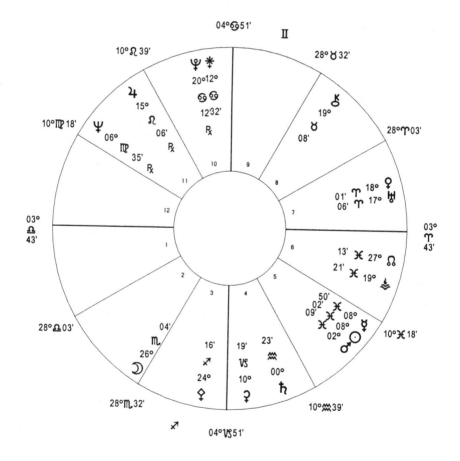

**Elizabeth Taylor**
February 27, 1932
7:56 PM GMT, London, England
51N31 00W06
Source: *Profiles of Women*, by Lois Rodden

I think we can safely say that Elizabeth Taylor is a most dedicated actress, as well. Not only has she persisted in the face of outrageous circumstances, ill health, and flaming gossip, but she also relates to her fellow actors like family members. Juno and Pluto together in Cancer can do their fair share of mothering, especially in light of a crisis. Her total commitment to AIDS research and fund raising is a perfect example of this. The trine to her natal Vesta in Pisces in the 6th helps her apply herself to her highest ideals, making sure she gets results.

It is wise to keep an eye on Juno. Thinking of her only as "the marriage asteroid," as we heard for so many years, can be misleading. "To what will we find ourselves married?" may be more appropriate phraseology. Where will the magnetic pull of Juno grab you below the belt and start reeling you in? Beware of the commitments you make, as Juno will surely exact payment. She can also reveal where your heart's delight really lies. No sense fooling yourself anymore. Strike up a relationship with this asteroid, and you will soon learn what "orgasm" really means.

## Vesta: The Inward Path

Vesta, the Greek Hestia, was the eldest sister in the family and the original vestal virgin, chosen to guard the hearth fire in the temple. Keeping the eternal flame alive was her sole responsibility, and she was completely devoted to the task. When given the option to leave the temple at the age of 30 (Saturn return?), and marry and raise a family, she chose to stay. Hence, her reputation as the "divorce asteroid" emerged.

This may lead us astray, however, for Vesta's total focus and dedication can be applied to anything. If she believes her role to be one of wife, mother, or corporate executive, she will give it 110%. Her nature can be likened to that of Pluto in Virgo. Intensity is her middle name, and duty is her calling. She can successfully focus so intently on one thing that she doesn't even notice what the costs may be.

Superhuman feats are possible wherever Vesta is found because of her amazing ability to concentrate on the purpose at hand. Tunnel vision might be a negative side effect, but a single-minded focus is often required to get the job done, and Vesta is the one to call. A client of mine has Vesta conjunct Mars and Mercury in Aries, and repairs cars as a hobby. His wife complained that he could spend 10-12 hours straight with his vehicles, never once taking a break for food, bathroom, or rest. Time vanishes when Vesta kicks in.

Her energy is the most inwardly directed of the asteroids. Her guarding of the eternal flame is meditative and sacred. Quietude and contemplation fill her aura. But deep within this extremely feminine being is the fire at the heart of it all. In addition to the flame itself, Vesta also guards a locked cupboard (the "penis!") at her altar. Inside the cupboard is a statue (the "Palladium") of another virgin goddess, Athena, in the shape of a phallus, the masculine, creative fire. The wisdom of the opposites seems inherent in Vesta, albeit hidden from public view. Ironically, Vesta is the only asteroid visible to the naked eye, as it is the brightest (the hearth/fire, no doubt).

A stressfully aspected Vesta can certainly bring forth patterns of fanaticism and extremity. Being too firmly tied to the plow keeps our nose in the dirt, rather than up in the air where it can sniff out the most worthy target for our dedication and commitment. Denying our inner truth whenever Vesta is involved is usually costly. Extreme behavior reaps extreme results.

Vesta in a fire sign may see herself as physically invincible and fail to take necessary precautions in dangerous situations. On the other hand, if positively focused, this combination could be extremely innovative and inspiring. A water sign Vesta is frequently artistically inclined, or at least motivated, to apply herself through feelings and intuition. She may be the one who can draw a picture to illustrate your story or compose a song to accompany your lyrics. Her compassion and understanding of the human condition runs deep; loyalty to the underdog might be expected.

## Zip Dobyns

Zip Dobyns, a mentor for many of us along our astrological pathways, may be a classic example of Vesta, with the asteroid natally conjunct her ASC. I didn't know her before she became an astrologer, but I do know she managed to have four brilliant children first and raise them on her own while she was getting her postgraduate degrees. Yes, she is a Virgo (quite!) with Taurus rising, so she would be expected to be conscientious. However, her actions have gone far beyond the call of duty, as only Vesta can.

I am convinced that no one spends as much time doing astrology as she does. She has been without a spouse for two or three decades now, and is "married to" astrology and the quest for related knowledge. May we all tip our hats to her for taking the time (zillions of hours) to do the research and exhaustive studies that have made our work so much easier.

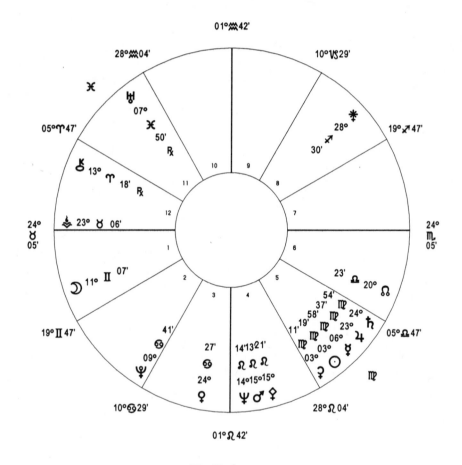

**Zip Dobyns**
August 26, 1921
9:47 PM CST, Chicago, IL
41N52 87W39
Source: *Profiles of Women*, by Lois Rodden

One of her sons, Mark Pottenger, was a pioneer in astrological software. I am not sure how much choice he had with his mother needing all those charts calculated, but without her, we might have been several years behind the 8-ball. Asteroids have almost become her claim to fame. Positions for hundreds of them are now available, thanks to her push.

Her 12th House Vesta is also quincunx an 8th House Juno in Sagittarius, which must have contributed to her focus on her relationship with astrology and her spiritual life at the expense of her personal social life. If you talk to her, however, I suspect she will not consider it much of a price to pay. Vesta's dedication runs so high, she usually doesn't know what you're talking about if you accuse her of being a workaholic or obsessed. But then, how are masters at anything made, if not by superhuman effort and unbelievably long hours of total commitment?

Zip's Sun/Ceres conjunction has also contributed greatly to her gift to us. She has been referred to as the Mother of Astrology and also the Nun of Astrology—an interesting combination. Maybe like the Mother Superior, she nurtures all her little fledglings until they are ready to fly on their own. Her mission is clearly a universal one, with Uranus opposing her Sun/Ceres/Mercury from the 11th House in Pisces, not to mention her Neptune conjoining Mars and Pallas Athena. Her libido could easily be sublimated to the spiritual realms. Whatever her internal story may be, we have all benefited immensely from her extraordinary research and her perpetual sharing of the findings.

There are two books I must mention that have brought me repeated illuminations about the asteroids. One is *Asteroid Goddesses*, by Demetra George, which is so thorough and profound it is an experience in itself. The other is *Goddesses in Everywoman*, by Jean Shinoda Bolemn, which is not an astrology book, but contains excellent examples of these goddesses' behavior (as well as three others), and is a treasure chest waiting to be opened. I highly recommend them both.

# K CHIRON: Path of the Shaman

**O** Can Chiron be seen as anything less than an enthusiastic guide into the Aquarian Age? His discovery in 1977 occurred during a transiting Saturn/Uranus square, and his orbit is between those same two planets. It is extremely eliptical, and at its innermost point dips inside the path of Saturn, linking it with our earthly reality. At its farthest reaches, it extends just beyond the trail of Uranus, tapping into the cosmic terrain of the outer planets.

Chiron was originally described by the astronomers as a "maverick," so appropriate for a venture into the Unknown: "When the student is ready, the Master appears." Does this mean humanity was ready to be shown the Way? Could Chiron hold the key to leaving the old, well-trodden path behind (Saturn) and embarking on an uncharted journey into the Great Beyond (Uranus)?

Chiron's position on the day it was discovered, Nov. 1, 1977, was 3:08 Taurus. The Sabian Symbol for the 4th degree of Taurus, according to Dane Rudhyar (in *An Astrological Mandala*) is a "pot of gold at the end of the rainbow," signifying "riches that come from linking the celestial (Uranus) and earthly (Saturn) nature."

Chiron lived *in* the mountain, not on top of it. We are reminded of Buddha's comment that his own enlightenment did not really occur until he came down from the mountain and re-entered the city. I have often mused how much easier it would be to achieve and maintain an enlightened state if we could stay in our own private Nirvanas. Mingling with the market rabble creates a much stiffer test.

*Living* our truth, "walking our talk," comes from deep inner experiences with Chiron. Honoring the body as the temple of the soul, honoring the soul as the ultimate purpose for the body, and using the human mind and heart to keep the two connected is a pretty tricky balancing act. No wonder it takes fifty years for a Chiron return.

His birth in the physical form of a centaur, half-man and half-horse, immediately evokes the image of the Sagittarian archer pointing his arrow into the sky. A sense of adventure and progress accompany this fellow. Chiron always seems to challenge us to our limits, and then just a little bit more. As a great teacher, healer, and sage, he inspired others to achieve their best, to stretch their boundaries, and to grow and learn continually.

His birth to Philyra, a mortal woman, was a shocking affair. Upon seeing her son's grotesque form, she threw him over the cliff in total repulsion. Thus, the young Chiron had received his initial rejection, the wounding that parallels our own, regardless of the details. He was fathered by a god, however, and had inherited his immortality, so he did not die.

Rescued by Apollo, the Sun God, and Diana, the Moon Goddess, twin brother and sister, he was raised to adulthood and allowed to develop into his full potential as a teacher of teachers and healer of healers. Chiron in the birth chart is the Shaman Within. It acts as a trigger point when we need reminding that our experience on Earth is threefold. Achieving a holistic synthesis among the animal, the human, and the Divine sides of our natures is Chiron's challenge.

Our "fall from Grace" in the Garden of Eden may have tainted us with Original Sin, but Chiron has come to redeem us. His mixed parentage, Divine father/mortal mother, parallels our own. His appearance into our conscious field of vision empowers us to reclaim our wholeness and disown our handicap. Once the primary wounds of childhood have been cleansed and healed, the psyche's innate tapestry can begin to weave itself into its own unique pattern of redemption.

As a messenger of Uranus, Chiron may be seen as the Second Coming, the Christ Consciousness within each individual. Chiron speaks to our highest Self and merely laughs uproariously at the antics of our egos who think they know so much and are so justified in behaving the way they do. Uranus was discovered over 200 years ago, but we obviously needed a wake-up call. Chiron got the job!

Another Aquarian Age connection to the myth of Chiron is his interaction with Prometheus (meaning foresight). When Chiron received a "mortal" wound from the sword of Hercules, his pain was excruciating. Being immortal he could not die, but a "mortal" wound cannot heal. Meanwhile, Prometheus had been eternally chained to a rock for stealing the fire of the gods (consciousness) for humankind. Eventually, a bargain was reached with Zeus/Jupiter who allowed Chiron to sacrifice his immortality to Prometheus, who was released and sent to live on Mount Olympus. Chiron was then free to die a peaceful death.

Aspects of transiting Saturn mark our progress in the maturation of the ego-self, but Chiron aspects ring the bell of the soul. Reconciliation of imbalances relative to the planet being aspected are insisted upon. The initial wounding of that part of the self must be reopened and cleansed in order to proceed forward in its intended evolutionary pattern. Consequently, Chiron transits, or even natal positions, are often experienced as painful crises, until the poison has been removed. Then, the fullness of Chiron's potential can begin to blossom, with the result that we become increasingly *conscious* of our higher purpose in our moment-to-moment realities.

In view of the fact that we have almost reached our *second* Saturn return by the time we have our first Chiron return (about fifty years), it would seem to me we had better pay attention to this little "maverick." He is surely up to something big. The Chiron return can be the point in our lives when we find out if we survived our mid-life crisis, and if so, who we are now!

Perhaps I should mention here that the phases of a Chiron cycle are not as predictable as most of the planets. Since its orbit is more like the eclipse of Pluto, it can take anywhere from five and a half to twenty-three years for the first transiting square of Chiron to occur. It is usually quite revealing to check back to the ages when Chiron squared, opposed and squared again your natal Chiron (or when it will).

Remember, regardless of rulership, Chiron is our link between Saturn and Uranus. He packs a powerful punch and demands that we look at reality with new eyes. A massive healing is underway on planet Earth, and Chiron is leading the way. He brings us out of the Piscean Age of saint/sinner consciousness and re-empowers us with the Christ Consciousness of the Aquarian Age. Breaking free (Uranus) of the past victimization also entails taking responsibility (Saturn) for one's own life.

The wounds cannot be healed by anyone else. Outer guidance is often helpful, but as with the Hierophant Tarot card, higher counsel inevitably comes from within. The myth of the Wounded Healer is exemplified in Chiron because of his self-healing character. Turning lemons into lemonade is his work. The stutterer becomes the speech therapist, or the drug addict becomes the detox counselor. The weak link in the chain, through hard work and many repair jobs, eventually becomes the strongest of all.

Look to Chiron for the secret talents hidden away for all those years under all those excuses/scars/reasons why we can't.

I had the opportunity to be one of four astrologers on the faculty of a Metaphysical Bead Game conference in Victoria, B.C., a few years ago. Since I was lecturing on Chiron, I had looked at the positions of Chiron in each of the other speakers' charts beforehand. I was both amazed and amused to find that all four of us had natal Chiron in the 12th House. Obviously, we had heard the urgent inner call to search out the Truth of our own spiritual origins (12th House) by being astrologers in the first place. In addition, we were "playing Chiron" for all those in attendance at the conference, by urging them on in their search for Life's meaning.

I can vividly recall my own rude awakening into Chiron's realm. One spring morning when I was seven years old, I found myself debating the issue of mortal sin with my little Catholic girlfriend. She insisted that committing a mortal sin would damn one to Hell forever. I said I didn't believe in Heaven and Hell, at least not as real places above and below the Earth. She became so exasperated with me that she called on her mother to come and set me straight.

I was then told all over again about the existence of Heaven, where God lived, and Hell, where the Devil lived. I replied that I didn't think God was just up in Heaven, but that He was everywhere: "in the sky, in the trees, in the animals, in us, and *even in that rock over there!*" That did it! Her hand flew out of nowhere and smacked me across the face, screaming about blasphemy and that I must *never* speak those words again.

My natal Chiron is conjunct Jupiter in Libra in the 12th House, squaring Mars and Saturn in the 9th. Obviously, I was already primed for religious confrontations. When transiting Chiron made its first square to itself that spring, it was accompanied by a transiting conjunction of Saturn and Neptune, conjunct my Chiron! It is not so surprising, then, that a jolt such as the one just described would be *my* wake-up call.

My 12th House sleep had ended. Unconscious no more, the spiritual purpose of my 12th House began to push its way through the fog. Regardless of how many lifetimes I had led being persecuted for speaking my truth, I could feel the pull of that karmic wheel, even at the tender age of seven. When the soul speaks, we listen. Age has nothing to do with it.

## Robert Hand

Rob Hand, well known to astrologers around the world, is my favorite Chiron personification. I don't know about his personal mythology, but for those of us who are recipients of his massive contribution to astrology, his natal Chiron at 29 Leo conjunct the North Node in the 3rd House says it all. His mind will never rest until he has crossed every conceptual threshold he can imagine. This inclination is initially stated in his Sagittarian stellium,

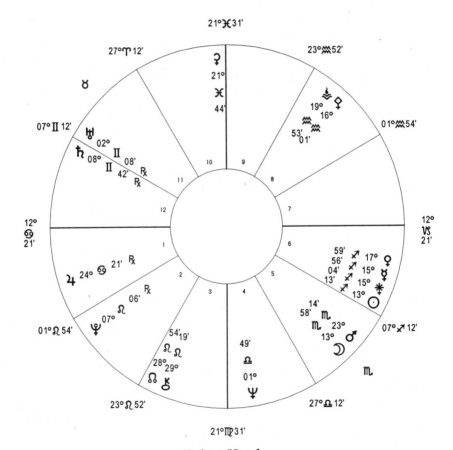

**Robert Hand**
December 5, 1942
7:30 PM EWT, Plainfield, NJ
40N37 74W25
Source: *Astro Data III* by Lois Rodden

but Chiron pulls back the bowstring and sets the arrow in motion. This teacher of teachers has written classic books, designed impressive astrological software, and dazzled us all with his brilliance in dozens of lectures over the years.

It is no secret that the 1990's are a decade of transition, to put it mildly. Complex times may require complex symbols. I see each of the asteroids as ruling, if we must, at least two signs. Chiron, being a spotlighted deity by virtue of his orbital position, holds larger sway. He perches his hand on the Wheel of Fortune, the mutable cross, sets it spinning . . . and "where she stops, nobody knows." We are leaving the static (fixed) reality behind and embarking on an entirely new adventure (cardinal). This is the role of the mutable signs. All four wiggle their way into Chiron's mythology. The more you look, the more you will find.

I heartily recommend Erminie Lantero's book, *The Continuing Discovery of Chiron* (even the title sounds mutable), for a comprehensive look at the varying depths of Chiron's influence. Her book was published in 1983, in the infancy stages of Chiron research, and is phenomenal in its scope. Four years later Barbara Hand Clow's book added another huge dimension to the significance of Chiron to astrology. Between the two of them your mind is likely to be blowing circuits left and right. The healing will have begun.

In closing, may I simply encourage you not to turn a blind eye to these recent additions to our astrological alphabet. Mother Earth and all her children are in crisis. The veils of the Heavens are lifting to allow us greater vision. May we all open our eyes, listen with our hearts, and say, "Thank You!"

### Michael Munkasey

Michael Munkasey has been an astrological researcher for over 23 years. He holds professional astrologer certifications from both the AFA (PMAFA) and The Astrologer's Guild. Michael has written hundreds of articles and letters on astrology, and maintains a busy and far-reaching lecture schedule. His books include *The Astrological Thesaurus, Book 1, House Keywords* (Llewellyn Publications, 1992), *Midpoints: Unleashing the Power of the Planets,* and *The Concept Dictionary* (both released in June, 1991).

Michael has served on the Board of Directors of NCGR since 1976, is currently the clerk, and was instrumental in writing their by-laws and organizational structure. He was NCGR's Director of Research from 1982 to 1985. He writes book reviews for NCGR and for *Dell Horoscope* magazine. Michael received the Professional Astrologer's, Inc. award for "The Outstanding Astrological Lecture of 1991," and the 1991 Matrix "Pioneer of Astrology" award.

Michael has degrees in engineering and management, is president of his own business, and has been an information processing consultant to the public transit industry since 1965. His public transit information systems are being used in such cities as Washington, New York, Chicago, and San Diego. He resides in Issaquah, WA, part of the greater Seattle metropolitan area.

# Psyche: The Planet of Consciousness

## Michael P. Munkasey

Psyche's story began long, long ago. Her famous myth takes various forms across many cultures. As with any myth, its allegorical truths work at many personality levels. What is new for *this* tale is what happens when we associate this wonderful story with a not-so-hypothetical planet and discover intriguing astrological inferences.

## The Myth of Eros and Psyche

Let me paraphrase Psyche's story (see Bullfinch's *Mythology*, et al.). Psyche, her sisters, and her family lived in an ancient and simple land. Awareness of the gods and daily respect to their presence were an integral part of life. Psyche's beauty far exceeded that of any other mortal, including her sisters. Ordinary people would go out of their way for nothing more than a glimpse of Psyche's face or a simple nod of recognition from her. This, of course, infuriated the goddess Venus, who could not understand how an ordinary mortal could steal homage from her. Deciding to put Psyche in her place, Venus called upon Eros (or Amor or Cupid), her son, won his attention, and persuaded him to play a trick upon Psyche.

    Eros was to make Psyche repugnant to all of mankind, despite her beauty, and at the same time to spread the story among the humans that she was destined to marry a loathsome and terrible beast who would eventually devour her. Eros began to carry out Venus' instructions but, in the process, as he gazed upon Psyche's beauty, nicked himself with one of his own arrows of love. Thus totally smitten, Eros became Psyche's foremost admirer. Unfortunately, Eros was a god and thus normally invisible to Psyche's human eyes unless he willed that his presence be known to her. Obviously, it was Venus' wish that Eros remain hidden from Psyche. So, what to do? How could Eros get Psyche to a meeting place unknown to Venus? He could admire Psyche from afar or incur the wrath of Venus.

As the years passed, Psyche's sisters all married and established good families. Psyche's parents despaired that the rumors about Psyche were true, and that she would come to a fearful end. They traveled to a powerful oracle and asked for guidance. Following instructions, they took Psyche to a mountain and prayed for the fates to take her in hand. Psyche was then transported to a beautiful valley, close to a magnificent castle, beautiful forest, running brook, waterfalls, and other wonders of nature. There the trees and the wind whispered to her that her *every* demand would be met; she had only to ask for what she wanted and it would be given to her, on one condition. Music, light, food, dancing, beauty, money—whatever, it was all hers for the asking. Her husband would come to her in the night and make love to her, but she was never to glance upon his face or question him about his identity. As long as she followed these instructions, her demands would be met.

Thus the years passed for her in total bliss. The days were hers to enjoy any wish or whim. The nights were spent with the most passionate and caring man. Both Psyche and Eros had found their love. As time passed however, Psyche began to think of her family, and expressed to her husband that she wished for a visit from them so that they could see that she had found total happiness. Eros was initially reluctant; then he relented and had the zephyrs carry Psyche's sisters in for a visit.

At first her sisters were amazed. They, themselves, had been reveling in how good their life was, but when they saw how well Psyche lived, they became very jealous. At first, Psyche explained her husband's absences with the story that he hunted by day and returned at night. The sisters saw through that deception and convinced Psyche that the rumors were true: that her husband was a loathsome beast who would shortly kill her. Then her sisters persuaded Psyche to take a lamp and a sharp knife to him as he slept and cut his throat before he murdered her.

After the sisters had returned home, one night as Eros lay asleep, Psyche took her knife and lamp and gazed upon his countenance for the first time. Seeing his golden ringlets, muscular body, white wings, and masculinity, Psyche recognized Eros immediately. But she also accidentally dropped some hot oil from the lamp on him in her surprise and woke him. "Oh, you foolish human," the God Eros cried, "now you have undone everything that I have created for you against Venus' wishes." Psyche fainted.

When she awoke, her fields, forest, and castle were gone and she lay in a place not far from her parents and sisters. Her world had vanished, and only a great empty yearning for the beauty of her home and her husband's delicate passions remained. For years she wandered, looking for Eros. Her emptiness and sorrow grew. In the meantime, Eros had retreated, deeply wounded by the loss of his true love. Venus kept him locked away in a dark room. Years of separation and loneliness passed for the two lovers. Finally relenting and consulting an oracle one day, Psyche was told to go directly to Venus, plead her case, and apologize for having offended the goddess.

She did just that, but Venus was *not* appeased. Venus demanded that Psyche prove her homage by performing certain difficult tasks. The first task was to sort a large pile of various mixed grains according to their kind, by sunset of that day. Psyche sat looking at the grain, not knowing what to do. She prayed for help. The ants and insects of the world took pity on her: they completed Psyche's task for her with the greatest of ease. When Venus returned at sunset and saw the grain perfectly sorted, she was enraged. "You could not have done this by yourself," she ranted, "you have had help." Venus was furious and assigned additional tasks to Psyche.

Psyche's second task was to go the place where the rams with the golden fleece lived. Psyche was to gather wool from each of their fleeces and return these precious threads to Venus for her use. These rams were well known for their ferocity. They would kill any human who approached them. As Psyche started to cross the river to go to the field where the rams lived, a wind came up and spoke through the reeds. The voice advised her to wait until the heat of the day had passed, and the rams had spent their daily fury. After their morning passion had passed, the rams would rest in the late afternoon. Their fury subsided, Psyche would then be able to gather their wool from the bushes and trees against which the rams had rubbed. She followed this advice and returned much wool to Venus. Venus again was enraged that Psyche had succeeded in a task designed for her failure.

Venus then demanded that Psyche travel to Proserpine's lair in Hades and bring back certain precious beauty aids which Venus required. Psyche, as innocent as she was, knew however that once in Hades it was not easy to return. Again, a friendly but unseen voice gave her instructions about how to complete this task. She descended into the depths, asked for and received the closed box of beauty supplies, and managed to return to the world of the living. As she was approaching Venus' place, however, Psyche began to wonder, "Why can't I have some of these beauty products for myself. Why must they all be for Venus?" she thought. The more she dwelled on this idea the more she knew that she must take some of the beauty aids. She opened the box but the box was empty except for a terrible demon. It leaped out and immediately proceeded to kill Psyche.

During the period of the impossible tasks, Eros still pined for his love. He was able to escape through a small crack in the wall of his prison. As luck would have it, he escaped *just* as Psyche released the demon which killed her: Eros witnessed the scene, immediately revived Psyche, and took her before Jupiter, the head of all of the gods. Eros plead his case for Psyche's love. Venus was enraged by this action and made her emotions felt. Jupiter listened patiently to all and decided that the only solution to the problem was to elevate Psyche herself to the rank of goddess. He did this by taking away some of Venus's power and domain. Then Eros and Psyche could live together. Jupiter decreed that Venus and Psyche share Venus's former domain. Venus was still enraged and could not fight the decision. This is how Psyche became the only human to be made a god or goddess. End of story.

## The Implications of the Myth

This is not really the end of the story. It is only the beginning. The story is psychologically complex and carries many implications. One good analysis of these implications can be found in

"An Interpretation of Apuleius' *Golden Ass*," by Marie-Louise von Franz, a renowned psychoanalyst and the daughter of Carl Jung. Let me share my own views of this many-faceted story; there is much that needs elaboration.

In terms of consciousness, here are some of the relevant themes of this myth:

- Acquiring and losing love
- Love as a means for inner self-fulfillment
- The role of beauty versus the role of love
- Woman-woman supremacy battles
- The role of fairness in life
- The role of material satisfaction versus the role of inner satisfaction
- The role of restrictions and discipline when loving another person
- Recognition that self is complex and exists at more than one level
- The role of loneliness in driving self to ask for spiritual help
- Tact and/or diplomacy used in mediating between different opinions
- The need for acquiring the ability to ask for spiritual help
- The role and use of (divine or common) justice systems
- Actual truth versus the representation of the truth that lies behind motives
- One person's view of truth versus another person's view of truth
- Confronting any inner restlessness about spiritual progress in life
- The fight between Venus and Psyche over a rulership of part of the heavens

As we ponder the themes contained in this myth, certain recurring ideas beg for further investigation. In no particular order, these concern the role of love and the self-fulfillment that true love can bring; the role of what is truth to you and what you want revealed about your motives; the need to recognize that no task is too difficult if you know how to tap into your higher potential(s); and woman versus woman, or woman versus system equality issues.

Love is a complex emotion. Many people seek a divine or cosmic love. We all seek the kind of marital bliss and personal interaction that Psyche enjoyed with Eros during the years at their mythical castle. Yet, behind that individually selfish love for self and love for just one person lay a terrible tragedy. Psyche was restricted from participating in one-half of her lover's world. What can that part of this allegory possibly mean to us as individuals in the everyday world? Could it mean that, no matter what we give to another of our externalized emotions, it is very difficult to share our true inner self? Could it mean that happiness can only be superficial if we do not get to know the hidden side of our self or partner? Could it mean that providing a satisfactory home and family life is only part of our obligation to inner fulfillment? Questions like these go on and on.

A question of predestination with love is also raised here. Is there only one truly cosmic love for any one person? Is there only one other person in the whole world who can provide the love you desire? Can curiosity about the life and means of another supplant love? Again, tough questions. I think what the allegory is saying is that *love is a driving emotion*. I think it is also saying that love is a basic urge that can control our lives and prevent us from looking at our real inner motives. I think that the story tells us that the search for a perfect love, and the use of externalized love as a substitute for inner consciousness and awareness, is folly. It can only lead to spiritual death.

Motives are often difficult to realize and explain. Venus' motive was to punish Psyche. Venus never intended to help or aid Psyche in any way. Venus purposely structured each task so that Psyche would either fail miserably and be humiliated, or be killed. There was no love or other motive on Venus's part. From the start of this story, Venus appears as the villain and Psyche as the innocent. Venus is so much the villain that we may secretly cheer for her downfall. Psyche is so much the innocent and the untouched pure person that she lies beyond human reality. Venus is depicted as materialistic, greedy, and grasping in the story.

There is little hint of kindness or warmth shown by Venus toward Psyche. To Venus, Psyche is a contemptible object.

Psyche, on the other hand, seems to be totally oblivious about what she has done to injure Venus' feelings. Psyche thinks that by her very existence she should share a part of Venus' domain. These feelings begin with her extraordinary beauty and the daily homage received from humankind. It later extends to the box of beauty aids. Venus resents having to give anything up to Psyche and feels that it is Psyche who must first earn her rights to Venus' power and magic. Venus's motives come from complacent power; Psyche's motives are directed toward that source of power. Psyche is more honest about her motives than Venus is honest. Venus imposes demands on Psyche; Psyche does Venus' bidding and finds that the tasks are fraught with pitfalls, danger, and death. Psyche is totally oblivious of this danger right up to the end. In complete innocence, she alternates through cycles of blunder, luck, blunder, luck, etc. It is hard to recall another story where two people's motives are so contrasted.

Psyche can not succeed with her primary task without spiritual guidance or divine intervention. Psyche does not even realize this. She goes through a great loss, and additionally must suffer the knowledge that she caused this loss through her own innocence. Her own seeds of doubt and her sisters' jealousy caused Psyche to confront Eros and break the magic spell. Without these seeds of doubt, Psyche could well have continued on forever in her self-centered bliss. It took an external event, the suggestion by someone else that all was not as it seemed, to arouse an inner deep-set fear, and to activate Psyche.

Psyche loses her material comfort, or at least discovers that materialism was only a sham cover for the realism behind everyday life. But still, Psyche in her innocence is not conscious enough to seek help outside herself. It is only after many years of isolation, loneliness, and sheer pining away, that she awakens within herself one day and says, "Oh, let me ask for help." So simple a concept, so simple a thing to do, but it takes the depths of despair and years of loss for her to realize how to ask for spiritual help. Psyche visits an oracle. "Confront your fear," directs the oracle. "Go directly to your attacker and apologize." Reason and practicality triumph over innocence. It takes despair and pain to cause Psyche to seek help outside herself.

The last part of the story that I want to touch on involves the woman-to-woman conflict. For some reason a woman, in a one-on-one verbal confrontation, will attack and seek to subdue another woman more easily than a man will attack another man. You can almost hear Venus saying something like "You mere mortal, how dare you desire part of my rightful due?!" Women seem to be more territorial about their rights than men. If a woman feels as if another woman is usurping her area of influence, she will attack. The normal outward purpose of this attack is to elevate self above others, or to help self regain something that has been wrongfully lost to another. Venus is careful not to place herself in any direct peril. Venus works from and covets her place of power. Venus intends to fight Psyche to the death. Venus screams and attacks. Psyche stands in innocence and deflects Venus's fury. Venus never apologizes for her rages and fury. Ultimately, it is Venus's single-minded revenge that betrays her. It is Psyche's innocence that wins Jupiter over. The concept of a woman attacking a woman to keep the other in her place is a central part of the myth.

Venus becomes enraged when she realizes that Psyche can transcend her demands. Venus becomes almost apoplectic when she finds that Eros, her son, has disobeyed her wishes. She tries just about every trick she knows to punish Psyche for whatever it is that Psyche did to Venus. Psyche was born with great beauty. Men showed appreciation for her beauty. Psyche reacted to the attention shown her. Psyche fell in love with Eros and vice-versa. All of this enraged Venus. Love and beauty are supposed to be Venus's domain. Psyche usurped some of Venus's power and Venus immediately sets off not only for revenge, but also adds a good dose of resentment, fury, rancor, and similar emotions. An impartial observer, Jupiter in the story, presumably would have allowed satisfaction for Venus, but Venus's hate and ill will go too far. Venus loses part of her domain for her ruthlessness. Why? It was still a woman-to-woman matter. Woman (Venus) tearing woman (Psyche) down. Woman (Psyche) fighting against the system or establishment (the gods). Throughout this myth, we see the persistence of innocence to have its due.

### Where's the Astrology in All of This?

Consciously, my involvement with what would become the planet Psyche began somewhere around 1970. It was just one sen-

tence, among thousands of sentences, in the Edgar Cayce readings at Virginia Beach, VA, which started a very long journey for
me. Edgar Cayce was an astonishing and renowned clairvoyant
and prophet who died in 1945. His thousands of psychic readings
are both transcribed and available to the public at "The Association for Research and Enlightenment" (ARE) in Virginia Beach,
VA. The important sentence that I found read *"(The fixed star) Arcturus is the Sun around which our Sun (Sol) revolves."* Could this be
true? Could our Sun be a planet in the Arcturan solar system?
Could the fixed star Arcturus astrologically work as a planet?
Could Arcturus be as astrologically important as Mars or Jupiter
or Saturn? What are the implications of Cayce's statement for our
astrology?

As with any statement questioning astrological validity, we
have two choices. We can test the statement by trying to forecast
with that hypothetical planet, and/or we can see what happens,
both to people and in the world, as the known planets transit the
body. Using astrology to forecast in the stock market was my chief
astrological avocation at that point in time, so that is where I started. I ran a normal two-month forecast for the Dow-Jones Industrial Average (DJIA), with and without the use of the fixed star
Arcturus acting as an eleventh planet. At the end of two months,
I compared both forecasts to what the stock market DJIA had
done, and *there was a noticeable improvement with the Arcturus data.*
I then ran my forecast to five or more years as I decided on my
next course of action. I watched that forecast and the accuracy
remained. The stock market, at least, thought that there was continuing truth in Edgar Cayce's statement about Arcturus acting as
an astrological body.

The next thing I did was to create an ephemeris for Arcturus
(Psyche-to-be). [This ephemeris is included at the end of this article.—Ed.] As a fixed star, Arcturus moves one degree in the sky
every seventy-two years. This rate of motion includes both the
precessional rate and the proper rate of motion for Arcturus. In
the year AD 1912, Arcturus entered 23 Libra 00, and in the year AD
1984 it entered 24 Libra 00. Using this ephemeris, I then hand-
calculated many dates when the known planets were transiting in
major aspect to Arcturus. I allowed almost no orb for this work; it
would either be an exact hit or not. With those dates in hand, I
went to the public library and researched and recorded the

essence of the more important newspaper stories on those dates. Primarily, I just copied the headlines of the stories. I then classified the newspaper headlines by keywords and keyword categories. With diligence, I acquired about eighty-eight pages of typed, single-spaced notes. Certain themes kept repeating throughout these notes. Of course, all of this took many, many months to accomplish. But the work was very rewarding.

The more I talked and wrote about these findings the better the feedback I got from people who had Arcturus prominent natally. But, one problem remained. Whenever I used the appellation "the planet Arcturus" people would say something like, "Oh, you mean the fixed star Arcturus." For some reason, astrologers could not shift from thinking of that point at 23 Libra as a fixed star. They treated it as an important fixed star, and I was thinking of it as a planet. I thought much about this dilemma. We needed both a name for this planet and we needed a symbol. Both arrived within a rather short period of time in 1973.

One day, while pondering this problem, a book containing the story of Cupid and Psyche literally fell off a bookstore's shelf into my hands. As I read the story I immediately recognized the astrological effects our group had been uncovering (the then fledgling NCGR chapter in New York center). Psyche! That was the theme. It wasn't the fixed star "Arcturus" we were seeking, it was the planet "Psyche!" I rushed to share this information with the group. They all agreed that this was indeed what we had been researching. Not too long after this, a thunderstorm followed one evening's research discussion. The storm finished around midnight and the clouds cleared. Dan Livingston suggested that we go up to the roof of the apartment building and do our standard meditation. Group meditation was something we had done together on many occasions, but that night, as we started our meditation, I felt as if I were being raised on an elevator to a very high level. A blackboard appeared before my eyes and a voice said something like, "I think this is the symbol you are looking for." I then saw this symbol:

That was it. There was our symbol. I immediately addressed the group and all agreed that this symbol was indeed symbolic of the "Psyche" which we had been studying for over two years. To this day I have continued using, talking about, and working with both this Psyche symbol and its astrological influences. I no longer refer to "the planet Arcturus," but I do make many references to "the planet Psyche." The planet Psyche has nothing in common (except the name) with the asteroid Psyche.

Below are many of the central key ideas which our group had intuited and tested about Psyche from both the newspaper exercise and working with Psyche in natal charts. These key ideas are listed in no particular order. Each of these ideas starts a long journey into more particular concepts that also define Psyche's astrological meaning.

**meaning**  (what is meaningful to you, versus what is meaningful to others)

**consciousness**  (the realization that you are a social being, and whatever it is that you do has impact upon the others who live around you; the emergence of either a personal, a social, or a spiritual consciousness)

**realization**  (understanding the social and personal impact of whatever it is that you are doing or thinking upon others or humanity)

**spiritual awareness**  (spiritual quests, or the awareness that further existence and meaning lie beyond that of the five human senses)

**meaningless**  (an inability to relate life's circumstances to personal desires)

**spiritual awakening**  (the realization that there is more to life than five senses)

**spiritual growth**  (a driving inner need to find spirituality)

**discovery**  (new knowledge relevant to spiritual awareness or development)

**fairness**  (applications of the test of fairness between you and others)

**compromise**  (adjustment of your principles and the principles of others to find commonalty)

**establishment of truth**  (truth as you see it, versus truth as another sees the same situation)

**justice** (justice meted as the consequence of prior actions)

**playing fair** (the application of equal rules for all participants)

**searches for the truth** (what really happened, versus what is believed)

**cooperation or non-cooperation**

**tolerance** (freedom from prejudice or bias)

**help and/or assistance requested** (seeking help outside of self)

**innocence** (simple and honest, straightforward, without guile or pretext)

**justification** (working beyond your own previously defined rules of conduct)

**harmony** (peaceful relations with another person, country, etc.)

**moral development** (your individual version of moral excellence)

**individual rights** (the realization that human society is both beyond and individually more significant than you personally)

**diplomacy** (tactful and considered responses and behavior)

**courtesy** (your way of acting around others)

**tact** (a sense of knowing what to say when)

### The Astrological Influence of the Planet Psyche

Good story, you say. Reads well. But, where's the proof?!? Grounded earth types are placed in our realm of existence to remind us that fire (enthusiasm) and air (ideas and expressions) alone are insufficient proof. For the earth types, a proof either works or it doesn't. I can not prove Edgar Cayce's statement that Arcturus is the fixed star around which our Sun revolves. But, try as I have, I am not able to disprove it either. Cayce's is a powerful astrological statement, but does Psyche *really* work as a planet? Does it exhibit a sign rulership? If Psyche does show affinity with a sign, does this sign affinity violate or reinforce existing astrological traditions? Does Psyche share any astrological commonalty with Venus?

Let me start with my favorite "earth" style proof for both the existence and the validity of Psyche as a planet. Psyche was positioned at 23 Libra between 1912 and 1984. Anyone born between 1912 and 1984 has Psyche in their natal chart at 23 Libra xx (where xx is some minute-value from zero to fifty-nine). People born between 1984 and 2056 have Psyche natally at 24 Libra. Psyche moves one degree, sixty minutes of arc, every seventy-two years. This rate of motion averages eight minutes of arc every ten years.

Let us start with the transit of the planet Uranus over Psyche. Uranus, the awakener. Uranus, the upsetter. Uranus, the one planet which shatters the illusions of Neptune quickly, abruptly, and decisively. According to my calculations, Uranus conjoined Psyche (exactly) on October 20, 1889, and then again on October 24, 1973. Uranus was also within fifteen minutes of orb of Psyche, at 22 Lib 41 between June 1 and July 29, 1890. The tightest of orbs focus our research keenly.

On January 31, 1974 Uranus turned retrograde, and in the summer of 1974 made a station very close to Psyche as Uranus turned direct. Psyche at that time was located at 23 Libra 53. Between May 29, 1974 and August 4, 1974 Uranus remained within a fifteen-minute orb of Psyche. Thus, for most of the summer of 1974, Uranus was conjunct Psyche within a very tight astrological orb. Let us begin with these and certain related astronomical facts, and then examine some of the events unfolding during that time.

During the transit of Psyche by Uranus in 1889 and 1890, the U.S. Government had sent troops to the area of the Rosebud Indian reservation in South Dakota to force the Native American people living near there to move back onto the reservation and give up their claims to sacred tribal lands in the nearby Black Hills where gold had recently been discovered. The Army troops eventually machine-gunned to death several hundred people—men, women, and children—who refused to comply with their orders. Dee Brown, in her book, *Bury My Heart at Wounded Knee*, describes the events.

At the time of the *next* transit of Uranus over Psyche, in October and November of 1973, Russell Means, on behalf of the Native American people who had lost their land, sued the U.S. Government for the return of this land. Note these dates carefully for they reveal astrology in action. On the first Uranus transit of Psyche, the land was illegally and forcefully taken from the Native American people. On the second Uranus transit of Psyche, eighty-four years later, a lawsuit for the return of this land was initiated. During the station of Uranus exactly on Psyche in the summer of 1974, the Native American people won their case against the government for the return of their tribal lands. From one exact station, plus one Uranus cycle, to a second station exact on Psyche. *That* reveals astrology in action.

In June, 1949, the transiting South Node conjoined Psyche. In May, 1977, the transiting North Node conjoined Psyche. At the time of the 1949 transit, Dr. John V. Atanasoff initiated a lawsuit against J. Presper Eckert and John W. Mauchley; at the time of the 1977 lawsuit, he won his legal case. Eckert and Mauchley, up until that lawsuit, were universally acknowledged by the scientific community as having built the first digital computer, Univac 1. They were granted U.S. patents for their computer circuitry. The lawsuit established that it was in fact Dr. John Atanasoff who had originally devised the circuitry for the modern digital computer. Eckert and Mauchley had "borrowed" and improved upon his original design. The lawsuit awarded Dr. Atanasoff official recognition (and unspecified monetary damages) of his patent claim for the invention of "the modern digital computer."

This story is typical of the way Psyche acts in our daily lives. The background presents two versions of the truth. There is the truth as seen by Dr. John Atanasoff and the truth as generally believed by the scientific community. A long and protracted law case finally resolved this truth in favor of one truth over the other. The commonly accepted truth fails. A hero in the background emerges. *You can see the parallel in this modern story with the myth of Psyche.* It is through such unfolding of daily events that we live through the ancient myths within our lives. The events of life portray these ancient truths, and we become their modern actors and actresses.

At some unknown time in the 1960s or 1970s, a carved wooden image, the Afo-A Kom, very sacred to the M'bang tribe of western Africa, was stolen from their central village. After this theft their land dried up, crops failed, babies were stillborn, the power of the people waned, tribal people dispersed, and the tribe suffered great distress. Around May, 1974, the wooden image was accidentally discovered in a second-hand store in New York City. During the summer of 1974, the King of Fom and elders of the tribe were flown to the United Nations in New York, and their deity, their soul, the very essence of their belief structures, was returned to them in a formal ceremony. Presumably, so was their prosperity.

So many events occurred during the 1974 Uranus station on Psyche that this is hardly the place to enumerate all of them. However, let us start with one word "Watergate." On May 30,

1974, the House Judiciary Committee formally notified President Richard Nixon that his refusal of their subpoena for the Watergate tapes "might constitute grounds for impeachment." On August 7, 1974, President Richard Nixon resigned as President of the United States. Many good books have been written on the "versions of truth" which flew back and forth during that summer. Those two particular dates also happen to coincide very closely with my fifteen-minute orb of Uranus conjunct Psyche. That whole time period happens to sit like a raw wound upon the American psyche. The very word "Watergate" has come to symbolize the futile, but persistent, effort of one group to force its version of truth upon another group. Even the word itself symbolizes our then Capricorn president. "Watergate," as a word, is very close in pronunciation to "water goat," an alternative term for the sign of Capricorn.

Banks, treaties, gold trading and gold standards, labor unions, peace efforts, Nobel prizes, lawsuits, etc., often figure prominently in Psyche-related mundane events. International treaties, especially those for which one side or the other does not intend to keep promises, invariably have strong Psyche astrological highlights. Obviously I could include hundreds of Watergate-related events in the following list, but I purposely choose not to do this here. Other interesting events related to the transit of Uranus over Psyche during the 1973 and 1974 time period follow.

October 6, 1973. Egyptian forces cross the Suez canal and a new Mideast war begins. The military war lasts but a few days, but the political war continues much longer.

October 12, 1973. Gerald R. Ford is named Vice-President of the United States, replacing Spiro Agnew who had resigned from the office after an alleged money-taking scandal.

October 17, 1973 (as the Sun is also conjunct Psyche and Uranus). The OPEC oil ministers vote to cut off oil shipments to the United States in retaliation for their support of Israel in the Mideast war.

Between May 10 and May 14, 1974, the Franklin National Bank, ranked twentieth in size of banks in the United States, fails. At that time it is the largest bank failure in modern history. Its proceeds are transferred to Chemical Bank of New York.

All during the month of May, 1974, U.S. Secretary of State Henry Kissinger (his natal Moon is conjunct Psyche, exact, in his natal Fifth house) continues his "shuttle diplomacy" in an effort to bring peace to the Middle East.

May 17, 1974. A very large international conference begins in Europe, which focuses on the role that gold should take in international trade.

May 17, 1974. Six members of "The Symbionese Liberation Army" are killed in a violent shoot-out in Los Angeles. See related items (outside the scope of this article) on events surrounding the kidnapping and conversion of Patty Hearst.

May 18, 1974. India explodes its first nuclear device. India claims at this time that its development of nuclear power will be solely for peaceful means.

May 18, 1974. Senior members of the U.S. Navy and U.S. Air Force reveal and discuss their attempts at waging weather warfare during the Vietnam war before a United Nations Assembly meeting.

May 23, 1974. The New York Times and the New York Daily News reach an agreement with their typographer's union. This ends a multi-year legal battle on the question of established union practices vs. automation in the newspaper industry.

May 23, 1974. The United States gives a pledge to the United Nations Conference on nuclear disarmament not to proceed further with the development of "mini-nuclear" battlefield weapons.

May 28, 1974. The "power-sharing" form of government in Northern Ireland fails, and the British take over governmental operations there.

June, 1974. Dr. John V. Atanasoff officially wins his court case in Minnesota concerning his patent for computer circuitry. Appeals drag the case out for three years.

June 1, 1974. Representatives of the Palestine Liberation Organization meet in Cairo to discuss their representation at the Geneva Peace Conference on the Middle East. They begin to map their plans for the new Palestinian state.

June 3, 1974. The U.S. Supreme Court rules that women performing in jobs on equal terms with men should receive the same pay.

June 5, 1974. The first formal talks begin between Portuguese representatives and the Mozambique rebels to end the war in Zambia. June 7, 1974. Ralph Nader makes public some documents which show that the "Cost of Living Council" authorized an oil price increase even though its staff recommended against such an action.

June 8, 1974. The governments of the United States and the Kingdom of Saudi Arabia sign a wide-ranging, multi-year military and economic cooperation agreement.

June 10, 1974. Saudi Arabia acquires a majority interest in Aramco, the oil consortium which operates their oil fields and equipment.

June 12, 1974. The International Monetary Fund sets new rules for the reform of international currency practices.

June 14, 1974. General Secretary Leonid Brezhnev of the Soviet Union announces that the Soviet Union is ready to agree to a limitation of underground nuclear testing.

June 25, 1974. The U.S. Supreme Court declares a Florida law unconstitutional. The law had stated that newspapers were required to print replies to political candidates who were criticized in the press.

July 3, 1974. The United States-Soviet Union summit ends with partial nuclear reduction accords.

July 20, 1974. Turkey invades Cyprus.

Literally hundreds of events of this nature continued during this active time period. The Vietnam peace accords were signed on strong Psyche aspects. So was the German non-aggression pact with Russia prior to World War II. So were the Greek and Turkish peace accords over Cyprus. The list goes on and on.

## Psyche and Consciousness

In *The Consciousness of the Atom*, (Lucis Printing Company, New York, 1961), Alice A. Bailey defines three levels of consciousness. Her three divisions suit Psyche-based consciousness well. Her divisions, paraphrasing her ideas, are

- The frankly materialistic. Involvement at the material level. Pure self-centeredness and self-interest. One's interests before those of others.

- The purely supernatural. Group coherency. The building and incorporating of one's self-interests into units which cooperate with others as a group whole and exhibit group cooperation.

- The idealistic. Unified existence. A blending of group needs and consciousness into an general perfected whole of consciousness exhibiting overall cooperation.

According to Bailey (of course, through supernatural contact with "The Tibetan," Djwhal Khul), in order to progress through the various stages of human development we need to become individually aware. We need to become self-realized and to learn not only personal maturity but also discrimination. We must learn to formulate our own thoughts and to manipulate our own mental processes. This goes on first at an individual level, then at a group or societal level, and then among groups of societies. The overall feeling and tone of her lectures is that the majority of mankind is somewhere to the left of step one, above.

Psyche's astrological role is concerned with this evolution of consciousness. First it works at the individual level. It describes personal circumstances which the individual faces. Often these circumstances involve great personal deprivation and hardship. They often involve loss. The purpose of these Psyche lessons is to open our eyes and to get us to ask for help. In the myth, Psyche had impossible tasks to do, but all she needed to do was merely wonder how she could transcend her circumstances *and the divine help came to her*. In a similar manner, when our planets progress or solar arc to important interactions with Psyche, then we too are faced with life's lessons. Often the lessons of Psyche help make us conscious that we should seek help outside ourselves. If you are born with natal planets in strong astrological interaction to Psyche, then you can be assured your life involves learning Psyche-based lessons.

The second level of Psyche-interaction occurs when we have evolved sufficiently to realize the effects of our actions on others. At the second stage of Psyche-based lessons, we face *group* lessons. Group lessons are designed to show us how to involve self with group consciousness efforts. Current group consciousness efforts concern the women's right movement, AIDS activism, help for starving people in the world, saving the whales, saving the ecosystem, and so forth. The particular mechanism of consciousness-raising is not as important as the effort to integrate the concept of consciousness-raising into one's background and over-all personality. Many members of the New Age movement seem to be at this level of Psyche awareness.

The third level of Psyche-interaction occurs when the groups realize that their individual group efforts must combine and harmonize with other group efforts. We do not see too much of that in the world these days, but it is a necessary part of the overall evolution of consciousness. Psyche doesn't ask us to be all things to all people, but it does ask us to become aware of how our individual needs can become group needs, and how our group needs can be combined into humanity's evolution. Right now we have individual groups, the New Age people, religious fundamentalists, ethnic rightists, etc., who work within their groups, and help to formulate group efforts. What the groups need to do is evolve to their next level, and that occurs when the groups begin to realize that all group efforts should become humanity's efforts. When will we see the various religious sects working in mutual cooperation?

Recently, I watched a television program where farmers were being interviewed on why they were cutting down (slash-and-burn farming) trees in the rain forest. The farmers were at Level One of the Psyche evolution of consciousness. All that they could see was their personal involvement. They wanted to make a living; they wanted sustenance for both their families and them-selves. Cutting and burning trees in the rain forest was a pretty cheap way of providing this. The ecologically oriented interview-er was trying to get the farmers to see the effects of their actions on world environment. The interviewer was trying to arrange a shift of consciousness from self (me, eat, warm, food, family) to ecology (saving trees helps alleviate global pollution or warming, etc.). When the ecology groups talk to the religious fundamental-ists, the business people (who only see corporate responsibilities and profits), the animal rights activists, whatever — then we have groups interacting at the third level of Psyche consciousness. The world seems to be pretty far from that goal right now.

## Psyche in the Natal Chart

Psyche can be a powerful factor. Placing Psyche in a natal chart is so much a part of my astrological practice that any chart without Psyche's symbol, at least mentally placed, appears naked to me. I have shifted my consciousness about Psyche: it is not a point; it is not a fixed star; it is not an asteroid; it is not something extraneous. I use it as a *planet*. I use it as the planet of consciousness. I use it as the planet *(not point) which opens us to certain lessons about how our consciousness should evolve.* Psyche has little to do with soul evolution, although to become an evolved soul you certainly must absorb Psyche's lessons. Psyche doesn't advocate eating meat or being a vegetarian. Psyche doesn't say that you have to be nice to others when you feel like being nasty. Psyche doesn't chastise you if you miss a meditation or a yoga session. Psyche doesn't care whether or not you went to church on Sunday or the synagogue on Saturday. Psyche doesn't care if your prayer rug is aligned exactly in the direction of Mecca. Those are *personal* matters.

Psyche *does* care if your orientation is into self, into self as part of a group, or into group as part of humanity. Those are the things that matter to Psyche.

People with their natal Sun (or Moon, or whatever), at 23 Libra often ask what the Psyche and planet interaction means in their personal life. It means that (insert your own appropriate keywords of the planet in question here, Sun = shining or male or important, or whatever keyword you care to use; Moon = female or basic things or changing circumstances; Saturn = solemn or reluctant or rigid; etc.) is applied to the list of Psyche key ideas given earlier. In general, interactions between natal planets and Psyche orient one toward the need for raising consciousness or social change, and this could be either one's personal consciousness or a group consciousness level. This is true in just about every planetary case, *except that of Venus.*

Any natal aspect between Venus and Psyche can be *very* difficult. The natal conjunction of Psyche and Venus presents the most difficult instance. This is especially true with women who have their natal Venus conjunct Psyche. They often find themselves in situations where they are giving abuse to other women, or they are on the receiving end of abuse from other women. This becomes a difficult problem for them to work through. It is even more difficult to work through than squares or semi-squares of Venus to Psyche. Please review the myth if you still don't understand the difficulty that Venus had with Psyche, and vice-versa. Their mutual interaction became a life and death struggle. Men with their natal Venus interacting with Psyche often have difficult lessons in life to face concerning the giving and receiving of love.

The first way to work through any Venus and Psyche combination is to become aware that all is not lost. You will be confronted with situations in life concerning love, the loss of love, fair treatment from others, etc. Restudy the Psyche key ideas listed earlier. No, things in life won't always work out the way you would want. Life will take its difficult turns. However, all situations presented to you of a Psyche nature are designed to help increase your self-awareness and your awareness of groups needed by self. One key to working through the Venus and Psyche turmoil is *to understand* (this is one of the Psyche keywords) the overall effect of your circumstances. Ask for spiritual guidance and help. Listen and heed that help (listening and heeding are also part of Psyche's lessons). Try to look beyond a self-centered position.

Interactions between Mars or Saturn and Psyche are some of the most gratifying aspects you may encounter. In over twenty years of testing Psyche and Mars connections in the natal chart I have found an amazingly high correlation between this combination and people who are interested in social causes. Mars conjunct, Mars square, Mars trine, etc. Psyche sets people to examining group needs. People with these aspects become law enforcers, social workers, teachers, firemen, firewomen, nurses, doctors, etc. These are the people who have a strong need to help others through their profession. These are often the people who leave one unrewarding profession to go back to school for academic credentials. They then use these credentials to obtain new jobs in social awareness-related positions.

Between Saturn and Psyche, much of the same can happen, but not with the high correlation that Mars-Psyche combinations bring. Often, if Saturn is in square or opposition to Psyche in the natal chart and if that person is also a New Age skeptic, then there is little that anyone can do to change their outlook that astrology, palmistry, yoga, or whatever, is just a bunch of horse balooey. Carl Sagan, the virulent anti-astrology astronomer, has a tight natal T-square involving Uranus, Pluto, *and* Psyche, with Saturn trine to Psyche. If Saturn is in strong natal aspect to Psyche and these people are New-Age practitioners, then they strive to carry ideas on the expansion of consciousness. Marion March, the co-author of *The Only Way to Learn Astrology* series of books has her natal Saturn conjunct Psyche. Neil Michelsen, the founder of Astro-Computing Services, had his natal Saturn square, and his Venus in opposition to Psyche. He was a pioneering New-Age advocate, but also had Psyche-type relationship problems.

Many people reading this article were born during the Saturn and Neptune conjunction with Psyche from 1952 to 1954. During those years, most people were born with both Saturn and Neptune in aspect with Psyche. Many of these people have a strong spiritual orientation. Many of these people are very interested in New Age concepts. Many of these people feel that immediate and effective social change is needed to reform the world. Many of these people feel that love is a strong and central issue in their life. Love given. Love received. What love advice should I accept? Why can't I find someone to love? These are important central issues for this group of people. Just behind love follows truth, harmony, cooperation, meaning, spiritual awareness, moral support, equality, the rights of self and the rights of others, etc., as life issues.

Saturn's keywords include burdens, inconvenience, delays, hardships, hesitation, or doing things correctly. Neptune's keywords include ideas like confusion, mistakes, dreaminess, inattention, mysterious actions, or regression. The ideas conflict with each other. Thus, people born at the Saturn and Neptune conjunction on top of Psyche face a key dilemma concerning how they choose to see and use love, meaning, support for another, tact, truth, etc., in their lives. The particular way this expresses itself in their lives will be colored by the natal House in which the triple conjunction occurs. In the 1st House people experience this directly on themselves, in the 2nd House they experience it through material values, in the 3rd House through communication with others or with siblings, in the 4th House through family matters.

### Psyche and Sign Rulership

The myth is particularly direct about the question of astrological rulership. Psyche and Venus fight. Psyche is a human and Venus is a goddess. Their battle is a draw. Jupiter elevates Psyche to the role of a goddess and gives Psyche part of Venus' domain of the heavens. What then does Psyche obtain from Venus? What part of the "sky" does Psyche gain dominion over? What is it that Venus has to relinquish to Psyche? According to astrological tradition, Venus rules both Taurus and Libra. So, which of these does Venus have to "give up" to Psyche? A part of both, is my answer.

In my book, *The Astrological Thesaurus, Book 1, House Keywords* (Llewellyn Publications, 1993), I present a yin and yang (or "day and night," to use older terms) concept of sign rulerships. If you were to write in the Psyche symbol for the yang (or day ruler of) Libra and for the yin (or night ruler of) Taurus, then my concept of how the rulership of Venus' domain was shared can be seen. I use Psyche as the yang ruler of the sign of Libra and as the yin ruler of the sign of Taurus. This scheme violates nothing from astrological tradition, but it does add much new information about how Venus and Psyche share a part of their astrological domain. As the day ruler of Libra, and being positioned in the sign of Libra from about the year 256 AD to the year 2416 AD, Psyche will be presenting humanity with challenges concerning truth, meaning, developing consciousness, etc. Before 256 AD, Psyche would have been positioned in tropical Virgo, according to my calculations, and about the year 2416 AD. Psyche will enter the tropical sign of Scorpio.

## Examples of Psyche Interactions in Famous People's Natal Charts

All birth data, chart and biographical information used for people in this section come from Lois Rodden's book on validated birth data, *Astro-Data III*. Philip M. Crane, an Illinois politician who campaigned for the 1979 Republican Presidential nomination, and who is an advocate of reduced government intervention, has his South Node conjunct Psyche. With this aspect he would tend to seek affiliations with others who had ideas similar to his. One stretch of this concept would be to have supporters vote for his candidacy. Another basic thrust would also tend toward advocating truth in government. Another person with a node and Psyche contact is Jerry Dumphy, the ABC news anchorman who was shot and wounded in an apparently aimless outburst of random street violence by youths in 1983. While I have no data specifically on the incident I assume that he used his position after this incident, to campaign strongly against violence, and for a more reasoned approach toward criminal justice. He also has a natal Mars conjunct Ascendant at 21 and 23 Gemini, trine Psyche.

With this position he would tend to use his Mars in Gemini (news of gunshots can be one interpretation of this aspect), trine Psyche (strong emphasis on a need for social justice) in his everyday work and life. Melvin Belli, the Los Angeles lawyer who specializes in headline-grabbing social and divorce cases, has his North Node at 23 Cancer square to Psyche. The Moon's Node uses keywords like connections, associations, contacts, and so on.

There are some people in *Astro-Data III* having Grand Air Trines involving Psyche. These include Dane Rudhyar, the humanistic astrologer who started an intellectual revolution with his progressive ideas in astrology. Dane Rudhyar has a natal Air Grand Trine involving the Moon trine Jupiter trine Psyche. Edward R. Murrow, the news commentator and broadcaster, also had an Air Grand Trine involving Psyche. His natal combination was Moon trine Pluto trine Psyche. He hosted a television news program for many years called "Person to Person," which certainly fits within the Psyche consciousness concept of exploring the truth. Harvey Milk, who was shot and killed along with San Francisco Mayor George Mosconi on Nov. 27, 1978 at City Hall in San Francisco also has an Air Grand Trine involving Psyche. His natal combination is Jupiter trine Ascendant trine Psyche. His natal Mars is also in opposition to Psyche. He was shot and killed by the man whom he had been hired to replace. The astrology of this grand air trine and Mars opposition speaks directly to this event. The clash of ideas and differences of opinion (Air Grand Trine) ended (opposition) with force (Mars).

Other politicians with Psyche interactions include Helmut Kohl, the Chancellor of Germany, and the youngest state governor in Germany's modern history. He has Venus conjunct his Ascendant in Aries in opposition to Psyche (on his Descendant). With this astrological combination, he would strive for *his* version of the truth, but face much opposition from women for his stand on rights issues.

Jean Drapeau, the Canadian politician, won a landslide victory in 1954 (at the height of the Neptune conjunction with Psyche) to become the youngest-ever Mayor of Montreal. His natal Sun at 28 Aquarius conjunct his MC at 26 Aquarius is trine to Psyche. In October, 1954, at the height of his campaign, a natal Jupiter and Uranus conjunction at 26 Cancer was square to Psyche at 23 Libra and transiting Neptune at 25 Libra. This Sun, MC, Jupiter,

Uranus, Neptune and Psyche involvement, all activated during this important political period in his life, lie at 23 to 26 degrees of the signs. His natal chart presents a rather powerful political and astrological statement.

Robert Muldoon, the former Prime Minister of New Zealand and Chairman of the World Monetary Fund and Money Bank, has his natal Mercury at 23 Libra conjunct Psyche.

The State of Israel officially began its existence with the degree of Psyche on its Ascendant.

United States President Bill Clinton has his natal Jupiter conjunct Psyche.

Ralph Nader, the Princeton graduate cum laude lawyer who has become a strong advocate for the cause of suppressed truth issues has his natal Jupiter retrograde at 22 Libra 34 conjunct Psyche. He also has a natal Saturn and North Node conjunction in the 1st House at 19 and 21 Aquarius, which places them trine to Psyche. His natal Pluto is at 22 Cancer 49 square to Psyche. These are powerful astrological statements which impel him to search for and try to correct social causes. Nader was instrumental in forcing the U.S. auto companies to change their ways of doing business. His public campaigns calling for increased auto safety forced an industry to build safer automobiles. He also is known for incurring ill-will from others for the stands he takes. (The myth we have studied is quite specific on this building of rancor in others for one's own personal causes. Nader is a person who is living proof that the myth of Cupid and Psyche is continuing to be perpetuated in our world.)

Dick Gregory, the former comedian, is another world-famous activist for various social causes. He became famous for his forty-day fast in protest of the Vietnam War. Since abandoning his successful career as a comedian, he has consistently worked for the improvement of the lot of the poor and downtrodden. His Sun at 19 Libra, is conjunct Psyche at 23 Libra, which is also conjunct his Descendant at 26 Libra and Mercury at 28 Libra. This powerful Sun, Mercury, Descendant, and Psyche combination fuels his thirst for social justice and helps direct him toward those who are disadvantaged.

Ralph Waldo Emerson had Venus in opposition to Psyche (his wife died early in their marriage), and Mercury trine to Psyche. His Equatorial Ascendant at 22 Libra was conjunct Psyche. This would indicate that Psyche-related issues were ever close in his mind. His writing reflects his concern for social justice and causes.

Dorothy Day, the political activist, feminist, and radical, had her natal Venus at 23 Libra, trine her Neptune conjunct Ascendant at 22 Gemini.

The people listed in *Astro-Data III* who have Venus and Psyche interactions make an interesting lot. While the short biographies provided there do not, in every instance, dwell on or mention how love did or did not manifest, there is sufficient other biographical material to make these people an interesting study. Michael Crichton, the writer, has a natal Mars conjunct Venus on top of Psyche, all at 23 Libra. His biography mentions a youthful marriage and divorce. Tony Curtis, the Hungarian-American movie actor, has his natal Venus at 23 Gemini, trine Venus. His biography mentions three marriages with bitter divorces. Bo Derek, who starred in the popular movie "10," which epitomized her in the leading role as the most beautiful woman in the world (again, go back to the myth!), has her natal Venus at 24 Libra conjunct Psyche. She was married at age sixteen to John Derek, 46, the movie producer who directed and produced her movies.

Alan Noonan, the UFO enthusiast, has his natal Venus at 22 Libra conjunct Psyche. His biography states that he claims to have made many trips to Venus in both flying saucers and by mental telepathy.

Perry Ellis, the woman's fashion designer, has his natal Venus at 24 Aries in opposition to Psyche. His fashions tend to de-emphasize women's figures with outsized, thrown-together looks. His biography notes that he lives alone in a New York brownstone with his dogs.

This list of people would not be complete without mentioning that Princess Diana of Great Britain has her 23 Libra MC conjunct Psyche. Her battle for women's issues and her children's rights has graced the front pages of the world's tabloid newspapers for years. The quest for love given and love received is a Psyche theme.

A number of notable people have their natal Moon in aspect to Psyche. These include Henry Kissinger, the U. S. Secretary of State during the Nixon Presidency, and the person who represented the United States during the Vietnam peace negotiations. He also negotiated a peace settlement between Egypt and Israel (with Psyche on its Ascendant) after the 1973 war in the Middle East. Others: Bob Fosse, the dancer and choreographer, who has his natal Moon at 24 Aries in opposition to Psyche; Francoise Mitterand, the French Premier in the early 1980s, has his North Node at 23 Saturn square Psyche, and his Moon at 23 Libra conjunct Psyche. He was the first French Socialist to win power from the center-right coalition. Ervin Nyiregyhazi, the violinist, has his natal Moon conjunct Psyche. He was married and divorced nine times. Al Unser, the race car driver, and Esther Williams, the movie actress noted for her water ballet movie roles, also have Moons at 23 Libra. Karen Kain, Canada's top prima ballerina, has her natal Neptune conjunct Ascendant conjunct Psyche. Her natal Mercury conjunct Mars at 20 and 23 Aries lie in opposition to her Neptune, Ascendant and Psyche conjunction.

# Conclusion *

The more you study astrology the more you realize that people live their lives in accordance with the ancient myths. The myths become the backdrop for many of the daily interactions we face in our lives. The myth of Cupid and Psyche is a very powerful one. It is repeated in many forms across many cultures. Its themes include the hidden lover, the need for cosmic love, the loss of love, the need to find help from beyond self, the need to fight for social causes, etc. The list goes on and on. In this article I have introduced you to some of the issues of consciousness which the astrological planet Psyche presents to you.

Consciousness. The very word carries hundreds of shades of meaning. Behind each of those meanings lies an astrological influence directly represented by Psyche. The word, psyche, comes from the Greek word for "soul." The astrological Psyche, whose ephemeris appears at the end of this article, epitomizes the various forms of consciousness which we face. I ask you to place *the planet* Psyche in all of the astrological charts that you study. Look for its interactions with the planets and the Angles. Use the same orb for Psyche that you would use for any other planet, like Mars, or Jupiter, or Saturn. If, in your work, you allow a five-degree orb for the Sun and a four-degree orb of Mars, then use a four-degree orb for Psyche also. Explore the interaction of Psyche with the other planets. Note and apply Psyche's shared rulership of Libra and Taurus. Dare to raise your consciousness!

# Ephemeris for "Psyche: The Planet of Consciousness"

Please note that the early entries are either in 5- or 10-year increments, depending on the century for which they were calculated. Later in the list, the interval between years varies even more. Longitude is zodiacal longitude.

| Year | Longitude | Declination | Latitude | Right Ascension |
|------|-----------|-------------|----------|-----------------|
| 2050 | 24 Lib 55 | 18 N 55 | 30 N 42 | 214° 29' 08" |
| 2040 | 24 Lib 47 | 18 N 59 | 30 N 43 | 214° 22' 18" |
| 2030 | 24 Lib 38 | 19 N 02 | 30 N 43 | 214° 15' 27" |
| 2020 | 24 Lib 30 | 19 N 05 | 30 N 43 | 214° 08' 36" |
| 2010 | 24 Lib 22 | 19 N 08 | 30 N 44 | 214° 01' 45" |
| | | | | |
| 2000 | 24 Lib 14 | 19 N 11 | 30 N 44 | 213° 54' 54" |
| 1995 | 24 Lib 10 | 19 N 12 | 30 N 44 | 213° 51' 29" |
| 1990 | 24 Lib 06 | 19 N 14 | 30 N 45 | 213° 48' 03" |
| 1985 | 24 Lib 01 | 19 N 16 | 30 N 45 | 213° 44' 38" |
| 1980 | 23 Lib 57 | 19 N 17 | 30 N 45 | 213° 41' 13" |
| | | | | |
| 1975 | 23 Lib 53 | 19 N 19 | 30 N 45 | 213° 37' 48" |
| 1970 | 23 Lib 49 | 19 N 20 | 30 N 45 | 213° 34' 22" |
| 1965 | 23 Lib 45 | 19 N 22 | 30 N 46 | 213° 30' 57" |
| 1960 | 23 Lib 41 | 19 N 23 | 30 N 46 | 213° 27' 32" |
| 1955 | 23 Lib 36 | 19 N 25 | 30 N 46 | 213° 24' 07" |
| | | | | |
| 1950 | 23 Lib 32 | 19 N 27 | 30 N 46 | 213° 20' 41" |
| 1945 | 23 Lib 28 | 19 N 28 | 30 N 46 | 213° 17' 16" |
| 1940 | 23 Lib 24 | 19 N 30 | 30 N 47 | 213° 13' 50" |
| 1935 | 23 Lib 20 | 19 N 31 | 30 N 47 | 213° 10' 25" |
| 1930 | 23 Lib 15 | 19 N 33 | 30 N 47 | 213° 07' 00" |
| | | | | |
| 1925 | 23 Lib 11 | 19 N 34 | 30 N 47 | 213° 03' 36" |
| 1920 | 23 Lib 07 | 19 N 36 | 30 N 47 | 213° 00' 10" |
| 1915 | 23 Lib 03 | 19 N 37 | 30 N 48 | 212° 56' 45" |
| 1910 | 22 Lib 58 | 19 N 39 | 30 N 48 | 212° 53' 20" |
| 1905 | 22 Lib 54 | 19 N 41 | 30 N 48 | 212° 49' 55" |

# Ephemeris for "Psyche: The Planet of Consciousness" (cont'd)

| Year | Longitude | Declination | Latitude | Right Ascension |
|------|-----------|-------------|----------|-----------------|
| 1900 | 22 Lib 50 | 19 N 42 | 30 N 48 | 212° 46′ 29″ |
| 1890 | 22 Lib 42 | 19 N 45 | 30 N 49 | 212° 39′ 39″ |
| 1880 | 22 Lib 34 | 19 N 48 | 30 N 49 | 212° 32′ 49″ |
| 1870 | 22 Lib 25 | 19 N 52 | 30 N 50 | 212°· 25′ 59″ |
| 1860 | 22 Lib 17 | 19 N 55 | 30 N 50 | 212° 19′ 09″ |
| | | | | |
| 1850 | 22 Lib 08 | 19 N 58 | 30 N 50 | 212° 12′ 18″ |
| 1840 | 22 Lib 00 | 20 N 01 | 30 N 51 | 212° 05′ 28″ |
| 1830 | 21 Lib 52 | 20 N 04 | 30 N 51 | 211° 58′ 38″ |
| 1820 | 21 Lib 43 | 20 N 07 | 30 N 52 | 211° 51′ 47″ |
| 1810 | 21 Lib 35 | 20 N 10 | 30 N 52 | 211° 44′ 57″ |
| | | | | |
| 1800 | 21 Lib 27 | 20 N 14 | 30 N 52 | 211° 38′ 09″ |
| 1790 | 21 Lib 18 | 20 N 16 | 30 N 52 | 211° 31′ 16″ |
| 1780 | 21 Lib 10 | 20 N 20 | 30 N 53 | 211° 24′ 26″ |
| 1770 | 21 Lib 02 | 20 N 23 | 30 N 53 | 211° 17′ 35″ |
| 1760 | 20 Lib 54 | 20 N 26 | 30 N 53 | 211° 10′ 26″ |
| | | | | |
| 1700 | 20 Lib 03 | 20 N 46 | 30 N 57 | 210° 29′ 51″ |
| | | | | |
| 1500 | 17 Lib 16 | 21 N 51 | 31 N 05 | 208° 13′ 23″ |
| | | | | |
| 1000 | 10 Lib 18 | 24 N 38 | 31 N 26 | 202° 32′ 26″ |
| | | | | |
| 0500 | 03 Lib 22 | 27 N 33 | 31 N 47 | 196° 50′ 48″ |
| | | | | |
| 0000 | 26 Vir 28 | 30 N 32 | 32 N 08 | 191° 07′ 15″ |

**A. T. Mann**

Tad Mann received his degree in architecture from Cornell University in 1966, then worked as an architect in New York City and Rome, designing award-winning buildings. Tad has been a professional astrologer since 1972, and has written, designed, and illustrated *The Phenomenon Book of Calendars* (1973–1980), *The Round Art* (1977), *Life Time Astrology* (1984 and 1991), *The Divine Plot: Astrology and Reincarnation* (1986 and 1991), *The Mandala Astrological Tarot* (1987), *Astrology and the Art of Healing* (1988), *The Future of Astrology* (1988), *Millennium Prophecies* (1992), *Sacred Architecture and the Elements of Tarot* (1993). He is also a graphic designer, having been associated with the design of many book covers, books, graphics, logos, radionic instruments, and computer programs.

Tad Mann is currently a member of AFAN and SAFA (Association of Scandinavian Professional Astrologers), and lives in Copenhagen, Denmark, where he teaches at the Unicorn School of Astro-Psychology. He is married to the astrologer Lise-Lotte Mann. He is currently editor of the International Sacred Arts Series of books published by Element Books, Ltd.

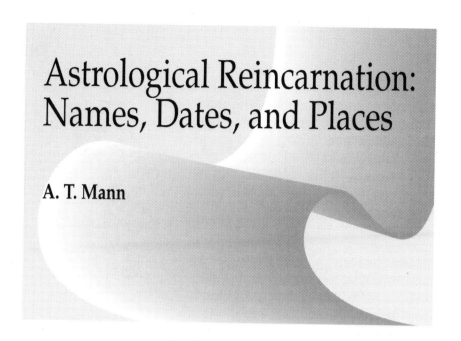

# Astrological Reincarnation: Names, Dates, and Places

## A. T. Mann

*As long as the experiences and sensations that stream through the consciousness of an individual remain untouched by any widening, devaluating vision, the perishable creatures that appear and vanish in the unending cycle of life (samsara, the round of rebirth) are regarded by him as utterly real. But the moment their fleeting character is discerned, they come to seem almost unreal—an illusion or mirage, a deception of the senses, the dubious figment of a too restricted, ego-centered consciousness. When understood and experienced in this manner, the world is Maya.*[1]

To its adepts and its multitude of students, astrology is the supreme science and art of life. From early historical times, the horoscope has been seen to symbolize all aspects of human reality, from the mundane to the transcendent. Its practitioners throughout human history have utilized the same set of symbols to achieve or justify myriad intellectual, emotional, or spiritual concepts. The beauty of astrology's dynamics is that the horoscope can be used in a virtually infinite number of ways, from the

---

1   Zimmer, Heinrich. *Myths and Symbols in Indian Art and Civilization*, 1946, Bollingen, Washington, p. 24.

statistical to the esoteric, from the mundane Sun-sign column to the sophisticated mythic-psychological. Sometimes I think that the most miraculous quality of astrology is its ability to "work" as a model for everyone, at every level.

Whereas in earlier times astrologers were forced to postulate some mystical rationale for explaining why and how astrology worked, in recent years an explanation has become available which is acceptable to both the scientific and the esoteric mind, and in some ways provides a missing link between them.

In my books, *The Round Art: The Astrology of Time and Space*[2] and *Life Time Astrology*, I presented the idea that the spiral path of the solar system through time resembles the structure of the genetic code DNA (figure 1: Spiraling Solar System and DNA). These two spiraling mechanisms have a similar mathematics, and to each is attributed the function of "creation of form" and "transmission of information." By virtue of the principle of resonance, these two similar forms transmit information instantaneously across time and space.

Every living cell contains a genetic "receiver" which resonates with the information carried by the movements of the solar system (and vice versa). Our

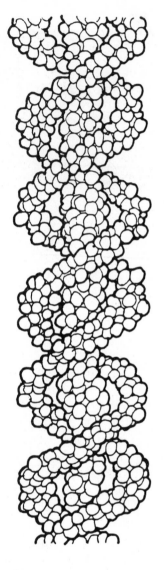

**Fig. 1a: The Spiraling Solar System and DNA** (From *Life Time Astrology*.)

---

2  Mann, A. T., *The Round Art: The Astrology of Time and Space*, Dragon's World/Paper Tiger, London, 1977, and reprinted 1991. These themes were subsequently taken further in *Life Time Astrology*, Allen & Unwin and Harper & Row, 1986, and *Astrology and the Art of Healing*, Unwin Hyman, 1988.

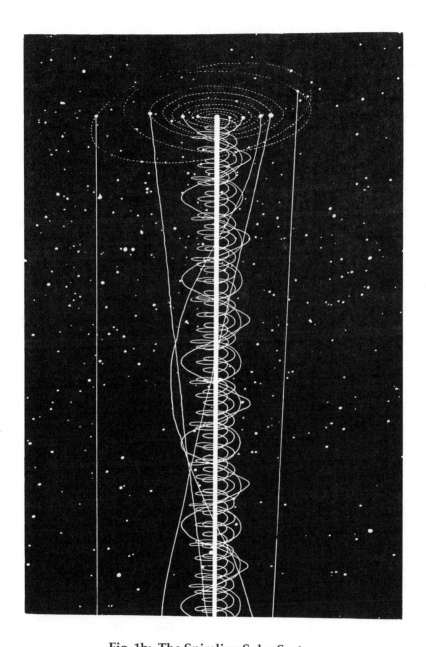

**Fig. 1b: The Spiraling Solar System**
The Central filament of the Sun hurtles through space, carrying the
planets along spiraling paths. The double helix of the DNA molecule
has a similar structure, both visually and mathematically.
(From *Life Time Astrology*.)

solar system, in turn, receives energy and information from the galactic center, and steps it down into quanta related to the planets, which can then be received by individual organisms on Earth through their genetic code. This is true for all creatures, bearing in mind that the structure of DNA is almost identical from the most primitive bacteria, planets, and animals to the most complex human.

Every living organism therefore has access to the universal intelligence *within itself*, and responds in its own way, at its own level. The bands received range from the most physical somatic and instinctive information for creating and maintaining the physical body, through many levels to the most subtle, spiritual vibrations. While the capability of receiving the correct channels is built into every organism, the biological intelligence of most creatures and the mechanism of consciousness of humanity typically censor all but the most mundane and mechanical bands. There is more information available than we choose to access.

It is in this way that the ancient axioms, "as above, so below" and "the microcosm is the macrocosm" can be seen as descriptions of reality rather than metaphors. We contain the entire universe (above) within us (below), and this information is always available if only we are able to understand the nature of the transmission and identify with its source. Because only astrology attempts to decode the significance of planetary movements, by extension, astrology is ideally suited to be a transformative medium for humanity, and the core of a spiritual science.

## Life Time Astrology

In traditional astrology, the horoscope circle is a symbolic representation of an individual. A "birth" horoscope will be read similarly, whatever the age of the subject, and is purported to provide an objective description of the person. Yet people change in time and see the birth pattern from successively different relative viewpoints. Introverted children become extroverted adults; adored children find loveless marriages. The underlying patterns remain, but within the unconscious. The two-dimensionality and lack of an inbuilt time sense of traditional and modern horoscope interpretation bothered me when I first learned astrology, and I attempted to rectify this inadequacy.

The analogy of a spiral solar system and DNA double-helix leads to a unique but obvious way of looking at astrology: *life as a process in time*. The birth horoscope is a plane slice through the spiraling solar system at birth, yet the spiral continues on into the future and *can be projected backward into the past*. The birth horoscope is therefore a reference plane amidst a process which begins at con-

**Fig. 2: Life Time Astrology Wheel**
When the logarithmic/biological time is superimposed on the horoscope, planets and house cusps may be dated using this wheel. This shows the archetypal sizes and qualities of the twelve houses, beginning with Aries on the Ascendant—actual horoscopes have unequal houses and hence variable developmental times through life. (From *Life Time Astrology*.)

ception and extends ahead to death. The birth horoscope artificially "freezes" the planetary continuum at an instant in time, but *continues its inexorable movement*. Because of the regular cyclical movement of the solar system, by extension forward and backward, it contains clues about the past and future of the person in question.

Each life encompasses a length of the spiraling solar system, reflecting a process of development from conception to death. Everyone alive at the same time sees an identical spiraling solar system from a succession of relative points of view, which they perceive to be different realities. At conception, our eternal soul enters a gestating physical body within this spiraling circus, and later, at death, leaves it, only to be reborn again, back into time. The timeless soul, together with its karma, incarnates into a body in gestation and lives its life bound by linear time and governed by the laws affecting the physical world of the solar system, as well as accepting the patterns of the genetic line into which it is born. This may be why the ancient sages considered the world to be the cross we bear and the tomb in which we confine ourselves. Since the movement of the solar system defines time for us, the entire life process within it *can be graded mathematically*.

We start life as a fertilized ovum which develops at a molecular rate, and, as our physical body grows within our mother, the rate of change slows down. This continual slowing-down of growth through life is reflected in our metabolism, the rate at which we live life. Biological studies[3] have proved that metabolism and time sense are inversely proportional: with a rapid metabolism time passes slowly, while with a slow metabolism time seems to pass quickly. Our time sense reflects our metabolic rate and determines the way we perceive the passage of time. This explains why time passes so slowly when we are children and then faster and faster the older we get, until in old age it literally flies by.

We all have physical, emotional, mental, and transcendent levels of being that exist in time and come into being in a preset sequence which can be mapped onto the wheel of the houses, and also a *spiritual* or *transpersonal* level that is beyond time. The resultant clock of life[4] illustrates a lifetime. (See Figure 2: Life Time Astrology Wheel) The divisions of the clock are divided by bio-

---

3   The work of the biologist Pierre Lecomte de Nöuy as referenced in Collin.
4   Collin, Rodney, *The Theory of Celestial Influence*, p. 156.

logical time, which is exponential or logarithmic, reflecting the fact that our perception of time changes as we age.

The biologically derived logarithmic scale divides an average human life of 77 years into three developmental octaves: *Gestation (physical body)*, *Childhood (emotional body)*, and *Maturity (mental body)*. In the log scale, the sequence 1, 2, 3, 4 is equivalent to 1, 10, 100, and 1,000 lunar months in life. One lunar month after conception, the fertilized ovum has attached to the uterine wall, and the development of the physical body begins; ten lunar months after conception we are born, the information required for the body has been received; 100 lunar months is about seven years old, when we have created our personality, an emotional body, and begin to leave the family system to go out into the world to create a mental body; and 1,000 lunar months is 77 years, the average life expectancy, and the time of death.

These three "octaves" are developmental stages experienced by everyone. Each successive (physical, emotional, and mental) body acts at a higher level of being, takes ten times longer to be created, and is less tangible. Perceptually, although each octave lasts ten times longer than the preceding octave, they have equal weight in our memory, and an equal amount of energy and awareness is manifest within them. Thus a child lives life more then ten times faster than an adult, and yet time seems to pass ten times longer to them. As we age, time passes faster and faster, and we have less and less energy to deal with it, until in old age time is passing faster than we can comprehend.

In this model of life, the earlier events register as the deeper, more potent and more formative in our lives, and yet, paradoxically, we are less likely to be conscious of them. Thus the early events of conception and gestation, which to a large extent determine our physical body, other inherited traits, our parental legacy, and our "collective unconscious," is a time about which we know virtually nothing. When critical events happened to our parents in these early stages, particularly the sexual facts of our conception itself, they were unlikely to tell us the truth about them, especially if they themselves were compromised by the events. So, we are the least likely to discover from the primary protagonists the true significance of this most important stage of our lives.

Life Time Astrology was derived by wrapping the circular biological, relative time scale around the horoscope and correlating it with the houses. When the three octaves are wrapped around a horoscope the accompanying diagram results. Each octave contains four houses (Houses 1–4, 5–8, 9–12), and the dates of each house can be determined.

In an unequal Placidean house system, each house varies in size according to the length of time it takes to experience its developmental stage. If the 3rd House is when we learn to talk, this can happen as early as one or as late as four or five years old. The planets are located in the life process at the times when they "register"and have primary significance. The coincidence of the conception and death points at the 9th cusp explains why the 8th House and the sign Scorpio represent decay and death, while the 9th House and the sign Sagittarius represent rebirth, higher mind (the brain is created in the first weeks after conception), and long journeys (starting with the journey of the sperm to fertilize the ovum and the fertilized ovum traveling up the fallopian tube).

Each planet is dated at its month and year of life, and qualified by its octave, Platonic body, and house, and therefore is interpreted at the appropriate time in life. Thus the Sun (the father) in the 10th house of Gestation means that your legacy from your father is largely inherited in your physical body, while the Moon (the mother) in the 3rd House of Childhood means that at two years old, when you started talking, you were emotionally influenced by your mother. Through your life, you move around the horoscope, beginning at conception at cusp 9, extending around the circle to the end of life. Because the process is not really circular, but a spiral, one can picture the cylinder of life from conception at the bottom to the end of life at the top. As we age, we progress around the circumference and the cylinder fills up with memories like water filling a glass. Our present age is the surface of this cylinder, and the deepest memories lie at the bottom of the cylinder. The cylinder is also the length of the spiraling solar system that encompasses our incarnation in this body.

Life Time Astrology allows the horoscope to grade and interpret the entire process of life from conception to the present, and beyond into the future. In no other system of astrology, except the extremely abstract idea of the prenatal epoch, is this essential period of life even referred to, much less focused upon. Yet, where in the traditional horoscope do we look to see the origin of attempted abortions, conception rapes, inherited family patterns or addictions, abuse during pregnancy, congenital defects, wartime, and the host of other gestation influences we carry into our lives? This unique aspect of Life Time Astrology itself makes it extremely valuable as a system for psychological interpretation.

The gestation influences, which form the launching pad from which we embark into incarnation, also signify the transcendent aspirations we will eventually manifest. The events of our mother carrying us are prototypes of our spiritual reality. It is therefore possible to reenter the gestation octave on a higher level by extending our reality beyond the physical, emotional, and mental levels of being. As Goethe stated, we must enter the "realm of the mothers." The process of entering the transcendent realm is an evocation of our own conception. The relationship between our father and mother at conception and during gestation reflects the relationship between our animus and anima, in the dance of the conjunction. The way our mother responds to gestation shows how we relate to our own higher self, in either love or rejection. Thus the circle is complete, and the ouroburos snake bites its tail to complete the life cycle.

The octave in which a planetary influence registers shows in which "body" the resultant affliction or dynamic lies, which is invaluable information both for diagnosis and treatment of life issues. Due to the integration of biological facts with the psychological structure of astrology, a new value can be placed upon both, and both viewpoints are seen to correspond. After all, there is no psychology without a body and a mind, and psychological patterns do not just manifest from the void; they are created by our parents, or inherited from our ancestors, or are the results of incarnative influences.

The horoscope of the first man on the moon, Neil Armstrong, illustrates the mechanism on an outer and inner level. His Sagittarius Moon in the 7th House registers at 38 years old (A. T. Mann, *Lifetime Astrology*), when he literally took a long journey (Sagittarius) to the Moon. The Moon's aspects show earlier events in Armstrong's life which prepared him for this great leap forward. The trine back to the Node in Aries in the 12th House of Gestation shows that just before his birth, while floating weightlessly in a small capsule (the womb), he attempted to control his mother. This aspect also represents the psychic nature of his experiences in space. The trine to Mercury and Neptune in Virgo in the

4th House shows both the radio and psychic communications used by these first astronauts to connect back with their base.

In the life process, we create four levels in sequence around the natal horoscope, which in essence is an integrating model for the Platonic, esoteric, biological, psychological, and traditional views of astrology.[5] It is a holistic matrix for the larger synthesis required by contemporary astrology. Our life cannot, however, be isolated from other lives.

# Deeper Levels

Planets in the birth horoscope activate particular qualities and describe subpersonalities we create in our lives, and they also have historical antecedents. Our attitudes, ways of behaving and thinking—our being—are based upon a foundation derived from stages of the development of humanity. Some of these layers and their associated memories are prehistorical, in which case they are called "instincts." Instinctive ways of acting are often seen as irrational or uncivilized, but they have their place in ensuring our survival, our need to mate, to find food, and the other actions we automatically rely upon. Our historical memories are concentrated at particular times in history when our planets have been activated. We all carry the panorama of history within our genes, and also by reverberation with the planetary movements through the soul, but we choose to access it in different ways, in the same way that we all contain similar genetic material, yet choose to have different bodies and inheritances. Some people act primarily from the instinctive levels of their being, while others have lost contact with these deeper, instinctive layers of being and feel disenfranchised. We all choose, whether consciously or unconsciously, a level of control over, and suppression of, instinctive influences. The twelve logarithmic phases of life (the houses) provide a key enabling us to extend the model into a system for grading historical time.[6]

---

5   See *Life Time Astrology* and *Astrology and the Art of Healing* for further details about the applications of this model.

6   This idea was first presented in *The Divine Plot: Astrology and Reincarnation*, Allen & Unwin, London, 1986 and recently republished by Element Books, Shaftesbury and Rockport, MA, 1991. Its elaboration will constitute *The Eternal Return: A Thinking Human's Guide to Reincarnation*, a manuscript awaiting publication.

When a planet registers in a particular house during the childhood octave, it represents a concentrated experience transmitted through an event, realization, or inner process occurring at that time, described by the meaning of the sign that qualifies the event, acting through the subpersonality quality of the planet or planets involved. As adults we are composed of a series of such critical events in our lives which we draw upon always, compacted into the present time. We carry our history within us, and our past is continually activated by present stimuli.

Freud formulated an extremely perceptive and powerful idea about human psychology: "Ontogeny recapitulates Phylogeny" means that an individual's life is a reactivation of the stages of development of the whole species. In our lives, *we relive human history*. Freud believed that the stage at which children learn to talk is a psychological reality similar to that of all humanity when language was developed. The stage of individual self-consciousness between seven and twelve years old is equivalent to the time in history when individuality first arose from tribal and mythological reality. Similarly, the time of gestation is an encoded history of humanity before the advent of consciousness.

The logarithmic scale of the life time does not start with 0, but with 1. We do not just "materialize" within our mothers; rather, we are the activation, the bringing-into-being of an ovum which existed within her from the time of her gestation. The ovum from which *she* was created lay within *her* mother in the same way. In this sense, we are the result of a continuous process of coming-into-being stretching back from mother to mother, back to the first humanity and to the first life. The ovum is eternal. The gestation time, during which we develop from a fertilized ovum to being a fully developed newly-born, is the time during which we relive, in highly compacted form, *the entire evolutionary process within the mother*. All our genetic and reincarnative memories come into being during this stage of the life process.

The gestation octave is what Jung called the "collective unconscious," the psychic substratum shared by all humans. Similarly, the Childhood octave from birth to about seven years is what Jung called the "personal unconscious," consisting of childhood memories, most of which are suppressed. This may explain why the women's and men's mysteries were abstractions and re-enactments of conception, gestation, and birth. Alchemy retained this symbolism in its "art."[7] Along the same lines, our father's sperm is derived from the primal sperm required to fertilize the primal egg. In this way each cell in our body contains a genetic record of all humanity.

The controversial biologist Rupert Sheldrake hypothesized the existence of a morphogenetic field for each species, which carries collective information, instinctive patterns, form-generating and genetic instructions and learned characteristics, and which can be accessed by all members of the species.[8] This hypothesis parallels the idea presented here.

This anti-Darwinian logic leads to the conclusion that everyone alive today is the result of a 100 percent successful genetic experiment, and that we contain within us, within our DNA, our brain structure, our very cells and molecules, a history of all life on Earth. In modern recombinant DNA research, the 97 percent of the human genome which is not apparently used for the creation and maintenance of the body is considered "junk," yet it is almost certainly the information derived from our previous history, available with every cell. This realization led to a deeper study of the Life Time model.

This logic also leads one to grade the history of humanity using the sequence of astrological signs, just as it was possible to grade an individual's life in *Life Time Astrology*. Since each sign of the zodiac, beginning with Aries, is a developmental stage in a process of achieving wholeness, it stands to reason that this sequence has and continues to operate within the historical process as well. By grading history into developmental stages corresponding to the astrological signs, it becomes possible to correlate the deeper, historical, and prehistorical root meanings of the signs with their activation in our birth horoscopes. This model is valuable for investigating our psychological development and also for discovering our previous incarnations. It is my feeling that these two quite different fields are converging and that a unified approach would be of benefit to both the astrological and psychological communities.

---

7  Fabricius, Johannes, *Alchemy, Rosenkilde and Bagger*, Copenhagen, 1976. This book shows the relationship of alchemical diagrams with electron microscope and intra-uterine photographs of the developing ovum in a very convincing manner.

8  Sheldrake, Rupert, *A New Science of Life*, Blond & Briggs, London, 1981.

# The Reincarnation Time Scale

It is important to understand the logic of the reincarnation time scale, in order to know how to modify or criticize it.

It is essential to postulate the "lifetime" of humanity. The starting point, 50,000 years ago, was chosen for a variety of reasons. From 500,000 years ago until about 50,000 years ago, Neanderthals were the most advanced species on earth. They were beetle-browed but with the brain capacity of contemporary humanity, and physically they were short, squat, hairy, and had sloped foreheads. They lived in tribal units, made tools, but seem never to have created language, which is a keynote of consciousness. About 50,000 years ago a new species arrived, descended from a different evolutionary line, previously unknown to anthropologists. The Cro-Magnons were taller, with straight foreheads, less hair, were more active and began to develop language. Over a period of about 15,000 years the Cro-Magnons destroyed the Neanderthals and inherited their role on earth.[9] We descend from Cro-Mzzagnon humanity, but also possess components of the Neanderthal with which they interbred. Therefore the beginning of our world age is 50,000 years ago.

It is also necessary to suggest the end point. This is determined by the duration of the reincarnation time scale world age, composed of two precessions of the equinoxes of 25,000 years each, a "night" and "day" of the world age. Starting at 48,000 BC, this brings us to the present time, which many say is the end of a world age, if not the end of the world. The year 2000 AD or thereabouts is generally considered the target date of the end of the present world (age) by people as diverse as Nostradamus, Edgar Cayce, Jose Arguelles (organizer of the Harmonic Convergence), the Seventh Day Adventists, cabalists, many fundamentalist Christian sects and the Hindus, Buddhists, and Brahma Kumaris, who see it as the end of the Kali Yuga, the age of misery.

The science-fiction writer H. G. Wells and historians Arnold Toynbee and Henry Adams believed that humanity is experiencing an acceleration which will become so extreme by the year

---

9   See *The Clan of the Cave Bear* and its sequels by Jean Auel, a series of novels about this transitory time in human history.

# The World Age

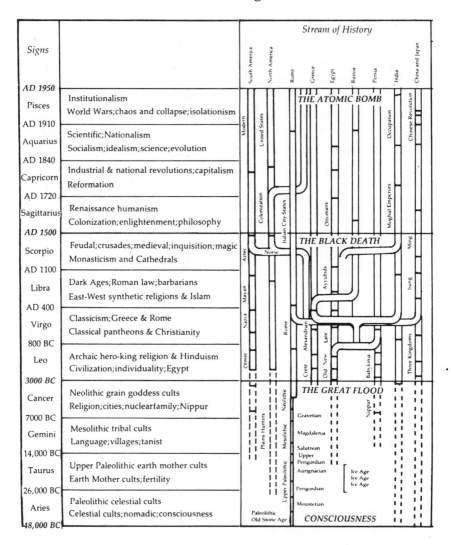

**Figure 3: The Reincarnation Time Scale**
The Reincarnation Time Scale describes a world age of 50,000 years, from the bottom to the top of the diagram. Each astrological sign governs a developmental stage in the historical process. The Stream of History illustrates schematically the development of continental cultures. The four demarcating historical events are Consciousness, The Great Flood, The Black Death, and The Atomic Bomb. (From *The Divine Plot: Astrology and Reincarnation*.)

258

2000 AD that history, meaning this development stage of our species, will end. Adams came to this conclusion by studying the exponential development of population, the use of energy, GNPs and a very wide range of diverse statistics. According to the ethnobotanist Terence McKenna: *"The twentieth century does not make any sense whatsoever unless it ends in a complete transformation of the [human] species."*[10] And: *"Human beings are therefore the natural agents for a compression that is building up in the temporal world toward transition into some higher dimension of existence. History is going to end."*[11] The idea of compacted evolution leading to a cataclysm or change of consciousness is known as "the acceleration of history."[12]

In order to grade the 50,000 year scale from 48,000 BC to 2000 AD, an important issue is the variable direction in which time compacts between the individual and the species. In our individual life, the early stages of development occur rapidly and are highly compacted, and as we age these stages become longer in time, but in the history of our species the opposite is true. In history, the early stages take a long time and history compresses as we move towards the present. In the last fifty years, we have developed as much as the previous 500, and in that 500 as much as the previous 5,000. Therefore the same logarithmic time scale is used for history, but *the direction of compaction is reversed.* Individual life is densest in the beginning, but history is densest at its end.

When history is graded into three "octaves' like the development of an individual life, they occupy the following time periods: -50,000 years is 48000 BC, -5000 years is 3000 BC, -500 years is 1500 AD, and -50 years, the basic *unit* of the time scale, is 1950 AD. (Figure 3: The Reincarnation Time Scale) The unit of 50 years is very interesting. In Hebrew mysticism, it is called the jubilee cycle (7x7+1), correlating with the 7000x7+1000 of the Shemitah cycle of the manifestation of the Torah, which is symbolized in the year as the Pentecost. It also appears in Christianity. The ancient Egyptians celebrated a fifty-year cycle (the golden section number phi [618] number of lunar months), and it also corresponds to the

10  McKenna, Terence, *The Archaic Revival*, Harper San Francisco, 1991.
11  Ibid, p. 18.
12  See the essays in *The Acceleration of History*, by Gerard Piel, Knopf, New York, 1972.

cycle of Sirius B around the star Sirius, which the Egyptians worshiped as the "Dog Star" and the "Sun of our Sun." It has been suggested that Sirius is the sun in the Milky Way galaxy around which our own Sun revolves.

Toynbee estimated that the number of people who will live between AD 1950 and the year 2000 will be approximately equal to the number of people who have lived from 50,000 years ago to 1950. This implies that in terms of the density of population, the last fifty years of our present century is a compacted version of all history. Indeed it is. When we die, our life passes before our eyes in an instant, an experience reported thousands of times as the "Near Death Experience," which was identified by Rodney Collin as the legendary "Last Judgment" of the Egyptian, Tibetan Buddhist, Christian, and other major religions. In a way, these fifty years are the Last Judgment of human history. We see around us the rediscovery and recreation of all former religions, philosophies, psychologies, arts, and crafts, and all of the various dimensions of human history, paraded before our eyes, and every soul incarnate during the world age is returning to crystallize its karma for the next cyclical world age of incarnations.

In describing the developmental stages in history which correspond to the sequence of astrological signs, it will be seen that *the root meaning of the signs within us is derived from their equivalent stages in history.* Traditional qualities attributed to the sign Taurus of pure physicality, love of agriculture and gardening, animals, a sense of security and stability can be easily correlated with the developments during the Taurean age between 26,000 and 14,000 BC when the Earth Mother cults reigned, agriculture was discovered, animals were domesticated, and humanity ceased being nomadic for the first time. Therefore, planets in zodiac signs are psychological qualities but they are also *layers of our primeval experience reactivated in this life.* It could be that we had an "incarnation" at that time, or that we simply contain particularly relevant memories from our genetic pool from that time.

There will also be given gods, goddesses, or historical individuals who symbolized each of the stages of the world age.

# The Era of Mythology

The earliest historically developmental octave, the Era of Mythology, is from the origin of consciousness 50,000 years ago (48,000 BC) to the Great Flood and the first civilizations 5000 years ago (3000 BC). Before 3000 BC we know only of mythological beings and legendary kings and queens. Humanity was governed by the divine direction of gods and goddesses who populated the heavens. Historical movements were symbolized by the battles, loves, and lineages of the gods and goddesses who preceded humanity, transmitted by stories which became myths. There were individuals, of course, but they do not exist in our known history of humanity. It is in this sense that we talk about "historical time."

A critical characteristic of consciousness during this earliest era of humanity was that *time perception was limited*. People lived one day at a time, existing in an eternal present. Days were repetitive, each one being like the preceding one. The longer monthly or yearly cycles were measured and marked on stones or monuments, but, in general, these cycles only served to identify phases of an eternal present. Past flowed into present, and the past and future were in the hands of the gods.

The Era of Mythology preceded the first civilizations, and, more importantly, was characterized by the gradual introduction of individuality. Sons were originally named after fathers and daughters after mothers for generation upon generation. Sons inherited and then carried the collected myths of their ancestors and inherited their prowess and understanding. At a certain point in their lives, *they became their ancestors*. In his marvelous book *Joseph and His Brothers*, Thomas Mann called this "open identity." People in such times had no clearly demarcated ego, in that they incorporated qualities, acts, and deeds which properly belonged to their ancestors. There was a lack of boundaries as generational stories or myths became a real part of their present lives. The telling of a dramatic and brave story invested them with qualities of the hero, and their peers and descendants attributed the bravery to them.

Incarnations during the Mythological Era are primal, instinctive, archetypal, and extremely powerful. Jungian psychology is primarily concerned with such mythological aspects of our personalities as expressed in our dreams. This period contains the origin of the collective unconscious in the historical process, although the collective unconscious stretches back before the first humans to the first life. The mythological incarnations alive within us are timeless and undifferentiated. They are our access to the wisdom of the primitive mind that drives us.

The primary characteristic of incarnations from the dawn of history is the quality of open identity, the ability to change and modify personality traits almost at will. The zodiac signs Aries, Taurus, Gemini, and Cancer occupy the Era of Mythology. *Goddesses in Everywoman and the Gods in Everyman* by Jean Shinoda Bolen describes the importance of discovering the primal forces that influence how women and men feel and act. The inner patterns of the myths transmit lessons which can be used to further integration and wholeness. The seven archetypal goddesses and gods Bolen presents are personality types with which most women and men can relate.

During this period of 45,000 years, humanity developed from Cro-Magnon hunter-gatherers to the creators of civilization. During the Aries time (48,000 to 26,000 BC) humanity was instinctive, tribal, nomadic, travelling with the seasons to find animals to hunt, and fruits and berries to eat. Their religion was Celestial worship: they found their gods in the elements and the sky, in the luminaries the Sun and Moon, in the planets, stars and constellations: the God Sky and the Goddess Night.

About 26,000 BC, the nomadic phase ended as humanity discovered agriculture and settled down in temperate climates in Taurus. The stability and security this provided led to the domestication of animals and the raising of cattle. The religious emphasis shifted from the sky to the Earth Mother who reigned over the fertility of the crops, the animals, and the hearth. The feminine qualities dominated as evidenced by cult objects such as the Willendorf Venus and the cattle painted at the Lascaux caves, the Goddesses Nature and Gaia.

Around 14,000 BC language became a focus of society, tribal organization became more complex and diverse, and instead of each man and woman doing all jobs, specialization emerged as a desirable trait. The division of labor meant some were priests, some farmers, some hunters or warriors, and some craftspeople.

Trade and commerce mutually affected wide ranges of tribes and life became richer and more elaborate. The religious beliefs of this time were symbolized by the Titans, mediators between the sky and earth, who participated more fully in the destiny of humanity. In a sense, language became a powerful tool of the priesthoods, who typically were its guardians: the God Helios and the Goddess Selene.

The first known city Jericho is dated at about 7,000 BC, at the beginning of the sign Cancer, and the nuclear family evolved during this time. Society was matriarchal and neolithic societies harnessed the movements of the planets and stars in the service of agrarian efficiency. Pottery, writing, and farming techniques became much more sophisticated, and many metals were found and worked. The religions were the Olympians and home gods, distilled from earlier more primitive cults, with a focus upon the grain goddesses such as Ceres and Demeter: the God Apollo and the Goddess Demeter.

# The Era of Civilization

The Era of Civilization began about 3000 BC, at the end of the Iron Age, which is a fascinating boundary point in history because *before that time there was no mention of individuals in history, only gods and goddesses.* The first historical rulers or sages were legendary descended gods and goddesses who possessed mythical being rather than historical, human being. The tribal leaders before this time carried generations of stories and traits and attained an almost godlike character which went beyond their actual exploits.

Incarnations in the Era of Civilization are aspects of the self that are bound up with one's sense of identity. People focused their entire lives upon specific areas of work, relationships, finding and attaining a position in society, ideas, and beliefs. Often there was a total personal identification with occupation or profession, religious beliefs, and other value systems that placed the individual within the society and were permanent and binding. The caste systems originated at this time as a hierarchical way of evaluating people. People alive now with prominent incarnations in this era are often identified by (and identify with) their position in society and tend to embrace the hierarchy of their society to support their position. Without a hierarchy, they have no identity.

History served primarily as a guide to behavior. Leaders from the past were emulated as models for their connections to the gods and goddesses, for the strategy, beliefs, and actions that led them to survival, success, and esteem. Learning from the lives of famous men and women provided models which were venerated to the extent that *they* became gods and goddesses incarnate, thereby bringing godlike spirit down to humanity. The Egyptian and Chinese cultures were notable examples of this principle. Their religions were initially god-worship, but gradually the pharaohs and emperors adopted their positions on Earth, until they supplanted them in the minds of the people. Also during this time, the first monotheistic religion, Judaism, developed in the Middle East.

Around 3000 BC, simultaneously with the foundation of the early civilizations of Chaldea, Egypt, Babylonia, and China, the cult of the individual began to evolve as a major force. During the early stages of this era, the only historical personages of whom we have records are pharaohs, emperors, kings and their queens. All others were considered mere extensions of, or secondary to, the divine rulers. Key figures were King Solomon and Helen of Troy.

At 800 BC, in the beginning of the Virgo time, what came to be known as the classical civilizations of Greece and Rome were founded. These pantheistic religions assimilated the gods and goddesses of the tribes and nations they conquered, and integrated them into a pantheon. Simultaneously, the Greeks and Romans reformed and created the classical organization of learning and culture. For the first time, art was created by individuals such as Homer and Phidias, rather than as the result of collective activities. The classical religions of Buddhism, Taoism, and Christianity came into being through their founders, who were themselves godlike men, culminating in the father-son relationship of the monotheistic God and Jesus. Toward the end of this time, the civilizations began decaying. Key figures were Plato and Cleopatra.

By 400 AD, the early Libran time saw the collapse of Greece and Rome, both invaded by barbarian hordes from the East, just as the Chinese civilization was invaded by mongols from the West. The Dark Ages came about as monastic societies replaced Roman Law and the power of the Church vied with the State, culminating in the reign of Charlemagne and the Holy Roman Empire. The religions of the time were the synthetic East/West Islam and mystic Christianity, symbolized by the Grail Legend and the Knights of King Arthur. In the East, a similar synthesis occurred in Zen Tibetan Buddhism. Key figures were Charlemagne and Queen Theodora.

By 1100 AD, the Scorpionic Crusades brought the birth of the Cathedrals and the Middle Ages. Feudal and monastic societies carried the fragmented learning, and the populace was racked by continual wars and church/state competition. Inquisition asserted the dominance of church over infidels. The Norman conquest of England marked the last time it was invaded.

The Papacy and religious orders became dominant. Buddhism was revived in China, Japan, and Tibet. Islamic Ottoman and Mamluk empires created high culture and art, and architecture flourished under the Medicis, Khans, and Mongols. The Black Death plague symbolized the death of classical civilization. Key figures were Genghis Khan and Eleanor of Aquitaine.

## The Era of Individuality

The Era of Individuality began in 1500 AD, with the Renaissance men and women who combined aspects of their revered ancestors but dissolved the rigid barriers of identification and freely traversed the entire domain of human understanding and art. Leonardo da Vinci, Michelangelo, Cosimo and Catherine de Medici, Queen Elizabeth I, and Shakespeare were patterns of such enlightened beings. Humanity explored outer and inner worlds: the long voyages of discovery were paralleled by inner travels into the domain of the spirit which led to the investigation of no less exciting lands/realms. The cross-fertilization of world ideas led to a new sense of self and to the ascendency of the individual. This era extends into our own lifetime, and represents the culmination of the "world age."

Incarnations in the Age of Individuality are those who shaped the modern world through their actions and ideas. The signs Sagittarius, Capricorn, Aquarius, and Pisces (the third octave) show the stages of development of the individual since the Renaissance. One's taste in literature, art, philosophy, politics, social systems, fashion, education, and the many other areas of modern civilization are determined by such incarnational influences. In recent years, you can observe the almost supreme influence of movies and the media upon attitudes and behavior. Our aspirations remain those of individuality and self-expression.

During Sagittarius beginning in 1500 AD, the voyages of discovery led to the first perception of the world as a whole. Renaissance humanism encouraged individual skills and knowledge, and the arts were furthered. Heliocentric astronomy and advanced mathematics transformed science and became accepted due to Galileo, Newton, and Kepler. Literature flowered in Elizabethan England and elsewhere. Religious beliefs were symbolized by the Protestant Reformation initiated by Luther and Calvin, which personalized an egocentric religious belief and worship that eliminated the intercession of the Pope. Key figures were Leonardo da Vinci and Queen Elizabeth I.

Beginning in 1720 AD, Capricorn brought materialism through the vehicle science, manifest through the Industrial Revolution. Electricity, machines, trains and explosives altered the world forever and initiated the modern era. Technology allied to war created colonial nationalism. The American and French revolutions chartered human rights and autonomy.

The arts reached a classical perfection in the work of Mozart, Bach, Beethoven, Goethe, Balzac, and many others. The Reformation was complete, and science replaced religion as the focus of humanity's beliefs and hopes for the future. Key figures were George Washington and Catherine the Great of Russia.

The Aquarian time began in 1840 AD, when there emerged the Utopian societies which embraced industrialism, such as the American and European nations. The American Civil War freed slaves and Czar Alexander freed serfs. Marxist Socialism and Darwinian evolution defined human progress and linked survival and future ideals to the state. Humanity abstracted and defined history, culture, and politics, which became opiates of the people as substitutes for religion. Key figures were Abraham Lincoln and Queen Victoria.

The Pisces time began in 1910 AD with the dissolution of the classical knowledge by the psychology of the unconscious, relativity, cubism, atonal music, Joycean literature, and medical science. The breakdown of civilization was heralded by the two

## Figure 4: Logarithmic Time Scale — Time Scale Dates from 48000 BC to 1950 AD

| Degree | Pisces | Aquarius | Capricorn | Sagittarius | Scorpio | Libra | Virgo | Leo | Cancer | Gemini | Taurus | Aries | Degree |
|---|---|---|---|---|---|---|---|---|---|---|---|---|---|
| 00 | Jan 1911 | Nov 1841 | Oct 1719 | Jan 1500 | 1109 AD | 419 AD | 811 BC | 3000 BC | 6891 BC | 13811 BC | 26117 BC | 48000 BC | 00 |
| 01 | Oct 1912 | Nov 1844 | Mar 1724 | Jul 1509 | 1128 | 449 | 758 | 2905 | 6722 | 13511 | 25583 | 47050 | 01 |
| 02 | Jun 1914 | Jun 1847 | May 1729 | Oct 1518 | 1143 | 478 | 705 | 2818 | 6557 | 13216 | 25059 | 46118 | 02 |
| 03 | Jan 1916 | Sep 1850 | Jul 1734 | Dec 1527 | 1161 | 507 | 654 | 2720 | 6394 | 12927 | 24544 | 45203 | 03 |
| 04 | Aug 1917 | Aug 1853 | Aug 1739 | Dec 1536 | 1177 | 536 | 604 | 2630 | 6234 | 12643 | 24040 | 44306 | 04 |
| 05 | Mar 1919 | May 1856 | Jul 1744 | Sep 1545 | 1192 | 564 | 554 | 2543 | 6078 | 12365 | 23545 | 43426 | 05 |
| 06 | Oct 1920 | Jan 1859 | May 1749 | May 1554 | 1208 | 591 | 506 | 2456 | 5924 | 12092 | 23059 | 42563 | 06 |
| 07 | Apr 1922 | Oct 1861 | Mar 1754 | Mar 1562 | 1223 | 618 | 458 | 2371 | 5774 | 11824 | 22583 | 41716 | 07 |
| 08 | Sep 1923 | May 1864 | Nov 1758 | Nov 1571 | 1237 | 644 | 412 | 2288 | 5626 | 11561 | 22116 | 40885 | 08 |
| 09 | Mar 1925 | Dec 1866 | Jun 1763 | Jan 1579 | 1252 | 670 | 366 | 2206 | 5481 | 11304 | 21658 | 40070 | 09 |
| 10 | Aug 1926 | Jun 1869 | Dec 1767 | Apr 1587 | 1266 | 695 | 321 | 2127 | 5339 | 11050 | 21208 | 39270 | 10 |
| 11 | Jan 1928 | Dec 1871 | Apr 1772 | Feb 1595 | 1280 | 720 | 277 | 2048 | 5200 | 10803 | 20767 | 38486 | 11 |
| 12 | May 1929 | May 1874 | Aug 1776 | Nov 1602 | 1294 | 744 | 233 | 1971 | 5063 | 10559 | 20334 | 37716 | 12 |
| 13 | Sep 1930 | Aug 1876 | Nov 1780 | May 1610 | 1307 | 768 | 191 | 1896 | 4928 | 10321 | 19910 | 36962 | 13 |
| 14 | Feb 1932 | Feb 1879 | Feb 1785 | Oct 1617 | 1320 | 791 | 149 | 1822 | 4797 | 10087 | 19493 | 36221 | 14 |
| 15 | Apr 1933 | Jun 1881 | Jun 1789 | Jan 1625 | 1333 | 814 | 108 | 1749 | 4668 | 9857 | 19085 | 35494 | 15 |
| 16 | Aug 1934 | Sep 1883 | Feb 1793 | Mar 1632 | 1346 | 837 | 68 | 1678 | 4501 | 9632 | 18684 | 34782 | 16 |
| 17 | Oct 1935 | Nov 1885 | Feb 1797 | Mar 1639 | 1358 | 859 | 29 BC | 1608 | 4417 | 9411 | 18291 | 34083 | 17 |
| 18 | Jan 1937 | Jan 1887 | Dec 1800 | Jan 1646 | 1371 | 881 | 10 AD | 1540 | 4295 | 9194 | 17905 | 33397 | 18 |
| 19 | Apr 1938 | Mar 1890 | Sep 1804 | Oct 1652 | 1383 | 902 | 48 | 1472 | 4175 | 8981 | 17527 | 32725 | 19 |
| 20 | Jun 1939 | Apr 1892 | Jun 1808 | May 1659 | 1394 | 923 | 84 | 1406 | 4058 | 8772 | 17156 | 32065 | 20 |
| 21 | Jul 1940 | Apr 1894 | Oct 1812 | Oct 1665 | 1406 | 943 | 121 | 1341 | 3943 | 8567 | 16792 | 31417 | 21 |
| 22 | Sep 1941 | May 1896 | Aug 1815 | Jun 1672 | 1417 | 964 | 157 | 1278 | 3830 | 8366 | 16435 | 30782 | 22 |
| 23 | Oct 1942 | May 1898 | Feb 1819 | Jul 1678 | 1428 | 984 | 192 | 1216 | 3719 | 8170 | 16084 | 30159 | 23 |
| 24 | Nov 1943 | Mar 1900 | Aug 1822 | Jul 1684 | 1439 | 1002 | 223 | 1155 | 3610 | 7976 | 15741 | 29548 | 24 |
| 25 | Dec 1944 | Feb 1902 | Dec 1825 | Jul 1690 | 1450 | 1021 | 260 | 1095 | 3503 | 7787 | 15404 | 28948 | 25 |
| 26 | Jan 1946 | Dec 1903 | Apr 1829 | May 1696 | 1460 | 1040 | 293 | 1036 | 3399 | 7601 | 15073 | 28360 | 26 |
| 27 | Jan 1947 | Oct 1905 | Jul 1832 | Mar 1702 | 1470 | 1058 | 325 | 978 | 3296 | 7418 | 14748 | 27783 | 27 |
| 28 | Jan 1948 | Aug 1907 | Oct 1835 | Jul 1707 | 1480 | 1076 | 357 | 921 | 3196 | 7239 | 14430 | 27217 | 28 |
| 29 | Jan 1949 | May 1909 | Sep 1838 | May 1713 | 1490 | 1094 | 388 | 866 | 3096 | 7064 | 14118 | 26662 | 29 |
| 30 | Jan 1950 | Jan 1911 | Nov 1841 | Oct 1719 | 1500 AD | 1109 AD | 419 AD | 811 BC | 3000 BC | 6891 BC | 13811 BC | 26117 BC | 30 |

## Figure 4: Reincarnation Time Scale Dates

Find the sign along the top and degree along the left side—their meeting will show the date in history of a particular incarnation of a planet or personal point. By reading across to left or right you can see Harmonic Incarnations in other times in history. (From *The Divine Plot: Astrology and Reincarnation*.)

Great Wars and the advent of the nuclear age. Artificial substitutes for culture and religion dominated in the form of cinema, telephone and the media, which idealized and formed mass reality. Alcohol, drugs and synthetics adulterated the natural world. The people had no beliefs, until it was understood that a new era in history began. Key figures were Adolf Hitler, Freud, Jung, and Marilyn Monroe.

With the end of the twelve-sign developmental stages in history, the entire scale repeats itself in highly compact form within fifty years. This is a "death memory" of the whole cycle of human development, during which time all history is recalled and synthesized as a prerequisite for the next cycle. All individuals who have lived during the world age return and their level of consciousness and ability to integrate the whole being determines the cycle of incarnations during the next world age. The coincidental nature of a time when great natural potential and man-made disasters look prepared to poison our planet while our species looks set for a complete transformation of consciousness shows that, at the end of world ages, there is a profound decision to be made individually and collectively.

In this sense, it is essential that we understand the various layers of historical being within us as indicated by our natal horoscope. They represent the origin and core issues of our psychological and evolutionary lives.

## Determining Our Past Lives

Each planet in the natal horoscope symbolizes characteristics, behavioral patterns, and archetypal ways of being which come into play during life. *The time when each planet registers in history determines the date of a past life.* Each component of our personality is derived from developments experienced by the human race at particular times in the past. *We bring the past into the present, without realizing it.* The obsession of modern psychotherapy with the archetypes and the gods and goddesses as they act through sub-personalities is a reflection of this primary historical principle of life. Its mechanism also explains why there is such an attraction to esoteric approaches to astrology and psychology throughout this century, particularly in the last fifty years.

The release of dance or vigorous exercise takes us back to early Stone Age freedom of movement typical of the Aries time; chanting or talking problems through evokes the Geminian time when language was developed, the attraction to mystery and the magic of rose windows reactivates the dynamic of the Scorpionic Middle Ages; while the enjoyment of a Beethoven concerto evokes the Capricornian sense of dominance over nature and the highest human expression of aesthetic order. We constantly evoke our history and respond to unconscious patterns of our past lives, just as we seek meaning in and through these roots of our life. The more we understand of our historical undercurrents, the richer and deeper is the sense of who we are and what we may be.

In order to determine the positions of the planets in history, the horoscope of birth must be calculated and the degree positions of the positions of the ten planets, Ascendant and Midheaven determined by the Reincarnation Time Scale (Figure 4). Each degree corresponds to a date in history and each planet can be dated within the twelve signs.

Just as each planet in natal astrology represents an archetype, a sub-personality or a dynamic within the whole of the Self, so it may be dated at a particular time in history when the same qualities originated in the collective development of humanity. The planetary qualities in reincarnation function as in the following example. The Sun sign represents the spiritual energy you possess. The position of the Sun is compared to a table showing the zodiac signs related to dates in history. The location of the Sun in history determines your energy and spiritual orientation. This may range from the self-assertive cave man to the detached Victorian gentleman.

## Planetary Incarnations

Each planet in your horoscope represents an aspect of your nature that has come into being *at a particular time in your life as well as in history*, determined by the sign of the zodiac in which it resides.

In your life, planetary influences are identified with people who influence you and the corresponding part of you that identifies with them, while reincarnational influences correspond to these personal identifications within the historical process. For example, the Sun is your father and symbolizes your relationships with him, to anyone who is fatherly to you, to men in general, to the masculine principle in yourself and others, as well as signifying the time in history when the masculine identification came into being. The Sun is also a metaphor for your qualities of consciousness, self-awareness and objectivity.

The Moon is initially your mother, but also symbolizes anyone who is motherly to you, to women in general and to the feminine aspect of your own nature. The Moon also indicates your feelings, emotional attachments, ability to nurture or support others, and your values.

The positions of the Sun and Moon by sign, as well as their relationship to other planets, determine the makeup of your masculine and feminine nature as well as the potential for their integration.

# Levels of Being

The planets are divided into three categories which represent levels of being. The planets closest to the Earth—the Sun, Moon, Mercury, Venus, Mars, Jupiter and Saturn—are the *inner planets* because they refer astrologically to personal character, usually based upon parents, siblings, family members, and friends. Our personality is shaped by qualities derived from people around us when we are young.

The *outer planets* beyond the orbit of Saturn represent qualities derived from the world, such as from friends and foes, the media, political movements and associations.

The *personal points*, the Ascendant (also called the rising sign) and the Midheaven, are not planets but positions in the birth horoscope corresponding to the sunrise and the noon point overhead. The personal points describe your personality (the Ascendant) and ego (the Midheaven). For example, infants born on the same day and year have different personal points reflecting their relative times of birth. The personal points are in different signs and have geometrical relationships to other planets.

It is possible to have each of the ten planets and two personal points in different signs of the zodiac, although in practice this almost never happens. Every person has a unique distribution of planets in signs. It is not unusual to have three or more planets in one or two signs, two planets in one or two signs, and the rest in separate signs.

The distribution of planets in signs determines the variety of, and intervals between, your previous incarnations. Planets grouped closely together imply a series of incarnations within certain periods of time. Planets spread around the horoscope imply broader coverage, a wider range of past life experiences and less concentration. No pattern is inherently good or bad, but it is helpful to understand which pattern describes your past lives in history.

Each planet represents a personality type that correlates to a past life. Each planet has its own specific quality and personality types. For example, we all contain all the planets, and therefore all have both the warrior Mars and the feminine Moon. *But when in history did they come into being?*

## Planetary Reincarnation Types

Each planet and personal point falls into one of the three Eras: of Mythology, Civilization, and Individuality (the historical octaves). The warrior in you may be a recent incarnation, while the woman in you may be an ancient goddess. Each planet describes a type that signifies an incarnation in one of the three Eras.

The **Sun** represents creator gods, sun gods, heroes, kings, patriarchs, emperors, czars, popes, lords, aristocrats, presidents, tyrants, autocrats, and refers to the masculine archetypes of the father and the wise old man. The Sun describes a masculine incarnation when you expressed your conscious and objective being, had a dominant spiritual direction, and led others.

The **Moon** represents the creator goddesses, earth mothers, lunar deities, earth goddesses, queens, empresses, heroines, significant women, matriarchs, and mothers. The Moon is an incarnation when you expressed feminine archetypes of the great mother, the wise old woman, and expressed your unconscious and subjective feelings.

**Mercury** represents titans, twin gods, intellectuals, thinkers, orators, authors, critics, mystics, alchemists, and magicians. Mercury is an incarnation when you developed your mental faculties, learned to communicate, concentrated on business, and expressed flexibility and breadth of interest.

**Venus** represents fertility and grain goddesses, deities of the arts and music, goddesses or gods of love, artists, musicians, architects, poets, playwrights, dramatists, lovers, actors or actresses, courtesans, and young women. Venus is an incarnation when your aesthetic and creative nature was embodied, when you had powerful loves, and were at your most attractive.

**Mars** represents gods and goddesses of war and strife, heroes, conquerors, generals, politicians, amazons, politicians, explorers, tyrants, martyrs, athletes, violent people, and young men. Mars is an incarnation when you aggressively expressed individual qualities, self-expression, separateness and tension.

**Jupiter** represents spiritual and procreative gods and goddesses: prophets, religious founders and leaders, philosophers, psychologists, sages and saints. Jupiter was an incarnation of expansive and wise archetypes, when your religious and spiritual life was developed.

**Saturn** represents paternal, rigid and orderly gods and goddesses, material deities, gods of order, scientists, great thinkers, doctors, mathematicians, academics, inventors and bankers. Saturn is an incarnation that determines your sense of tradition and order, a lifetime when your limitations and ability to concentrate were formed.

### The Outer Planets

The outer planets represent more collective characteristics and incarnations:

**Uranus** represents dominant, individualistic gods and goddesses, dramatic transformers of shape and character, eccentrics, intuitives, freedom fighters, inventive scientists, individuals, creative and independent people. Uranus symbolizes an incarnation when you expressed your individuality and uniqueness, and fought for freedom.

**Neptune** represents gods and goddesses of the psyche, of inner spiritual processes, of fantasy, imagination, romance, idealistic spirituality, mediums, mystics, dreamers, and addicts. Neptune symbolizes an incarnation when you expressed your highest ideals and wishes, and allowed your spiritual higher self to be in control.

**Pluto** represents underworld gods and goddesses, transformers, revolutionaries, violent tyrants and rulers, mass murderers, warriors, statesmen, and politicians. Pluto symbolizes an incarnation when you expressed dramatic and far-reaching changes, wanted to change the world, and carried a grand, impulsive energy for transformation.

### The Personal Points:

**The Ascendant** represents your personality, personal characteristics, often physical appearance and taste in art and other environmental qualities, ways of acting, and general milieu. The Ascendant is an incarnation when your self-expression was formulated, a milieu which defines the way you act and see yourself.

**The Midheaven** represents your spiritual awareness, ego-consciousness, objectives, sense of purpose in life, and goals of incarnation. The Midheaven is an incarnation which embodies your aspirations and soul direction in life.

## A Renaissance Odyssey

An example will show how the Reincarnation Time Scale works in practice. My Ascendant (Personality) is at 6° Sagittarius. The Sagittarius time was the Renaissance from AD 1500 to 1720, during the "Age of Humanism."

I wanted to be an architect from an early age, without knowing anyone who was. It led me to draw buildings in childhood, and to an architecture degree from Cornell University. While at Cornell, I traveled to Europe for the first time, wandering alone by motorcycle. When I visited Florence, Venice, and Rome, *I immediately recognized them from before.* Upon seeing some of the architecture of the 16th century, not only did I feel comfortable with the structures, but I could have designed them myself.

After working as an architect in New York City for a few years, in 1968 I traveled through northeastern Italy and lived in Rome for a year. Friends lived in an apartment above the Campo de Fiori, and from my first visit I was bewitched by the piazza: it was dark, it terrified me, and made me feel in mortal danger. I looked closely at the buildings for some familiar sign. I noticed a statue at the end of the piazza, but didn't recognize the name.

When I later became interested in metaphysics and astrology, I was fascinated by and studied the astrologers, mystics, and magicians of the sixteenth century; men such as John Dee, Robert Fludd, Nostradamus, and Giordano Bruno. I felt as though I knew how their minds worked and understood their humanist and mystical aspirations. This was especially true of Giordano Bruno, a philosopher considered heretical because of his worship of the Sun and his support of heliocentricity. Reading *Giordano Bruno and the Hermetic Tradition*,[13] I instinctively understood his ideas, his deepest emotions about the mysteries of the cosmos, and felt as though I knew Bruno's mind. I then discovered *that Bruno had been burnt at the stake in Campo dei Fiori in the year 1600.* The statue in the Campo commemorated Bruno's burning!

When my Reincarnation Theory was first developed, I was shocked to see that my Ascendant registered in 1554, early in the lifetime of Bruno. Many of the architects and mystics I had been attracted to lived at that time. It felt as though I had a previous incarnation at that time in Italy, and the correlation of that time with my Ascendant confirmed the connection.

Similarly, planets in the sign Taurus would indicate an incarnation during the time of the Earth Mother cults, tens of thousands of years ago. This would explain why qualities such as an interest in agriculture or gardening, a love of the pure natural world, a veneration of sculpture and colorful art, physical beauty, and an appreciation of the mature feminine are associated with Taurus, as well as casting new light on its Venusian rulership and exaltation by the Moon. Having the Moon in Taurus would accentuate the need for deep, emotional, primal, and possessive emotional relationships which would lie deeper than formal marriage contracts or more sophisticated communication.

The distribution of planets by octave or era indicate the depth and balance of subpersonalities throughout history. Many planets in the early signs will show archetypal and basic qualities in this life, and the aspect connections between planets obviously indicate the connections between various lives and their qualities. Trines and sextiles between planets indicate harmonic times in history, while squares and oppositions highlight opposing histor-

---

13  Yates, Frances, *Giordano Bruno the Hermetic Tradition,* University of Chicago, 1964.

ical movements. For example, the hero-king personality derived from the Leo time would naturally have tension by opposition, with the trend toward Socialism and communal holding of property and wealth of the opposite Aquarius time. A person with

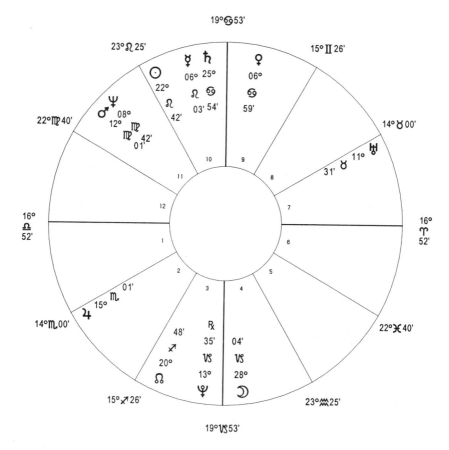

**Napoleon**
Aug. 15, 1979, Ajaccio, Corsica
9:15 AM GMT
8E44  41N55

### Figure 5: The Horoscope of Napoleon
Napoleon's Mars-Neptune conjunction in Virgo correlates with the life-time of Alexander the Great and his Libra Ascendant with the life of Charlemagne. (Horoscope according to *The Astrological Who's Who*, by Marc Penfield, reproduced from *The Eternal Return*.)

opposing planets in these signs would essentially act out an historical drama within their personality, with a deeper sense of the kingly right opposing the more recent socialist idealism. Close observation of ourselves, friends, and clients yield much validity to this hypothesis, but the best proof is through case histories.

## The Incarnations of Napoleon

One of the most interesting examples of an historical figure who believed he had previous incarnations was Napoleon. He believed that he had previously incarnated as Alexander the Great and Charlemagne, which he used as justification for having himself crowned the second Holy Roman Emperor in 1804.

It must be noted that there is a margin of error in the determination of reincarnation dates. A variation of three degrees in planetary position represents a spread of a mere 1 percent on either side of its resultant date. The dates derived from planetary positions can only be approximate, because a lifetime occupies many degrees, and it is impossible to know when during the life of an incarnation the dated influence actually registers.

Napoleon believed that he had previous incarnations as Alexander the Great (356-323 BC) and Charlemagne (742-812 AD). The lifetime of Alexander the Great is from 9 to 10 degrees of the sign Virgo (see figure 4, page 267), and the lifetime of Charlemagne is from 12 to 15 degrees of the sign Libra. In Napoleon's horoscope, Neptune and Mars are conjunct in Virgo. Neptune occupies 8 of Virgo, which is translated as 377 BC. Neptune in Virgo is "psychic connections and abilities, high spiritual aspirations, dreams, and fantasies, and the ability to see the future." Mars registers at 12 Virgo, which translates as 233 BC. Mars is the incarnation of the warrior and soldier. These planets therefore bracket the lifetime of Alexander, and together describe the significance of these qualities in Napoleon's life. In a sense, Napoleon was a spiritual warrior in the truest sense, and certainly derived great inspiration from these former incarnations.

The Ascendant (personality) in Napoleon's horoscope is at 16 Libra, which corresponds to 837 AD. Napoleon modeled his own quest in Europe on Charlemagne's creation of the Holy Roman Empire. His personality is therefore based on qualities derived from his previous incarnation as Charlemagne. It seems that Napoleon was justified in believing that he had indeed led past lives as Alexander and Charlemagne.

It is interesting also to look at the horoscope of Alexander the Great, and to discover that he has a connection *ahead to Napoleon*. Alexander has Uranus at 10 Capricorn, equivalent to March 1754, just 15 years before the birth of Napoleon! The relationship between their horoscopes demonstrates that Napoleon recognized his former life as Alexander. We could even hypothesize that Alexander could have had a premonition of his future life as Napoleon.

Such reincarnation relationships exist in history and form a spiritual or psychic fabric which underlies outer events.

## Creativity and Reincarnation

Past lives embedded within the horoscope have a deep symbolism. They may tell you something about the kind of setting in which you choose to live or work, your hobbies, secret dreams, taste in music, art, drama, literature, or architecture. All figure in the nature of your past lives. Often the job or function you performed in previous times is the reason why you choose the focus in life that you do, or the relationships you attract.

Creative or enquiring people need continually to rediscover themselves, going deeper into their inner truths. Reincarnation theory is a tool for directing access to the creative function, particularly heeding the call to deeper layers of the self in a search for its expression. Previous historical eras can activate higher levels of inspiration.

The creativity of reincarnation may be demonstrated in the horoscopes of authors, musicians, historians, and other creative people. Almost by definition, authors of fiction express themselves through characters that are either autobiographical, imaginary, fictitious, or in some combination. It is fascinating to see how clearly historical interests may be identified in the work of creative people. The German Nobel Prize-winning novelist, Thomas Mann, knew Freud, and had a deep appreciation of the history within himself, as well as the process in the psyche. His novels correlate with the location of planets in his horoscope. His

Uranus in Leo corresponds with *Joseph and His Brothers*, while Saturn in Aquarius corresponds to the analysis of his own family in *Buddenbrooks*. The creative tension derived from the prophetic vision of a Joseph figure contrasted with the stern and paternal German family structure was the keynote of Mann's personality, and he worked with it in his art.

Gore Vidal has his MC in Virgo, corresponding to the time of his novel *Julian*, about the Emperor Julian the Apostate, while his Jupiter in Capricorn corresponds to his great interest and numerous novels about the founding and founding fathers of America, such as *Washington, DC*, and *Burr*. What is amusing is that his novel about the transsexual Myra Breckenridge corresponds to his Uranus in Pisces and overlaps his own life, possibly implying that "Myra" is an original and autonomous aspect of Vidal's personality.

A musician such as Wagner exerted a powerful and archetypal influence upon his audiences and continues to do so today. It is then appropriate that his Ring cycle of operas is evoked by his Venus and Mercury in Taurus, showing a mythological creative quality and unique musical language that evokes deep and mystical layers of the unconscious. His opera *Parsifal* is extremely impelling, and therefore it is not accidental that Wagner's Uranus in Scorpio registers in 1470, when the Grail legends were being first printed and popularized by Malory's *Le Morte d'Arthur.*

Among creative influences, you can expect to see the times in history when Venus, Jupiter, Uranus, and Neptune are significant, activated by emotional qualities when the Moon is involved by aspect to them.

### Soul Mates and Karmic Links

Because relationships constitute such an important area of our lives, and are also so synchronistic and magical, the depth of our ties to others is a fruitful path to follow. Knowing the historical periods of our ties with others can show the kind of relationships we have had with others in past lives. When planets in synastry are conjunct, it implies that we shared an incarnation time with another. It would therefore be quite important to realize that as a man, my previous Medieval incarnation as a Venusian woman in thrall to the Saturnian wise old man of my female partner, would constitute a change of sexual values.

The unusual and brief relationship between the actress Shirley Maclaine and the psychic channeler J. Z. Knight is worthy of our attention. J. Z. Knight was a California housewife who discovered that she could channel an entity called Ramtha, who was a wise being from 35,000 BC, and Shirley Maclaine became an avid follower of the wisdom of Ramtha. As we would expect, both have Mercury, the planet of intelligence and intellect, in the middle of the sign Aries, and Maclaine has it at 15 degrees, which corresponds to 35,000 BC. So, despite the claims of disrepute directed at both women, they seem to have strong and deep links at the time they claimed.

In the horoscopes of Katherine Hepburn and Spencer Tracy, there are no less than three conjunctions at different times in history, showing that their relationship was a strong one, but also with variable aspects. Two of the conjunctions are in Aries (her Saturn, his Sun) and Scorpio (her Sun, his MC), at times in history when relationships were combative, flamboyant, and intensely sexual, as well as being secretive, which characterized their contacts in this life. The last conjunction in Pisces (her Pluto, his Moon), happened during their lifetimes, and accurately describes their compulsive, yet separate, lives in the glare of the Hollywood film business.

Relationships carry historical qualities, and the times activated by our relationships may have an intense and valuable significance in our ability to understand and empower ourselves and our partners.

## Potential Applications

The potential applications of the Reincarnation Time Scale (figure 4, page 267) are innumerable. While the model presented here and in *The Divine Plot* in more depth, is extremely accurate when tested against the dates of the historical process and individual horoscopes, as a lone investigator I have seen many applications of the idea.

Since the Reincarnation Time Scale (RTS) determines the time in history for an incarnation, it would stand to reason that techniques such as Local Space or AstroCartoGraphy could determine *their location*. When the horoscope of Napoleon is tested with a Local Space map, the line corresponding with Mars and

Neptune passes near Macedonia and the areas of the world where Alexander the Great was born and performed his military feats. Much research can be done using individuals who have concrete memories of past lives and can therefore correlate the time scale.

The series of books written by Rudolf Steiner called *Karmic Relationships* contains an idea which can be verified by the RTS. Steiner describes reincarnative chains of individuals, people who throughout history reappeared periodically and made an impact upon our world. When the dates of such successive incarnations, derived psychically by Steiner, are checked against the RTS, it is found that they conform to aspects within the RTS, i.e., their correlative time periods can be found by moving horizontally along a degree line, such as the square from 15° Libra (lifetime of Caliph al Mamun) to 15° Capricorn (the lifetime of the astronomer Laplace, whom Steiner said carried the scientific spirit of the Arab philosophers into the West).

Similarly, the RTS can be used to cross-check channeling experiences and also regression therapy experiences. It can often be seen that the equivalent times in history correspond to significant planets in the individual's horoscope.

It is also obvious that once a reincarnative influence is discovered and dated from the horoscope, reading or putting oneself back into the appropriate time in history can build a greater sense of historical wholeness and solidify karmic tasks and lessons as aids for this valuable but elusive field.

## The Future is Now

The objectives of the "consciousness expansion movement" of the latter twentieth century provide an antidote to the materialist-mechanist scientific world view that is destroying our planet. The discovery of the past within us can bring us closer to our brothers and sisters on our earth. The core of our behavior, our deepest urges and instincts, originates with our common history. This may in part explain the phenomenal popularity of astrology and its progression of zodiac signs: they are expressions of our own development throughout the maze of history. Similarly, it may be that astrology, as the manifest foundation of the Reincarnation Time Scale, is the threat of Ariadne which will allow us to navigate through the labyrinth of time.

When explored with the potential for wholeness in mind, Reincarnation Theory is a bridge across which humanity can journey into the future. In the same way that our past is the common inheritance of all humanity, so our future is the only common future for all the world. Nothing is lost and nothing is gained in "The Eternal Return."

## STAY IN TOUCH

On the following pages you will find some of the books now available on related subjects. Your book dealer stocks most of these and will stock new titles in the Llewellyn series as they become available. We urge your patronage.

To obtain our full catalog, to keep informed about new titles as they are released, and to benefit from informative articles and helpful news, you are invited to write for our bimonthly news magazine/catalog, *Llewellyn's New Worlds of Mind and Spirit*. A sample copy is free, and it will continue coming to you at no cost as long as you are an active mail customer. Or you may subscribe for just $10.00 in the U.S.A. and Canada ($20.00 overseas, first class mail). Many bookstores also have *New Worlds* available to their customers. Ask for it.

*Llewellyn's New Worlds of Mind and Spirit*
**P.O. Box 64383-391, St. Paul, MN 55164-0383, U.S.A.**

\* \* \*

## TO ORDER BOOKS AND TAPES

If your book dealer does not have the books described, you may order them directly from the publisher by sending the full price in U.S. funds, plus $3.00 for postage and handling for orders *under* $10.00; $4.00 for orders *over* $10.00. There are no postage and handling charges for orders over $50.00. Postage and handling rates are subject to change. We ship UPS whenever possible. Delivery guaranteed. Provide your street address as UPS does not deliver to P.O. boxes. Allow 4-6 weeks for delivery. UPS to Canada requires a $50.00 minimum order. Orders outside the U.S.A. and Canada: Airmail—add retail price of book; add $5.00 for each non-book item (tapes, etc.); add $1.00 per item for surface mail.

## FOR GROUP STUDY AND PURCHASE

Because there is a great deal of interest in group discussion and study of the subject matter of this book, we offer a special quantity price to group leaders or agents. Our special quantity price for a minimum order of five copies of *Exploring the Values of Consciousness in the Horoscope* is $44.85 cash-with-order. This price includes postage and handling within the United States. Minnesota residents must add 6.5% sales tax. For additional quantities, please order in multiples of five. For Canadian and foreign orders, add postage and handling charges as above. Credit card (VISA, MasterCard, American Express) orders are accepted. Charge card orders only ($15.00 minimum order) may be phoned in free within the U.S.A. or Canada by dialing 1-800-THE-MOON. For customer service, call 1-612-291-1970. Mail orders to:

**LLEWELLYN PUBLICATIONS**
**P.O. Box 64383-391, St. Paul, MN 55164-0383, U.S.A.**

# HOW TO USE VOCATIONAL ASTROLOGY
# FOR SUCCESS IN THE WORKPLACE
### edited by Noel Tyl

Announcing the most practical examination of Vocational Astrology in five decades! Improve your astrological skills with these revolutionary NEW tools for vocational and business analysis! Now, in *How to Use Vocational Astrology for Success in the Workplace,* edited by Noel Tyl, seven respected astrologers provide their well-seasoned modern views on that great issue of personal life—Work. Their expert advice will prepare you well for those tricky questions clients often ask: "Am I in the right job?" "Will I get promoted?" or "When is the best time to make a career move?"

With an introduction by Noel Tyl in which he discusses the startling research of the Gauquelins, this ninth volume in Llewellyn's New World Astrology Series features enlightening counsel from the following experts:

- Jayj Jacobs: The Transits of Experience/Career Cycles, Job Changes and Rewards
- Gina Ceaglio: Money Patterns in the Horoscope
- Donna Cunningham: Attitudes and Aptitudes in the Chart
- Anthony Louis: Void-of-Course Moon Strategies for Doing Business, Retrograde Planets, and Electional Astrology
- Noel Tyl: Special Measurements for Vocational Guidance, and How to Evaluate Personnel for Profit
- Henry Weingarten: 12 Principles of Modern Astro-Vocational Guidance, Planetary Rulership and Career Guidance, and The 21st Century Astrologer
- Bob Mulligan: How to Advance *Your Own* Career as a Professional Astrologer!

Read *How to Use Vocational Astrology* today, and add "Vocational Counselor" to *your* resume tomorrow! Includes the complete 1942 classic by Charles E. Luntz *Vocational Guidance by Astrology*

**0-87542-387-6, 384 pgs., 6 x 9, illus., softcover**     **$14.95**

## HOW TO MANAGE THE ASTROLOGY OF CRISIS
### edited by Noel Tyl

More often than not, a person will consult an astrologer during those times when life has become difficult, uncertain or distressing. While crisis of any type is really a turning point, not a disaster, the client's crisis of growth becomes the astrologer's challenge. By coming to the astrologer, the client has come to an oracle. At the very best, there is hope for a miracle; at the very least, there is hope for reinforcement through companionship and information. How do you as an astrological counselor balance a sober discussion of the realities with enthusiastic efforts to leave the client feeling empowered and optimistic?

In this, the eleventh title in Llewellyn's New World Astrology Series, eight renowned astrologers provide answers this question as it applies to a variety of life crises. *How to Manage the Astrology of Crisis* begins with a discussion of the birth-crisis, the first major transition crisis in everybody's life—their confrontation with the world. It then discusses significant family crises in childhood and healing of the inner child . . . mental crises including head injuries, psychological breakdown, psychic experiences, multiple personalities . . . career turning points and crises of life direction and action . . . astrological triggers of financial crisis and recent advances in financial astrology . . . astrological maxims for relationship crises . . . and the mid-life crises of creative space, idealism, and consciousness.

**0-87542-390-6, 224 pgs., 6 x 9, charts, softcover** $12.00

## ASTROLOGICAL COUNSELING
### The Path to Self-Actualization
### Edited by Joan McEvers

This book explores the challenges for today's counselors and gives guidance to those interested in seeking an astrological counselor to help them win their own personal challenges. Includes articles by 10 well-known astrologers:

- David Pond: Astrological Counseling
- Maritha Pottenger: Potent, Personal Astrological Counseling
- Bill Herbst: Astrology and Psychotherapy: A Comparison for Astrologers
- Gray Keen: Plato Sat on a Rock
- Ginger Chalford, Ph.D.: Healing Wounded Spirits: An Astrological Counseling Guide to Releasing Life Issues
- Donald L. Weston, Ph.D.: Astrology and Therapy/Counseling
- Susan Dearborn Jackson: Reading the Body, Reading the Chart
- Doris A. Hebel: Business Counseling
- Donna Cunningham: The Adult Child Syndrome, Codependency, and Their Implications for Astrologers
- Eileen Nauman: Medical Astrology Counseling

**0-87542-385-X, 304 pgs., 5 1/4 x 8, charts, softcover** $14.95

## HOW TO PERSONALIZE THE OUTER PLANETS
**The Astrology of Uranus, Neptune & Pluto**
**Edited by Noel Tyl**

Since their discoveries, the three outer planets have been symbols of the modern era. They also take us as individuals to higher levels of consciousness and new possibilities of experience. Explored individually, each outer planet offers tremendous promise for growth. But when taken as a group, as they are in *Personalizing the Outer Planets*, the potential exists to recognize *accelerated* development.

As never done before, the seven prominent astrologers in *Personalizing the Outer Planets* bring these revolutionary forces down to earth in practical ways.

- Jeff Jawer: Learn how the discoveries of the outer planets rocked the world
- Noel Tyl: Project into the future with outer planet Solar Arcs
- Jeff Green: See how the outer planets are tied to personal trauma
- Jeff Jawer: Give perspective to your inner spirit through outer planet symbolisms
- Jayj Jacobs: Explore interpersonal relationships and sex through the outer planets
- Mary E. Shea: Make the right choices using outer planet transits
- Joanne Wickenburg: Realize your unconscious drives and urges through the outer planets
- Capel N. McCutcheon: Personalize the incredible archetypal significance of outer planet aspects

**0-87542-389-2, 288 pgs., 6 x 9, illus., softcover**       **$12.00**

## INTIMATE RELATIONSHIPS
**the Astrology of Attraction**
**edited by Joan McEvers**

Explore the deeper meaning of intimate relationships with the knowledge and expertise of eight renowned astrologers. Dare to look into your own chart and confront your own vulnerabilities. Find the true meaning of love and its place in your life. Gain new insights into the astrology of marriage, dating, affairs and more!

In Intimate Relationships, eight astrologers discuss their views on romance and the horoscope. The roles of Venus and the Moon, as well as the asteroids Sappho, Eros and Amor, are explored in our attitudes and actions toward potential mates. The theory of affinities is also presented wherein we are attracted to someone with similar planetary energies.

Is it a love that will last a lifetime, or mere animal lust that will burn itself out in a few months? Read *Intimate Relationships* and discover your *natal* attractions as well as your *fatal* attractions.

**0-87542-386-8, 240 pgs., 6 x 9, softcover**       **$14.95**

**PLANETS: The Astrological Tools**
**Edited by Joan McEvers**
This is the second in the astrological anthology series edited by respected astrologer Joan McEvers, who provides a brief factual overview of the planets. Then take off through the solar system with 10 professional astrologers as they bring their insights to the symbolism and influences of the planets.

- Toni Glover Sedgwick: The Sun as the life force and our ego
- Joanne Wickenburg: The Moon as our emotional signal to change
- Erin Sullivan-Seale: Mercury as the multifaceted god, followed with an in-depth explanation of its retrogradation
- Robert Glasscock: Venus as your inner value system and relationships
- Johanna Mitchell: Mars as your cooperative, energizing inner warrior
- Don Borkowski: Jupiter as expansion and preservation
- Gina Ceaglio: Saturn as a source of freedom through self-discipline
- Bil Tierney: Uranus as the original, growth-producing planet
- Karma Welch: Neptune as selfless giving and compassionate love
- Joan Negus: Pluto as a powerful personal force

0-87542-381-7, 384 pgs., 5-1/4 x 8, softcover
$12.95

**THE ASTROLOGY OF THE MACROCOSM**
**New Directions in Mundane Astrology**
**Edited by Joan McEvers**
Explains various mundane, transpersonal and worldly events through astrology. The perfect introduction to understanding the fate of nations, weather patterns and other global movements.

- Jimm Erickson: A Philosophy of Mundane Astrology
- Judy Johns: The Ingress Chart
- Jim Lewis: Astro*Carto*Graphy—Bringing Mundane Astrology Down to Earth
- Richard Nolle: The SuperMoon Alignment
- Chris McRae: The Geodetic Equivalent Method of Prediction
- Nicholas Campion: The Age of Aquarius—A Modern Myth
- Nancy Soller: Weather Watching with an Ephemeris
- Marc Penfield: The Mystery of the Romanovs
- Steve Cozzi: The Astrological Quatrains of Michel Nostradamus
- Diana K. Rosenberg: Stalking the Wild Earthquake
- Caroline W. Casey: Dreams and Disasters—Patterns of Cultural and Mythological Evolution into the 21st Century

0-87542-384-1, 420 pgs., 5 1/4 x 8, charts, softcover          $19.95

## FINANCIAL ASTROLOGY
### Edited by Joan McEvers

Money . . . investment . . . finance . . . speculation. The contributors to this popular book in Llewellyn's New World Astrology Series have vast financial and astrological experience and are well-known in the field. Did you know that new tools such as the 360 dial and the graphic ephemeris can help you spot impending market changes? You owe it to yourself to explore this relatively new (and lucrative!) topic. Learn about the various types of analysis and how astrology fine-tunes these methods. Covered cycles include the Lunar Cycle, the Mars/Vesta Cycle, the 4 1/2-year Martian Cycle, the 500-year Civilization Cycle used by Nostradamus, the Kondratieff Wave and the Elliot Wave.

- Michael Munkasey: A Primer on Market Forecasting
- Pat Esclavon Hardy: Charting the United States and the NYSE
- Jeanne Long: New Concepts for Commodities Trading Combining Astrology and Technical Analysis
- Georgia Stathis: The Real Estate Process
- Mary B. Downing: An Investor's Guide to Financial Astrology
- Judy Johns: The Gann Technique
- Carol S. Mull: Predicting the Dow
- Bill Meridian: The Effect of Planetary Stations on U.S. Stock Prices
- Georgia Stathis: Delineating the Corporation
- Robert Cole: The Predictable Economy

0-87542-382-5, 368 pgs., 5 1/4 x 8, illus., softcover          **$14.95**

## WEB OF RELATIONSHIPS
### Spiritual, Karmic & Psychological Bonds
### edited by Joan McEvers

The astrology of intimacy has long been a popular subject among professional astrologers and psychologists. Many have sought the answer to what makes some people have successful relationships with one another, while others struggle. *Web of Relationships* examines this topic not only in intimate affiliations, but also in families and friendships, in this eighth volume of the Llewellyn New World Astrology Series.

Editor Joan McEvers has brought together the wisdom and experience of eight astrology experts. Listen to what one author says about the mythological background of planets as they pertain to relationships. Discover how past life regression is illustrated in the chart. Consider the relationship of astrology and transactional analysis.

*Web of Relationships* explores the karmic and mystical connections between child and parent, how friends support and understand each other, the significance of the horoscope as it pertains to connections and much more. Each chapter will bring you closer to your own web of relationships and the astrology of intimacy.

0-87542-388-4, 240 pgs., 6 x 9, softcover          **$14.95**

## THE HOUSES
### Power Places of the Horoscope
### Edited by Joan McEvers

The Houses are the departments of experience. The planets energize these areas—giving life meaning. Understand why you attract and are attracted to certain people by your 7th House cusp. Go back in time to your 4th House, the history of your beginning. Joan McEvers has ingeniously arranged the chapters to show the Houses' relationships to each other and the whole. Various house systems are briefly described in Joan McEvers' introduction. Learn about house associations and planetary influences upon each house's activities with the following experts.

- Peter Damian: The First House and the Rising Sun
- Ken Negus: The Seventh House
- Noel Tyl: The Second House and The Eighth House
- Spencer Grendahl: The Third House
- Dona Shaw: The Ninth House
- Gloria Star: The Fourth House
- Marwayne Leipzig: The Tenth House
- Lina Accurso: Exploring Your Fifth House
- Sara Corbin Looms: The Eleventh: House of Tomorrow
- Michael Munkasey: The Sixth House
- Joan McEvers: The Twelfth House: Strength, Peace, Tranquillity

**0-87542-383-3, 400 pgs., 5 1/4 x 8, illus., softcover** **$12.95**

## SPIRITUAL, METAPHYSICAL & NEW TRENDS IN MODERN ASTROLOGY
### Edited by Joan McEvers

This is the first book in Llewellyn's New World Astrology Series. Edited by well-known astrologer, lecturer and writer Joan McEvers, this book pulls together the latest thoughts by the best astrologers in the field of Spiritual Astrology.

- Gray Keen: Perspective: The Ethereal Conclusion
- Marion D. March: Some Insights Into Esoteric Astrology
- Kimberly McSherry: The Feminine Element of Astrology: Reframing the Darkness
- Kathleen Burt: The Spiritual Rulers and Their Role in the Transformation
- Shirley Lyons Meier: The Secrets Behind Carl Payne Tobey's Secondary Chart
- Jeff Jawer: Astrodrama
- Donna Van Toen: Alice Bailey Revisited
- Philip Sedgwick: Galactic Studies
- Myrna Lofthus: The Spiritual Programming Within a Natal Chart
- Angel Thompson: Transformational Astrology

**0-87542-380-9, 264 pgs., 5 1/4 x 8, softcover** **$9.95**

## PREDICTION IN ASTROLOGY
**A Master Volume of Technique and Practice**
**by Noel Tyl**
No matter how much you know about astrology already, no matter how much experience you've had to date, you'll be fascinated by *Prediction in Astrology*, and you'll grow as an astrologer. Using the Solar Arc theory and methods he describes in this book, the author was able to accurately predict the Gulf War, including the actual date it would begin and the timetable of tactics, two months *before* it began. He also predicted the overturning of Communist rule in the Eastern bloc nations nine months in advance of its actual occurrence.

Tyl teaches through example. You learn by doing astrology, not just thinking about it. Tyl introduces Solar Arc theory in terms of "rapport" measurements, which you begin to do immediately, without paper, pencil, or computer, dials, or wheels. Just with your eyes! You will never look at a horoscope the same way again!

Tyl, in his well-known, very special way, also gets personal. He presents 30 Aphorisms, the keenest of maxims, the most practical of techniques, to create predictions from any horoscope. And as if this were not enough, Tyl then presents 20 Aphorisms for Counseling. Look for Tyl's "Quick-Glance" Transit Table, 1940-2040, to which you can refer more quickly than a computer. The busy astrologer will use this Appendix every day for many years to come.
**0-87542-814-2, 360 pgs., 6 x 9, softcover** **$14.95**

## NAVIGATING BY THE STARS
**Astrology and the Art of Decision-Making**
**by Edith Hathaway**
This book is chock full of convenient shortcuts to mapping out one's life. It presents the decision-maker's astrology, with the full range of astrological techniques.

No other one source presents all these cutting edge methods: Uranian astrology, the 90° dial, astro-mapping, Saturn quarters, hard aspects, angular relationships, the Meridian House System, secondary progressions, solar arc directions, eclipses, solstice and equinox charts, transiting lunation cycles, monthly kinetic mundascope graphs, among others.

To illustrate the immediate applications of the techniques, the author examines many charts in depth, focussing on study of character, destiny, timing cycles, and geographical location. She draws form 45 wide-ranging personal stories, including famous figures from history, politics, show business, the annals of crime, even corporations.
**0-87542-366-3, 320 pgs., 6 x 9, softcover** **$14.95**

## THE ASTROLOGICAL THESAURUS, BOOK ONE
## House Keywords
## Michael Munkasey

Keywords are crucial for astrological work. They correctly translate astrological symbols into clear, everyday language—which is a never-ending pursuit of astrologers. For example, the Third House can be translated into the keywords "visitors," "early education" or "novelist."

*The Astrological Thesaurus, Book One: House Keywords* is a the first easy-to-use reference book and textbook on the houses, their psychologically rich meanings, and their keywords. This book also includes information on astrological quadrants and hemispheres, how to choose a house system, and the mathematical formulations for many described house systems.

Astrologer Michael Munkasey compiled almost 14,000 keywords from more than 600 sources over a 23-year period. He has organized them into 17 commonplace categories (e.g., things, occupations and psychological qualities), and cross-referenced them three ways for ease of use: alphabetically, by house, and by category. Horary users, in particular, will find this book extremely useful.

0-87542-579-8, 434 pgs., 7 x 10, illus., softcover                    $19.95

## ASTROLOGY FOR THE MILLIONS
## by Grant Lewi

First published in 1940, this practical, do-it-yourself textbook has become a classic guide to computing accurate horoscopes quickly. Throughout the years, it has been improved upon since Grant Lewi's death by his astrological proteges and Llewellyn's expert editors. Grant Lewi is astrology's forerunner to the computer, a man who literally brought astrology to everyone. This, the first new edition since 1979, presents updated transits and new, user-friendly tables to the year 2050, including a new sun ephemeris of revolutionary simplicity. It's actually easier to use than a computer! Also added is new information on Pluto and rising signs, and a new foreword by Carl Llewellyn Weschcke and introduction by J. Gordon Melton.

Of course, the original material is still here in Lewi's captivating writing style all of his insights on transits as a tool for planning the future and making the right decisions. His historical analysis of U.S. presidents has been brought up to date to include George Bush. This new edition also features a special In Memoriam to Lewi that presents his birthchart.

One of the most remarkable astrology books available, *Astrology for the Millions* allows the reader to cast a personal horoscope in 15 minutes, interpret from the readings and project the horoscope into the future to forecast coming planetary influences and develop "a grand strategy for living."

0-87542-438-4, 464 pgs., 6 x 9, tables, charts, softcover                    $12.95

## PLUTO
### The Evolutionary Journey of the Soul
### by Jeff Green

If you have ever asked "Why am I here?",or "What are my lessons?," then this book will help you to objectively learn the answers from an astrological point of view. Green shows you how the planet Pluto relates to the evolutionary and karmic lessons in this life and how past lives can be understood through the position of Pluto in your chart.

Beyond presenting key principles and ideas about the nature of the evolutionary journey of the Soul, this book supplies practical, concise and specific astrological methods and techniques that pinpoint the answers to the above questions. If you are a professional counselor or astrologer, this book is indispensable to your practice. The reader who studies this material carefully and applies it to his or her own chart will discover an objective vehicle to uncover the essence of his or her own state of being. The understanding that this promotes can help you cooperate with, instead of resist, the evolutionary and karmic lessons in your life. Green describes the position of Pluto through all of the signs and houses, explains the aspects and transits of Pluto, discusses Pluto in aspect to the Moon's Nodes, and gives sample charts and readings. It is the most complete look at this "new" planet ever.

**0-87542-296-9, 384 pgs., 6 x 9, softcover** **$12.95**

## URANUS
### Freedom From the Known
### by Jeff Green

This book deals primarily with the archetypal correlations of the planet Uranus to human psychology and behavior to anatomy/physiology and the chakra system, and to metaphysical and cosmic laws. Uranus' relationship to Saturn, from an individual and collective point of view, is also discussed.

The text of this book comes intact in style and tone from an intensive workshop held in Toronto. You will feel as if you are a part of that workshop. In reading *Uranus* you will discover how to naturally liberate yourself from all of your conditioning patterns, patterns that were determined by the "internal" and "external" environment. Every person has a natural way to actualize this liberation. This natural way is examined by use of the natal chart and from a developmental point of view.

The 48-year sociopolitical cycle of Uranus and Saturn is discussed extensively, as is the relationship between Uranus, Saturn and Neptune.

**0-87542-297-7, 192 pgs., 5 1/4 x 8, softcover** **$7.95**

# HORARY ASTROLOGY
## The History and Practice of Astro-Divination
### by Anthony Louis

Here is a how-to guide for the intermediate astrologer on the art of astrological divination. It's the best method for getting answers to questions of pressing personal concern based on the planets' positions at the time of inquiry. Delves deeply into the heritage and the modern applicability of the horary art. Author Anthony Louis is a practicing psychiatrist, and he brings the compassion and erudition associated with his field to this scholarly textbook.

Written beautifully and reverently in the tradition of William Lilly, the book translates Lilly's meaning into modern terms. Other features include numerous case studies; tables; diagrams; and more than 100 pages of appendices, including an exhaustive planetary rulership list, planetary key words and a lengthy astrological/horary glossary. Dignities and debilities, aspects and orbs, derivative houses, Arabic parts, fixed stars, critical degrees and more are explored in relation to the science of horary astrology. Worksheets supplement the text.

**0-87542-394-9, 592 pgs., 6 x 9, illus., softcover**           **$18.95**

# PLANETS IN LOCALITY
## Exploring Local Space Astrology
### by Steve Cozzi

When you or your clients desire practical and personal help in planning your next move, vacation, or just in rearranging the furniture, look to Steve Cozzi's pioneering book *Planets in Locality*.

Time remains frozen but space/place can change. This is the primary truth underlying the whole field of locational astrology. *Planets in Locality* is the first and only book to explore "local space" techniques and their practical applications. Every road you drive, every meeting you attend, every place you move has a different energy based on its relationship to the planets, to the time, and to you.

Locality Astrology shows you what influences are at work anywhere you may be on Earth. You learn how the directions you travel and where you live affect your psychological and physical health. The improvements that follow will certainly make your home life more comfortable and enjoyable.

**0-87542-098-2, 320 pgs., 6 x 9, illus., softcover**           **$12.95**

# COMPUTERIZED ASTROLOGY REPORTS

**Simple Natal APS03-119:** Your chart calculated by computer in the Tropical/Placidus House system or the House system of your choice. It has all of the trimmings, including aspects, midpoints, Chiron and a glossary of symbols, plus a free booklet! . . . . . . . . . . . . . . . . . . . . . . . . **$5.00**

**Personality Profile Horoscope APS03-503:** Our most popular reading! This ten-part reading gives you a complete look at how the planets affect you. Learn about your general characteristics and life patterns. Look into your imagination and emotional needs. It is an excellent way to become acquainted with astrology and to learn about yourself. Very reasonable price! . . . . . . . . . . . . . . . . . . . . . . . . . . . . . . . . . . . . . . . . . . . . . . . . . . **$20.00**

**Transit Forecasts:** These reports keep you abreast of positive trends and challenging periods. Transit Forecasts can be an invaluable aid for timing your actions and decision making. Reports begin the first day of the month you specify.
**3-month Transit Forecast APS03-500** . . . . . . . . . . . . . . . . . . . . . . . . . **$12.00**
**6-month Transit Forecast APS03-501** . . . . . . . . . . . . . . . . . . . . . . . . . **$20.00**
**1-year Transit Forecast APS03-502** . . . . . . . . . . . . . . . . . . . . . . . . . . . **$25.00**

**Life Progressions APSO3-507:** Discover what the future has in store for you! This incredible reading covers a year's time and is designed to complement the Personality Profile Reading. Progressions are a special system with which astrologers map how the "natal you" develops through specified periods of your present and future life, and with this report you can discover the "now you!" . . . . . . . . . . . . . . . . . . . . . . . . . . . . **$20.00**

**Personal Relationship Reading APS03-506:** If you've just called it quits on one relationship and know you need to understand more about yourself before you test the waters again, then this is the report for you! This reading will tell you how you approach relationships in general, what kind of people you look for and what kind of people might rub you the wrong way. Important for anyone! . . . . . . . . . . . . . . . . . . . . . . . . . . . . **$20.00**

**Biorhythm Report:** Ever have one of those days when you have unlimited energy and everything is going your way? Then the next day you are feeling sluggish and awkward? These cycles are called biorhythms. This individual report will accurately map your daily biorhythms. Each important day is thoroughly discussed. With this valuable information, you can schedule important events with great success. This report is an invaluable source of information to help you plan your days to the fullest. Order today!
**3-month Biorhythm Report APS03-515** . . . . . . . . . . . . . . . . . . . . . . . . **$12.00**
**6-month Biorhythm Report APS03-516** . . . . . . . . . . . . . . . . . . . . . . . . **$18.00**
**12-month Biorhythm Report APS03-517** . . . . . . . . . . . . . . . . . . . . . . . **$25.00**

**Compatibility Profile APS03-504:** Find out if you really are compatible with your lover, spouse, friend or business partner! This is a great way of getting an in-depth look at your relationship with another person. Find out each person's approach to the relationship. Do you have the same goals? How well do you deal with arguments? Do you have the same values? This service includes planetary placements for both individuals, so send birth data for both and specify the type of relationship (i.e., friends, lovers, etc.). Order today! ........................ $30.00

**Numerology Report:** Find out which numbers are right for you with this report. It uses an ancient form of numerology invented by Pythagoras to determine the significant numbers in your life. Using both your *full* birth name and date of birth, this report will accurately calculate those numbers which stand out as yours.
**3-month Numerology Report APSO3-508** ..................... $12.00
**6-month Numerology Report APSO3-509** ..................... $18.00
**12-month Numerology Report APSO3-510** ................... $25.00

**Tarot Reading APS03-120:** Find out what the cards have in store for you! This reading features the graphics of the traditional Rider-Waite card deck in a detailed 10-card spread, and as a bonus, there are three pages explaining what each Tarot card means for you. Specify a short question that you would like to have answered as well as the number of times you wish the deck to be shuffled. Order this exciting tarot reading today! ................................................. $10.00

**Lucky Lotto Report (State Lottery Report):** Do you play the state lotteries? This report will determine your luckiest sequence of numbers for each day based on specific planets, degrees and other indicators in your own chart. Provide your full birth data and middle name, and specify the parameters of your state's lottery: i.e., how many numbers you need in sequence (up to 10 numbers) as well as the highest possible numeral (up to #999). Indicate the month you want to start.
**3-month Lucky Lotto Report APS03-512** ...................... $10.00
**6-month Lucky Lotto Report APS03-513** ...................... $15.00
**12-month Lucky Lotto Report APS03-514** ..................... $25.00

**Ultimate Astro-Profile APS03-505:** This report has it all! Receive over 40 pages of fascinating, insightful and uncanny descriptions of your innermost qualities and talents. Read about your burn rate (thirst for change). Explore your personal patterns (inside and outside). Examine the particular pattern of your Houses. The Astro-Profile doesn't repeat what you've already learned from other personality profiles, but considers the often neglected natal influence of the lunar nodes, plus much more! .... $40.00

# THE LLEWELLYN ANNUALS

**Llewellyn's MOON SIGN BOOK:** Approximately 400 pages of valuable information on gardening, fishing, weather, stock market forecasts, personal horoscopes, good planting dates, and general instructions for finding the best date to do just about anything! Articles by prominent forecasters and writers in the fields of gardening, astrology, politics, economics and cycles. This special almanac, different from any other, has been published annually since 1906. It's fun, informative and has been a great help to millions in their daily planning. **State year $4.95**

**Llewellyn's SUN SIGN BOOK:** Your personal horoscope for the entire year! All 12 signs are included in one handy book. Also included are forecasts, special feature articles, and an action guide for each sign. Monthly horoscopes are written by Gloria Star, author of *Optimum Child*, for your personal Sun Sign and there are articles on a variety of subjects written by well-known astrologers from around the country. Much more than just a horoscope guide! Entertaining and fun the year around. **State year $4.95**

**Llewellyn's DAILY PLANETARY GUIDE:** Includes all of the major daily aspects plus their exact times in Eastern and Pacific time zones, lunar phases, signs and voids plus their times, planetary motion, a monthly ephemeris, sunrise and sunset tables, special articles on the planets, signs, aspects, a business guide, planetary hours, rulerships, and much more. Large 5-1/4 x 8 format for more writing space, spiral bound to lay flat, address and phone listings, time-zone conversion chart and blank horoscope chart. **State year $6.95**

**Llewellyn's ASTROLOGICAL CALENDAR:** Large wall calendar of 48 pages. Beautiful full-color cover and full-color paintings inside. Includes special feature articles by famous astrologers, and complete introductory information on astrology. It also contains a Lunar Gardening Guide, celestial phenomena, a blank horoscope chart, and monthly date pages which include aspects, Moon phases, signs and voids, planetary motion, an ephemeris, personal forecasts, lucky dates, planting and fishing dates, and more. 10 x 13 size. Set in Central time, with fold-down conversion table for other time zones worldwide. **State year $9.95**